THE BATTLE FOR
CREATION

ACTS/FACTS/IMPACTS VOLUME 2
edited by HENRY M. MORRIS/DUANE T.GISH

CREATION-LIFE PUBLISHERS
SAN DIEGO, CA 92115

ISBN 0-89051-020-2

Library of Congress Catalog Card Number 74-75429

Copyright © 1976
CREATION-LIFE PUBLISHERS, INC.
San Diego, California 92115
ALL RIGHTS RESERVED

Printed in the United States of America

First Printing 1976
Second Printing 1977

contents

Preface 1
Chapter I: The Great Debate .3
The Campus Debates (March 1974) 3
University of North Carolina Hosts Creation
  Debate (February 1974) 5
Panel at Wyoming Debates Creation (March 1974) 6
Televised Debate Draws Overflow Crowd (April 1974) 7
Dr. Gish Debates in Canada (April 1974) 8
1500 Hear Ft. Lauderdale Debate (May 1974) 10
Origins of Life Theories Debated Before Packed
  House (October 1974) 12
"Flood Geology" Debated at Wheaton College (December 1974) . . . 15
Gish, Morris Debate Leading Scientists in
  Tennessee (February 1975) 18
Texas Tech. Debate Draws Record Crowd (March 1975) 22
Debates Generate Vigorous Response (Impact #24,
  May 1975) 24
University Debates Feature New Orleans Seminar
  (March 1975) 53
Overflow Audience Hears University of Manitoba
  Debate (April 1975) 55
Gish Debates Anthropology Chairman (December 1975) 57
San Diego Newspaper Features Creation Debate
  (November 1975) 60

Chapter II: Creation Goes to College 68
Creation on the Campus (December 1975) 68
Case for Creation Reaches Fullerton (January 1974) 69
Morris Lectures at L.S.U. Shreveport (February 1974) 71
University of Florida Hosts Creation Lecture
  (April 1974) 71
ICR Staff Scientist at Peoria (July 1974) 72

Creationist Interest Continues on Oklahoma Campuses
  (November 1974) 73
University of Oregon Seminar Draws Record
  Attendance (February 1975) 73
Minnesota Colleges Hear Dr. Morris (March 1975) 74
Astronomy — Geology Lectures Given in Colorado
  (April 1975) 74
Morris Speaks at Fairleigh-Dickinson (June 1975) 75
New Mexico Seminar Reaches Students and
  Scientists (June 1975) 75
ICR Scientist Speaks at U.C. Berkeley (July 1975) 76
University Meetings in Kansas Make Impact (December 1975) ... 77
Wisconsin University Students Hear Gish, Morris
  (December 1975) 78
Evolution in Christian Colleges, Morris (December 1974) 79

Chapter III: Creationism and the Public Schools .83

The Christian Creationist in the Classroom (July 1974) 83
Creation Workshop Sponsored by School District
  (April 1974) 86
Poll Strongly Favors Creation in California School
  District (July 1974) 88
The Book of Genesis (September 1974) 90
Citizens Committee Holds Oregon Rally (September 1974) 91
Evolutionary Smog (October 1975) 92
Introducing Creationism into the Public Schools
  Impact #20, December 1974) 94
Resolution for Equitable Treatment of Both Creation
  and Evolution (Impact #26, July 1975 104

Chapter IV: Confrontation with Scientists 115

Scientific Establishment Alarmed at Creationism Rise
  (June 1974) 115
Creationism Theme of Louisiana Science Teachers
  Convention (January 1974) 116

Morris, Gish Speak to Professional Geologists
(March 1974) 117
Stanford Research Institute Hears ICR Director
(June 1974) 121
Blick Brings Creation Message to Engineering
Educators (November 1974) 122
Professional Engineers Hear Creation Message (March 1975) 122
Dr. Lester Speaks to National Science Teachers (May 1975) 123
Gish, Morris Confront Miami Geologists (June 1975) 124
Hughes Scientists Hear Evidence for Creation
(November 1975) ....

Chapter V: Creation Research

Careers in Creationism (November 1974) 126
ICR Research Team Studies "Overthrust" Areas
(November 1974) 128
Noah's Ark: Status 1975 (Impact #22, March 1975) 130
New Flood Tradition Discovered (April 1975) 140
Turkey Closed to 1975 Ararat Expedition (July 1975) 141
Oil Seepage Rates Indicate Young Age for Earth's
Crust (September 1975) 144

Chapter VI: Creation International 147

ICR Staff Scientist Tours Canada (December 1974) 147
Creation Literature Society Formed in New Zealand
(September 1974) 149
Newton Scientific Association Active in England
(September 1974) 149
University of Toronto Hears Creation Lectures
(November 1974) 150
Creation Scholarships Established in Taiwan
(November 1974) 150
Scientific Creation Group Established in Brazil
(May 1975) 151
ICR Speakers Featured at Muskoka Conference
(September 1975) 151
ICR Scientist Tours New Zealand and Australia
(October 1975) 152

Chapter VII: Creation in the City 157

600 Attend Canton-Akron Seminar (February 1974) 157
Seminar Reaches Winter Visitors in Florida (April 1974) 158
First New England Seminar in Bridgeport (June 1974) 158
Meetings Held in Georgia's Top Southern Baptist
    Church (May 1974) 159
Creation-Evolution Institute Held in Historic
    Church (October 1974) 159
Lutheran Workers Study Creationism at
    Minneapolis (March 1975) 160
Miami Seminar Sets Records (June 1975) 161
New York City Has First Creation Seminar (June 1975) 161
First Creation Seminar Held in Las Vegas
    (November 1975) 162
Gish at Missouri Creation Seminar (December 1975) 162
Dallas-Fort Worth Seminar Reaches 3000 (December 1975) 163
New England Seminar Attracts Wide Interest
    (December 1975) 164
Grand Rapids Seminar Has Record Registration
    (December 1975) 164

Chapter VIII: ICR and the Media 165

Ararat Project Featured on NBC "Today Show" (June 1974) 165
Creation Receives National TV Coverage (July 1974) 166
ICR Ararat Project Featured on Nationwide TV in
    Canada (November 1974) 166
Church of Satan Opposes Creationism (December 1974) 167
Scientist Backs Human Creation Claim (July 1975) 168

Chapter IX: Creation and the Christian Life 171

Creation and Family Life (April 1974) 171
Ecumenical Creationism (October 1974) 173
The Importance of Creationism (October 1974) 175
Creation and Christian Witnessing (April 1975) 178
Give Attendance to Reading (May 1975) 180
A Testimony (June 1975) 182

Chapter X: The Impact of Creation—Scientific and
          Biblical 184

Impact Series Articles

The Stars of Heaven (Impact #10, January 1974) 184
Richard Leakey's Skull (Impact #11, February 1974) 193
Interpreting Earth History (Impact #12, March 1974) 201
Creation and the Environment (Impact #13, April 1974) 209
Planet Earth: Design or Accident? (Impact #14, May 1974) 215
The Solar System — New Discoveries (Impact #15, June 1974) 223
Physics: A Challenge to Geologic Time (Impact #16,
   July 1974) 230
The Young Earth (Impact #17, September 1974 238
Mimicry (Impact #18, October 1974) 249
Clues Regarding the Age of the Universe (Impact #19,
   November 1974) 253
Evolution and the Population Problem (Impact #21,
   February 1975) 259
The Amino Acid Racemization Dating Method (Impact #23,
   April 1975) 269
Some Recent Developments Having to Do with Time
   (Impact #27, September 1975) 278
Language, Creation and the Inner Man (Impact #28,
   October 1975) 286
Multivariate Analysis: Man, Apes, Australopithecines
   (Impact #29, November 1975) 298
Creation and the Virgin Birth (Impact #30, December 1975) 303
The Gospel of Creation (Impact #25, June 1975) 312

**ADDITIONAL IMPACT SERIES ARTICLES
ON THE FOLLOWING PAGES:**

Chapter I, Page 24: Debates Generate Vigorous
                    Response (Impact #24, May 1975)

Chapter III, Page 94: Introducing Creationism into the
                      Public Schools (Impact #20, December 1974)

Chapter III, Page 104: Resolution for Equitable Treatment of
                       Both Creation and Evolution
                       (Impact #26, July 1975)

Chapter V, Page 130: Noah's Ark: Status 1975 (Impact #22,
                     March 1975)

preface

In this book are contained all the "Impact" articles, as well as all the news reports, columns, and special features of continuing interest, that were published in *Acts and Facts* during the years 1974 and 1975. The modern revival of creationism is being documented month-by-month in this popular and unique publication of the Institute for Creation Research, so that this book provides a convenient compendium of the developments of these two significant years.

The ICR intends to issue a similar volume every two years; the first (published in 1974) incorporated the major items published in *Acts and Facts* during 1972 and 1973. This one covers 1974 and 1975.

In the present volume, articles are grouped together in terms of similar subject matter, rather than in chronological order of publication. This arrangement makes for easier reading and reference use.

Thus, Chapter I describes the various university creation-evolution debates that have taken place during the past two years, with their impact and effects. Chapter II details all the seminars and other types of creationist meetings on secular college and university campuses during this period.

Chapter III treats the continuing drive to restore creationism to the public schools of the nation and Chapter IV describes various creationist meetings held by invitation of different professional scientific and educational organizations. Chapter V discusses some of ICR's creation research projects, including the ongoing search for Noah's Ark.

The extension of the creationist movement to other lands is sketched in Chapter VI. The wide-ranging geographical outreach of ICR in our own land is described in Chapter VII, in terms of seminars and other meetings held in numerous cities across the country. The increasing interest of the news media is outlined in Chapter VIII. The impact of creationism in many aspects of personal Christian living is emphasized in Chapter IX.

Finally, the balance of the popular "Impact Series" articles not included with subjects in previous chapters are reprinted in Chapter X. These deal helpfully with a wide range of topical studies in both the scientific and theological aspects of creationism.

The authors and publisher believe that this book will serve as a very helpful reference volume and witnessing medium, as well as providing hours of fascinating reading to those who are newcomers in this important field of creation studies.

chapter I

THE GREAT DEBATE

THE CAMPUS DEBATES

Henry M. Morris

Few developments in the creationist movement have stirred as much interest as have the creation-evolution debates that have been held on various campuses the past two years. Some may question the value of such engagements, but there is no doubt that these serve to get the creationist message heard by more non-Christians and non-creationists than almost any other method. Other things being equal, one can be sure a debate will draw a larger audience than a regular lecture. Maybe it's like the crowds in ancient Rome anticipating a bloody confrontation between the Christians and the lions!

We personally much prefer to give a straightforward lecture or message, perhaps followed by questions from the audience, since this gives more time for our own material (and we do need all the time we can get, to give an adequate presentation of creationism to people who have never heard it). Also the debate format, in the nature of things, tends to generate heat as well as light, although we do try diligently to "let our speech be always with grace" (Colossians 4:6), and not to use bitterness or sarcasm, nor to respond emotionally when our opponents use it.

Because of this, we normally do not attempt to promote or arrange such debates ourselves. The one exception to this policy was an unsuccessful attempt to arrange a debate with Dr. William Mayer, of the Biological Sciences Curriculum Study Center, as reported in June, 1973 issue of ACTS AND FACTS.

However, when others arrange them, naturally we try to accept if possible. It is interesting that we get reports from campus after campus that the student and faculty sponsors of our meetings have found it almost impossible to find evolutionist professors — no matter how outspoken they may be in favor of evolution in their own classrooms — who are willing to debate the issue with creationist scientists in a public meeting! They use various excuses, some even admitting they are afraid of losing a debate with such "professional debaters" as Gish and Morris (can you imagine!); but in any event, very few will agree to participate.

Well, we are anything but professional debaters. Neither of us ever participated in a debate before we began to take part in these debates, and we certainly have had no training in preaching or public speaking — as anyone who has ever heard *me* speak, at least, will no doubt agree. One thing we have learned, however, from such confrontations is that the creationist position can stand up against the best arguments of top evolutionist scientists. Whether or not we can convince others, we ourselves have certainly become convinced of this. The arguments of such men often seem incredibly naive and frequently reveal that they are not up to date, even in the field of evolutionary theory that they teach. We certainly would not question their competence in their particular scientific specialties, however, and there are, of course, many unresolved problems in the detailed application of our own creation "model," but we do become personally more confident of the basic scientific validity of creationism every time we encounter such men and their arguments. The very best arguments they have been able to bring are trivial in comparison to the strength of the evidence for creation.

We do not know what the future may hold. Unless the Lord returns first, however, we believe the case for scientific creationism is so sound that, by His grace, we may yet see a real nationwide re-introduction of creationism as a viable alternative into our schools and colleges. The ultimate results, in terms of a revival of Biblical Christianity in our national life and in individual lives, are exciting to contemplate.

And something to pray for!

University of North Carolina
Hosts Creation Debate

The main campus of the University of North Carolina at Chapel Hill, widely known as one of the most "liberal" university centers in the South, was the site of a creation-evolution debate on January 21, 1974 between Dr. Pollitser, Professsor of Anatomy and Anthropology, and Dr. Henry Morris, Director of I.C.R. Although the debate had only been scheduled a few days before, the 400-seat auditorium was more than filled with students and faculty with many standing. Audience interest seemed very keen throughout the evening.

Dr. Pollitser gave an excellent illustrated lecture summarizing the evidences for evolution from various fields. Dr. Morris showed that the same evidences (mainly various types of similarities) could be interpreted as well within the creation model and that the systematic gaps in the fossil record, the deteriorative nature of mutations and the law of increasing entropy gave strong evidence of special creation. In his rebuttal, Dr. Pollitser stressed that, regardless of the efforts of creationists, evolution was "here to stay" and that one could still believe in both God and evolution (citing Teilhard de Chardin), urging students to remain committed to evolution. Dr. Morris again stressed the unanswered creationist testimony of the Second Law of Thermodynamics, showed the creationist implications of the latest finds related to man's origin, alluded to the theological problems in postulating a god who uses an evolutionary process to produce man (while pointing out that the debate was supposed to relate only to scientific aspects of the problem) and finally stressed the statistical impossibilities inherent in the

5

concept of the naturalistic evolution of life from non-life. A short period of audience questioning followed.

Panel At University of Wyoming Debates Creation

An overflow audience of 450 students and faculty sat for over three hours as the creation message was given at the University of Wyoming, February 8, 1974, by Dr. Duane Gish and Dr. Henry Morris, and then an attempt at refutation by three prominent faculty members there. The panel of evolutionists consisted of Dr. Don Boyd, Professor of Geology, Dr. George Gill, Professor of Anthropology, and Dr. Robert George, Professor of Biology. A lengthy question and answer period from the floor followed the panel discussions.

The panel "debate" seemed to follow the typical trend for such confrontations. The panelists attempted to bring an answer to the evidence that had been presented supporting the creation model from the principles of thermodynamics and the systematic absence of transitional forms among living organisms and in the fossil record. Dr. Boyd's main argument was that Dr. Gish had failed to deal with several specific supposed transitional fossils (the main of which, the crossopterygian fish, had indeed been discussed at length by Dr. Gish and shown to be no possible transition at all). Dr. Gill attacked the academic credentials of Richard Leakey (whose recent fossil discoveries have so upset previous theories of human evolution), cited the long-discredited embryological recapitulation theory and "vestigial organs" such as human goose-bumps as proof of evolution, and stressed that students should trust the judgment of paleontologists rather than creationist biochemists as to the validity of evolution. Dr. George's response consisted mostly of jokes and criticisms of the Bible and fundamentalist religion (although the creationists had not mentioned the Bible or religion at all), while at the same time protesting that he believed in God and had a completely open mind toward creationism. A visiting campus lecturer, Dr. Stephen Stanley, an invertebrate paleontologist on the faculty at Johns Hopkins

University, in the first comment from the audience, attacked Dr. Morris' use of the Second Law as evidence against evolution since no "law" could be regarded as absolutely proved in science. He also insisted Archaeopteryx was a true transitional fossil since, if the fossil feathers of this creature had not been discovered, it would have been identified as a dinosaur instead of a bird (maybe, then, dinosaurs were really big birds whose feathers didn't get fossilized!).

Though the audience was predominantly evolutionist, at least before the meeting, almost unanimous applause greeted Dr. Gish's query, following the panel discussion, whether they believed this kind of open discussion on a scientific level of the creation-evolution issue was desirable and helpful on a university campus.

Televised Debate Draws Overflow Crowd

Approximately 800 crowded into a 600-seat auditorium, with an undetermined number unable to get in at all, to see and hear WJTV, Tampa's Television Channel 13, film a three-hour debate between two evolutionist professors from the University of South Florida and two I.C.R. scientists, on Saturday night, March 2, 1974. Taking the affirmative on the topic "Resolved that evolution is a better model than creation with which to explain the scientific data related to origins" were Dr. Evelyn Kessler, Professor of Anthropology, and Dr. John Betz, Assistant Professor of Biology. Defending creationism were Dr. Henry Morris and Dr. Duane Gish. The debate was arranged by Pat Colmenares, hostess of one of Florida's most popular television talk shows, and was scheduled for regional broadcast the following week.

The debate had been publicized in the local high schools and on the University of South Florida campus, and most of the 800 in the audience were students. Reaction slips turned in after the meeting indicated that practically everyone enjoyed the debate and a large majority thought creation had "won."

7

Both professors were popular figures in the area. Dr. Kessler is a widely-known anthropologist and archaeologist, and Dr. Betz is one of Florida's leading environmentalists. In their presentations, both laid strong emphasis on their respective faiths, Dr. Kessler stressing her commitment to secular humanism and Dr. Betz his belief in theistic evolution. Dr. Kessler's scientific evidence consisted mainly of a discussion of the supposed hominid ancestors of man, especially Australopithecus and Homo erectus. Dr. Betz did not cite any scientific evidence but confined his presentation to philosophic and religious considerations, stressing that evolution was a better scientific model because it was naturalistic, insisting that, although he believed in God, one should only allow God to create where it was impossible to conceive of a naturalistic explanation of the data.

In the creationist presentation, Dr. Morris defined the two models, discussed briefly the questions of similarities, variation and selection, and especially emphasized the impossibility of evolution in light of the laws of thermodynamics. Dr. Gish documented the systematic absence of evolutionary intermediates in the fossil record and the newer discoveries of Leakey and others which had made the traditional interpretations of human evolution obsolete. He noted in particular that fossils of Australopithecus, Homo habilis and Homo erectus had been found in the very same layer by Dr. Louis Leakey and that, below all of them, had been excavated a circular stone habitation constructed by early man. Dr. Betz attempted to coounter this by suggesting that if his sister had died and been buried before his father, it would not prove that she was older than her father (!) Dr. Kessler suggested that the circular stone structure was only a "windbreak" constructed by the Australopithecines. Neither attempted to refute the evidence from the laws of thermodynamics, except to assert that the two laws had not been proven. Dr. Betz admitted that evolution was a "bad" scientific theory since it could not be falsified, but nevertheless insisted that creationism should not be taught in the schools since it involved a supernatural Creator.

Dr. Gish Debates in Canada

Dr. Duane Gish, under the sponsorship of the Alberta Committee for True Education, lectured and debated in the cities of Calgary, Edmonton, Lethbridge, and Grand Prairie, February 20-23, 1975. Rev. Neil Unruh, Director of the Committee, had attempted to arrange debates at each location, but only Dr. Job Kuijt, a graduate of the University of California, Berkeley, and Professor of Botany, University of Lethbridge, accepted the challenge.

Dr. Gish presented an evening lecture to a general audience at Calgary on Wednesday, February 20. On Thursday noon before a large audience of students and faculty of the University of Calgary, he presented the case for creation. A panel of three professors, which included a semicreationist (direct creation of the first cell not certain what happened after that) and two evolutionists, offered a critique of Dr. Gish's presentation. An interaction with the audience followed. This discussion was very favorably received.

A capacity audience of about 300 attended the Thursday evening debate in Lethbridge. Before the debate, Dr. Kuijt asked assurance that no Christian testimony would be given, asserting that if any were given he would walk out. He was assured that so such testimony would be given, but, as agreed upon, only scientific evidence would be presented.

Dr. Gish, the first speaker, presented the case for creation, emphasizing the irrefutable contradiction between the theory of evolution and the Second Law of Thermodynamics, and the fact that the fossil record is in accord with the predictions based on special creation, but contradicts the predictions of evolution. Dr. Kuijt read a prepared statement in which he declared that all leading scientists believe in evolution, and that the creationists documented their case by quoting statements out of context.

The remainder of Dr. Kuijt's prepared statement consisted of a diatribe against the Bible, Christianity, and Christians! Thus Dr. Kuijt, although specifically demanding that no Christian testimony be given, spent the bulk of his time giving his own atheistic religious testimony. He did not present any scientific argument in support of evolution, nor did he attempt to refute any of the scientific evidence presented by Dr. Gish, either in his opening statement or in his rebuttal. His presentation thus uniquely illustrated Dr. Gish's claim, made in his opening statement, that evolution was as religious as creation.

1500 Hear Ft. Lauderdale
Creation-Evolution Debate

About 1500 people attended the debate between evolutionist Dr. Joel Warren, professor of microbiology at Nova University, and Dr. Gish, which was held at the Coral Ridge Presbyterian Church, Ft. Lauderdale, Florida, on March 14, 1974. Dr. D. James Kennedy, pastor of this rapidly growing evangelical Presbyterian church, (attendances at the two Sunday morning services total 4,000) called nine other universities in Florida attempting to obtain a second evolutionist willing to debate the creation-evolution question, but could find no one else who was willing to defend the evolution position!). Dr. Kennedy was amazed at the reluctance of these professors, who teach evolution to their students as an established fact year in and year out, to publicly face a challenge from creationists on the comparative scientific validity of the creation and evolution models.

The main thrust of Dr. Warren's formal presentation was that while a belief in the Bible and a literal creation did serve a useful, in fact a necessary, purpose at a particular stage in the history of Western civilization, to hold such beliefs in the present scientific age is anti-intellectual and harmful. He compared creationists with the anti-intellectuals of the Middle Ages.

About the only specific scientific evidence Dr. Warren cited in his formal presentation in support of evolution was his reference to what he believed to be vestigial organs in the human body (the so-called vestigial organs are organs which are now supposed to be completely without function or purpose but which were useful or functional in the past in our hypothetical evolutionary ancestors). He referred specifically to two organs — the appendix and the coccyx, or tailbone.

About a hundred years ago, evolutionists maintained that there were almost 180 vestigial organs in the human body, including those already mentioned, as well as such vital organs as the pituitary, thyroid and pineal glands. Scientific and medical research since that time has discovered the true function of these organs, including the function of the appendix and coccyx, and consequently, that list has been reduced almost to zero.

To hear a scientist in 1974 claim that the coccyx and appendix are useless organs is astounding, indeed. It is known that the appendix includes lymphatic tissue which produces agents which actively participate in fighting diseases, particularly those which affect the intestinal tract. The coccyx is certainly not a useless organ, but serves as the anchor for important muscles of the pelvic region and, furthermore, a person cannot sit comfortably without it. If Dr. Warren believes the coccyx is a useless organ, he should try getting along without it!

In Dr. Gish's formal presentation, he pointed out the contradiction between evolutionary theory and the Second Law of Thermodynamics. He also emphasized the fact that the fossil record accords amazingly well with that predicted on the basis of creation, but that the fossil record contradicts the major predictions based on evolution theory, citing numerous examples.

In his presentation on the Second Law of Thermodynamics, Dr. Gish was careful to point out that merely having an open system and an adequate outside supply of energy were not sufficient conditions for the formation of complex systems from simple matter. Two other vital conditions are necessary: energy transforming mechanisms and a system to control and to maintain these systems. These conditions are satisfied in the green plant, for example, by photosynthesis and other energy transforming mechanisms, and the incredibly complex genetic system found in these plants. Without this pre-existing machinery and control system, the energy coming to the earth from the sun could not be harnessed to build up the complex from the simple, but would, on the other hand, be destructive.

Dr. Warren, in his rebuttal, referred rather derisively to Dr. Gish's argument on evolution and the Second Law of Thermodynamics, saying that these naive creationists apparently were not aware of the fact that the Second Law applies only to closed systems, and that all that is needed to build up complex systems from simple matter is an open system! Apparently Dr. Warren was just not listening when Dr. Gish presented the details of his argument, since he had in some detail pointed out that an open system and an energy supply were necessary *but not sufficient* conditions for complex systems to arise from simple matter.

In a conversation with Dr. Gish the day after the debate, a high school student expressed his amusement at Dr. Warren's failure to grasp the full implication of his argument on the Second Law of Thermodynamics. When Dr. Gish expressed the possibility that perhaps he had not expressed his argument in an adequately clear fashion, the high school student quickly assured Dr. Gish that *he* had no difficulty understanding his argument!

As has so often been the case, it was the creationist who based his arguments strictly on the scientific evidence, while the evolutionist dealt extensively with philosophical and religious considerations. Although evolutionists present their product in the guise of pure science while claiming that special creation is simply a religious position, it seems clear to creationists that evolution is just as religious as creation and that creation is actually more scientific than evolution.

Origins of Life Theories
Debated Before Packed House

"The 'missing link' could have surfaced unnoticed Thursday night in a packed Flint Center in Cupertino as two speakers debated theories on the origin of life before a rapt audience of 2,000 people . . ." This was the beginning of an article in the PALO ALTO TIMES newspaper which aptly described the turnout for the debate at De Anza College, in Cupertino, on August 29, 1974.

Actually, some 2,300 people, many of whom were teenagers, swarmed into the auditorium carrying Bibles, notebooks, and tape recorders, to hear Dr. Duane T. Gish and Dr. Sheldon Matlow debate creation and evolution. Reports in the San Jose newspapers compared it to the famous Scopes Trial fifty years ago. One reporter wrote, "Man, his origin and development has been the subject of controversy for centuries, and interest here has not diminished with time, the size of the audience indicated."

Dr. Matlow, who has his degree in Physical Chemistry from the University of Chicago, is a math instructor at West Valley College and is managing director of the Scientific Mining and Manufacturing Company in Santa Clara. He is a member of the American Physical Society, the American Chemical Society, and is a Fellow of the Chemical Society (London). He has published numerous papers in physics and chemistry. In his case for evolution he avoided the biological evidence and focused on the chemical and physical aspects. He stated that creation is not scientific, nor is it even good philosophy or theology.

One of the most powerful arguments against evolution, and one of several which Dr. Gish stressed, is the universal tendency of all spontaneously occurring natural process to go toward disorder (the Second Law of Thermodynamics, also known as the law of increasing entropy, or disorder). Dr. Matlow tried to answer this argument by implying that a change in temperature might reverse this tendency. He said, for example, that garbage decomposes rapidly at ordinary temperature, but that this process is retarded at low temperature, and implied that at sufficiently low temperature this tendency toward disorder might reverse!

Dr. Gish pointed out that Dr. Matlow was confusing thermodynamics with kinetics. Thermodynamic considerations determine the direction a reaction will take, while kinetics deals with the rate at which the reaction proceeds. Since building complex molecules from simple ones requires the *input* of energy, an *increase* of temperature would be expected to favor such a process. On the other hand, decomposition *releases* energy, and a *lowering* of temperature should favor that process thermodynamically. However, an increase in temperature may accelerate the rate in just the opposite direction predicted on the basis of these considerations, because energy must be used to overcome what might be called chemical inertia (activation energy). The latter is most often the most important factor. Thus an *increase* of temperature actually *increases* the rate of decomposition of complex compounds (and of garbage), and even though this process of decomposition releases energy, a lowering of temperature retards the process.

Since the formation of the complex compounds necessary for life would require the input of energy, it is obvious that lowering the temperature would never bring about their formation. On the other hand, raw, uncontrolled energy, be it heat energy or any other kind of energy, causes the destruction of chemical compounds far in excess of their rate of formation, just as predicted on the basis of the Second Law of Thermodynamics. Neither Dr. Matlow, nor any other evolutionist, has ever been able to refute the contradiction between evolution and this universal law of science.

Dr. Matlow's other arguments were equally weak. He argued, for example, that the link between the reptile and the bird might have been something like an ostrich, since an ostrich could be considered to be a feathered reptile rather than a bird! Not even many evolutionists would accept that argument.

In his presentation, Dr. Gish argued that evolution is no more scientific than creation, but even less so, and that it is just as religious, being fundamental to a non-theistic, humanistic religion. In addition to the evidence from thermodynamics, Dr. Gish also presented a series of slides illustrating the systematic gaps in the fossil record between all basic kinds of plants and animals. Dr. Gish closed by showing slides of several creatures which evolutionists once argued were our ancestors, but now have been abandoned as such.

These included Nebraska Man (he turned out to be a pig!), Piltdown Man (an ape's jaw!), and Neanderthal Man (now considered fully human).

An opinion questionnaire was offered to those entering the auditorium until the supply of 1,600 was expended. A total of 695 forms were returned after the debate. The results showed that the audience distribution was: 83%Creationists, 8% Evolutionists, 3% Other, and 6% Undecided; 74%of the creationists report their creation beliefs were strengthened by the debate, while 22% of the evolutionists said their evolution beliefs had been strengthened; another 22% of the evolutionists said they now believe in creation, where only 1% of the creationists were swayed over to the evolution side; 45% learned about the debate through local churches, 28% through a friend or relative, 13% from a flier or poster, 10% learned about the debate in newspapers, and 3% responded to radio or television announcements.

"Flood Geology"
Debated at Wheaton College

A unique quasi-debate (no rebuttals) on so-called "flood geology" was the highlight of a week of creation-oriented meetings in the Wheaton (Illinois) area, November 19-24, 1974. The "debate" was held in the Science Auditorium on the Wheaton College campus on November 19, with Dr. Frank Roberts (Ph.D. in Geology from Bryn Mawr College, now on the staff of the Delaware County Christian High School near Philadelphia) opposing flood geology, and Dr. Henry Morris (I.C.R. Director) defending it. Attendance, which was limited to Wheaton students and staff, was approximately 300. The panel was sponsored by the Wheaton College Science Division (Dr. Howard Claassen, Chairman), with Dr. James Kraakevik (Professor of Physics) serving as moderator.

Each speaker was allotted 45 minutes to present his case. Dr. Morris was asked to speak first. Since it had been agreed that the presentation would not deal with any Biblical aspects of the question, the main thrust of his argument was a documented demonstration that most of the significant formations in the geologic column had been deposited by processes operating at catastrophic intensities. Further, he showed (from principles of hydraulics, as well as the actual physical character of the boundaries between successive strata and formations) that, since each unit of the column had been formed rapidly and since each unit could be shown to grade gradually into another unit above it, the necessary conclusion was that the entire column had been formed continuously, and therefore rapidly, Thus, instead of representing slowly-changing forms of life over many ages of time, the geologic column much more likely represents a rapid destruction of the different ecological communities of life all over the world in one specific period of time.

In his presentation, Dr. Roberts did not deal with the above argument. Instead, he stressed that the Biblical record of the flood could not explain the actual phenomena found in the sedimentary rocks. He pointed out that some sedimentary rocks contain fragments of rocks from earlier periods. He especially emphasized the great periods of time required to produce evaporite beds, coral reefs, banded deposits, and deposits of fine-grained sediments. He also stressed that most of the fossils are of marine organisms, whereas the Genesis record indicates that only land animals died in the Flood.

Dr. Roberts summarized by stating that the Biblical record of the Flood had no bearing on the fossil record and the sedimentary rocks. Furthermore, he felt that flood geology was such an embarrassment to him and other Christian scientists that they had to dissociate themselves altogether from creationists who held such views, lest they turn students and other scientists away from Christianity. He also assured the audience that the Biblical record could be interpreted either as a local flood or as a flood of relatively unimportant geological significance.

Since no rebuttals were permitted, Dr. Morris had no opportunity to respond to most of these points. However, Dr. Kraakevik did permit a brief period of questions from the audience. Since all of these questions were directed to Dr. Morris, he did speak to two of the points made by Dr. Roberts. He noted that the violent sub-marine upheavals of the "fountains of the great deep" (Genesis 7:11) necessarily would entomb great numbers of marine organisms. The Bible did not mention these since it was not necessary to preserve representative marine organisms on the Ark. The Bible says that "everything in the dry land died," but said nothing about how many of these land animals were preserved as fossils.

In reply to a question about evaporite beds, especially the Castile formation of New Mexico described by Dr. Roberts, Dr. Morris noted that recent geological studies had shown that large bodies of salt and similar evaporites must have had a juvenile origin (eruption and precipitation from deep-seated sources) rather than by the traditional concept of evaporation from shallow inland seas. Other questions had to do with Biblical chronology, the stability of the Ark and other topics unrelated to the main theme of the debate.

Dr. Morris also met with the Wheaton College Science Division faculty members at two luncheon meetings. At the first of these, most of the discussion centered on the use by Dr. Morris and other creationists of the second law of thermodynamics as an argument against evolution. The Wheaton scientists all felt that this argument was invalid since the earth is an open system. Dr. Morris mentioned, on the other hand, that the argument was sound and compelling, since the evolutionary process did not possess the necessary additional criteria of a self-contained program for directing growth and an energy-conversion system to empower the growth.

At the second luncheon meeting, Dr. Morris assured the faculty that literal creationism and flood geology was *not* a hindrance to Christians, as Dr. Roberts had maintained, but that it was receiving far more attention and winning far more converts on university campuses than the compromising positions of theistic evolution and progressive creation had ever been able to do. He also stressed that, regardless of geological questions, the global cataclysm approach to geological interpretation was required by sound Biblical exegesis. However, in explanation of the apparent Bible teaching that the floodwaters covered the mountains for most of a year, Dr. Claassen suggested that the antediluvian world was inside a large extinct volcanic crater and the mountains which were inundated for a year were actually various mounds of the floor of the crater! Several faculty members said the early chapters of Genesis were not intended to give detailed scientific and historical data but primarily to convey the truth that God was Creator. All of these men, as well as Dr. Roberts, did assure Dr. Morris (many times, in fact) that they were creationists.

Gish, Morris Debate
Leading Scientists in Tennessee

Two of the nation's best-known promoters of evolution were their opponents as I.C.R. scientists, Duane T. Gish and Henry M. Morris, debated the question of evolution versus creation in the largest auditorium on the campus of the University of Tennessee in Knoxville on January 14, 1975. Dr. George Schweitzer and Dr. Arthur Jones had the affirmative side on the resolution: "That evolution is a more satisfactory scientific explanation for the origin and history of life than creation," with Dr. Gish and Dr. Morris on the negative side. An outstanding paid attendance of 2200, over half of whom were students, stayed through the four-hour session, with relatively few leaving before the end of the question periods. In addition to the local students and faculty, delegations attended from four nearby states, as well as numerous other cities in Tennessee.

Dr. Schweitzer is one of the nation's best-known campus lecturers, having spoken on over 400 college and university campuses. As a University of Tennessee Distinguished Professor in Chemistry, he has two earned doctorates (in Chemistry and in Philosophy of Religion). He is a Southern Baptist layman and strong proponent of a form of theistic evolution. He authored one of the chapters (advocating cosmic evolution) in the symposium volume *Evolution and Christian Thought Today*, produced by the ostensibly evangelical American Scientific Affiliation.

Dr. Jones is a long-time Professor of Biology at the University of Tennessee. As a mechanistic-evolutionist, he published a very negative review of the Creation Research Society's high school biology textbook, *Biology: A Search for Order in Complexity* in a recent issue of *American Biology Teacher*. He says he is particularly proud of having been the leader among Tennessee scientists in getting Tennessee's anti-evolution law (made famous by the Scopes Trial) repealed. More recently, he was able to get the 1973 Tennessee law requiring equal time for creationism declared unconstitutional. He is a recent past President of the Tennessee Academy of Science.

Although the topic of the debate had to do with the *scientific* evidence for evolution and creation, Dr. Schweitzer as first affirmative speaker and closing rebuttal speaker, made practically no attempt to present scientific evidence, relying mainly on the argument that, since the majority of both scientists and theologians accepted evolution, it must be true. With considerable eloquence and sarcastic humor he discussed various philosophies of origins, describing believers in special creation as "zappers" and evolutionists as either "oozers" or "jumpers." He describes himself as a combined "oozerjumper." He briefly repudiated the argument against evolution from the entrophy principle by saying that entropy applied only in a closed system and had nothing to do with the question. He also briefly referred to the commonly-known arguments from radiometric dating that the earth is very old. His closing rebuttal speech was entirely devoted to citing passages (out of context) from Dr. Morris' book *The Twilight of Evolution* referring to evolutionary philosophy as the basis for communism, fascism, and other harmful systems. He considered such a position to be not only wrong in its conclusions but divisive and hurtful, making an impassioned plea for tolerance and openmindedness. Although there was no opportunity for Dr. Morris to respond to these statements, which were of course outside the range of the actual question being debated, it is well known that such ideas were not original with him. The first man to claim that communism was based on evolution was Karl Marx, and two of the first to claim an evolutionary basis for fascism and nazism were Benito Mussolini and Adolph Hitler. Whether or not such philosophies are indeed false and harmful, as most Christians and creationists do believe, of course, is apparently an open question among many evolutionists.

Dr. Jones spent most of his time in a low-key defense of the methods of evolutionists in developing their system and in expressing his opinion that the difficulties cited by creationists relative to evolution did not really constitute serious problems. His only positive evidence was a reference to new strains of viruses and bacteria, and mutations of fruit flies. Neither Dr. Jones nor Dr. Schweitzer included any documentation with their talks, with the exception of the latter's references to *Twilight of Evolution*.

As first speaker for the negative, Dr. Morris first posed that, although evolution was commonly taught as scientific fact, it was actually not possible either to prove or disprove, in a scientific sense, either concept of origins and, therefore, the proper approach to the question was a comparative evaluation of the predictive and explanatory capabilities of the two *models* of origins. He then showed that, as predicted by the creation model, the observed changes in the organic world were always "horizontal" rather than "vertical," showing lateral shifting within kinds but never emergence of a new and more complex kind.

He next showed that the second law of thermodynamics was in serious conflict with the evolution model and that the "open system" response of the evolutionists was no answer at all, since a system that grows in complexity must also have an innate information program to direct its growth. In his rebuttal time, he pointed out that the horizontal variations cited by Dr. Jones were not evidence for evolution but were actually predicted by the creation model as a mechanism established by the Creator to enable the organism to adjust (within limits) to changing environments without becoming extinct. He then discussed briefly the subject of geochronometry, showing that uranium dating was subject to tremendously greater errors than claimed by Dr. Schweitzer, often giving billion-year ages for lava rocks known to be only a few centuries old. Furthermore, there were more reliable processes (e.g., the magnetic-field decay calculations developed by Dr. Tom Barnes), which showed the earth to be only several thousand years old.

Dr. Gish presented a slide-illustrated discussion of the fossil record, demonstrating the systematic and regular absence of transitional forms between all the basic kinds of organisms in the fossils, a fact directly predicted from the creation model but posing a serious problem to the evolution model. In his rebuttal period, since the evolutionist speakers had presented no further scientific evidence to rebut, he continued his slide lecture showing the absence of ape-human intermediates and the evidence that man was created as fully-developed man, with no evolutionary ancestors. He also demonstrated, from a probabilistic argument, the impossibility of any specific protein molecule in living systems ever arising by naturalistic processes. All of the arguments presented by both Dr. Gish and Dr. Morris were documented by relevant publications of qualified scientists.

Following the formal debate, which was moderated by Dr. Glenn of the University of Tennessee Speech Department, a number of written questions from the audience were answered in terms of 3-minute responses from each side. Dr. Schweitzer was asked how he would meet the requirement that the evolutionary system have a code and an energy converter in order to enable it to overcome the tendency toward decay implicity in the second law of thermodynamics. He replied by agreeing that there was no naturalistic answer to this problem, but that, as a theistic evolutionist, he believed that God provided continuous direction and energy to evolution to meet this need. To this idea, Dr. Morris replied that God would indeed be necessary to make evolution work, but that He is too wise, powerful and gracious to use such an incredibly inefficient, wasteful and cruel process as evolution as His method by which to produce men and animals.

Dr. Gish was asked why the fossils were found in a certain chronologic framework in the rocks suggesting evolution from simple to complex. He answered that the apparent order was primarily one of ecological zonation rather than evolutionary development and that, also, there were many exceptions to the standard order, mentioning especially the discovery of spores and fragments of woody plants in Cambrian rocks. This statement elicited a cry from the audience charging him with falsehood. After the meeting, the unscheduled speaker, Dr. Robert McLaughlin, Professor of Paleontology, rushed to the stage to challenge him personally. Dr. Gish, however, quickly produced documentation from the authoritative evolutionary literature supporting his statement. Dr. McLaughlin then challenged the validity of the latter, accusing Dr. Gish of ignorance and deception, also questioning several of his other points relative to the fossils. Dr. Gish, however, produced authoritative documentation for each point challenged. Dr. McLaughlin never apologized, but finally desisted making further charges.

Dr. Morris was asked a question about radiocarbon dating, and he was able to show briefly that the non-equilibrium model of radiocarbon development supported a very recent origin of the earth's atmosphere.

Many people attending the debate expressed surprise that it was the creationists who used scientific arguments and evidence and the evolutionists who repeatedly used religious and philosophical arguments, as well as unsupported generalities. The debate was co-sponsored by the New Life organization of Knoxville and by the University's Issues Program.

Texas Tech Debate
Draws Record Crowd

What is believed to be the largest attendance yet at a creation-evolution debate almost filled Lubbock's municipal auditorium on the campus of the Texas Technological University (Texas Tech to football fans) on February 9, 1975. Approximately 2700 people — the large majority being Tech students — listened for over three hours as two Tech professors, Dr. Rae Harris and Dr. Robert Baker, debated Dr. Henry Morris and Dr. Duane Gish of I.C.R. Dr. Harris is a Professor of Earth Sciences and Dr. Baker, who teaches the Tech course on human evolution, a Professor of Biology.

As usual, the creationist debaters stressed the second law of thermodynamics and the systematic gaps in the fossil record as explicit predictions of the creation model and as serious difficulties to the evolution model, the one showing evolution is impossible at present and the other that evolution has not occurred in the past. It was obvious that there is no answer to this evidence except a statement of faith that there probably is an answer, since the earth is an open system and since certain indeterminate factors may have prevented discovery of the missing transitional fossils.

Dr. Harris devoted his time to listing a number of geological evidences which (on uniformitarian assumptions) indicate the earth to be very old. This was not the topic of the debate, of course, and both Dr. Gish and Dr. Morris pointed out that evolution was impossible regardless of the age of the earth. Dr. Baker's main argument was that certain "homologies" in structure and embryologic development, as well as observed changes in living organisms, argued in favor of evolution. In rebuttal, it was pointed out that such similarities have been exaggerated and actually indicate design according to a common plan and that the observed changes in organisms were very trivial compared to the unbridgeable gaps between the basic kinds, actually representing the Creator's genetic provision for adapation to changing environments.

The debate was sponsored by the Baptist Student Union on the Tech campus and by the University Ministry of Lubbock's First Baptist Church. Rev. Barry Wood is the Church's University Pastor, and was in charge of arrangements. The debate had been officially approved by the administration of Texas Technological University.

The First Baptist Church of Lubbock provided over-all direction and financing for the project. This is an outstanding church of over 5700 resident and active members, and is considered to be the second largest church in the Southern Baptist Convention. Dr. Jaroy Weber, pastor of the church, is also current President of the Southern Baptist Convention.

In addition to the debate, the First Baptist Church sponsored a Creation Seminar on Saturday, February 8, with 300 attending. On Sunday morning, Dr. Morris spoke in all three morning services of the church, to a total of over 3300. One of these services was the university "church-within-a-church," with nearly 1000 university students present. Dr. Gish spoke to two morning services and a combined Sunday school class at the Highland Baptist Church of Lubbock. For the evening services, Dr. Gish spoke at the Lubbock Bible Church, where Charles Clough is pastor, and Dr. Morris spoke again at First Baptist.

A significant impact was made on the Lubbock area for creationism. The debate was also broadcast on FM radio and a videotape was made for future televising. Extensive newspaper coverage was given.

DEBATES GENERATE VIGOROUS RESPONSE*

The creation-evolution debates on the University of Tennessee campus on January 14 (*Acts and Facts*, February 1975) and on the campus of Texas Tech on February 9 (*Acts and Facts*, March 1975), not only generated considerable excitement on these campuses, but also inspired a series of totally unsupportable and false charges against Dr. Morris and Dr. Gish, particularly Dr. Gish, by their opponents and other faculty members on these campuses. The creationists have been accused of misquoting sources, quoting out of context, distorting evidence, mislabeling slides, and other questionable tactics. Dr. Morris and Dr.

* Impact Series #24, (May 1975)

24

Gish, on the other hand, have always assumed that their opponents were men of integrity and sincerity. ICR scientists have never publicly accused their opponents of dishonesty or of deliberately distorting evidence. Perhaps these attacks on the creationists have been inspired by the poor showing the evolutionists have made in these debates.

To give our readers an insight into the impression these debates have left on some of those present and to acquaint our readers with the nature of the charges against the ICR scientists, as well as their defense, we are publishing in this issue some newspaper stories about the debates on the University of Tennessee and Texas Tech campuses, as well as a series of letters published in the Knoxville Courier-Times and in the campus paper of Texas Tech. Publication of these letters and articles in their entirety will not only give our readers a full report, but also will protect ICR from further charges of quoting out of context. Other articles and letters may have been published concerning these debates, but these are the only ones which have become available to ICR.

The debate at the University of Tennessee was between Drs. Morris and Gish and evolutionists Drs. George Schweitzer and Arthur Jones, both members of the UT faculty. Neither Schweitzer nor Jones made any accusations against the ICR scientists, but Dr. R.E. McLaughlin, UT Professor and paleobotanist, apparently enraged by the debate, made a series of charges against Dr. Gish on the evening of the debate and later in a letter to the editor of the Knoxville Courier-Times. The following include the newspaper articles and the exchange of letters inspired by this debate.

Zappers Outshine Oozers in the U.T. Debate

By Lois Thomas, Staff Writer
The Knoxville News-Sentinel,
Knoxville, Tennessee   January 15, 1975

The oozers debated the zappers at UT Tuesday night, and although no winners were officially acclaimed, it was quite obvious the large audience was very heavily pro-zapper.

"Zapper" was the name used by Dr. George K. Schweitzer, UT chemistry professor and a debater, to describe those who believe the creation theory of life.

"They just say 'Zap!' It all was created, just like that," he explained.

Back Evolution

The zappers in the debate entitled "The Textbook Controversy — evolution or Religion?" were Dr. Henry Morris and Dr. Duane Gish, director and associate director, respectively, of the Institute for Creation Research in California. They debated against the hypothesis that had been set for discussion: "Evolution is a more satisfactory scientific explanation of life than is creation."

Dr. Schweitzer and Dr. Arthur Jones, UT zoology professor and former president of the Tennessee Academy of Science, were oozers, or at least they debated for the evolutional theory.

Dr. Schweitzer said, actually, he is more of an oozer-jumper. "Jumpers," he described are those who believed things came about through little spurts, or jumps, rather than oozing or zapping.

Emphasizes View

He described another category (and there are still others that could have been mentioned, he said) as "five-second-agoers."

"There are people who say that everything came about five seconds ago," he explained.

Dr. Schweitzer used his terms to emphasize his view that there are many ways to look at the way the world came about, and that persons should not shut their minds to any views.

It was quite obvious that many in the almost full Alumni Gym did not share his views. They very obviously believed the creation theory and showed it with cheers, applause, and some hoots and hissing at times appropriate to them.

Cites Evidence

Dr. Gish was well received for his presentation based generally on discrediting scientist's theories or findings regarding fossils. He said there has not been a single instance of a fossil that is a transition form between major species. He said this proves that each species was created separately. He also cited some evidences of scientific errors in theories regarding early mankind. However, he said students received these theories as truths in textbooks.

He received considerable applause for his view that "creation is unbelievable to an atheist. But it is believable for those who believe in God."

Dr. Morris maintained that the creation theory does not receive fair treatment in today's educational institutions. He said evolution is taught almost exclusively.

"We want to have a hearing granted equally for creation," he said.

Doesn't Mean Rejection

Dr. Jones joined Dr. Schweitzer in arguing that scientific research to date shows that more than likely man evolved from a lower form. They both admitted there are errors in science, but urged that an open mind be maintained.

Dr. Schweitzer maintained that believing in evolution does not mean rejection of God.

"We must not base our religion on whether a scientific theory is true or not," he said, urging that the difference be realized between mechanism and meaning. "Regardless of which theory you hold, you are still free to interpret it to fit your religion," he said.

The debate was sponsored by the UT ISSUES lecture committee.

Evolution Debate No Debate At All

By J.G. Williams, Minister and
Larry Barnickle, MTSU Graduate Student
Rutherford Courier, Tennessee
January 30, 1975

On the evening of January 14th the campus of the University of Tennessee at Knoxville was the occasion of a momentous event. On that night, for almost four hours, four scientists debated the theory of organic evolution. To our

27

knowledge this is the first time in the history of Tennessee that evolution has been publicly debated between scientists.

The Alumni Gymnasium was crowded with over 2,500 people, the large majority of whom were U.T. students.

Dr. Arthur Jones and Dr. George Schweitzer of the University of Tennessee defended the theory of evolution, while Dr. Duane Gish and Dr. Henry Morris of the Institute of Creation Research, San Diego, California, defended the creation viewpoint.

We, along with two other men, attended the debate anticipating a thorough discussion of the scientific evidences; however, we were sadly mistaken. During over 1½ hours of discourse between them the two U.T. professors failed to present one single argument favoring the evolution theory. Mind you, they introduced not one affirmative argument which defended evolution! It was thoroughly disappointing! One would expect, as we did, that men with Ph.D. degrees and supposed specialists in their fields, could give at least some defense of the theory.

However, their speeches abounded with broad generalizations completely evading the real issue. They constantly strayed into philosophical and religious areas, when the debate was supposed to be centered around scientific information. In fact, they made fun of conservative Biblical interpretation and tried to cast reflection on anyone not believing in evolution. Yet, the whole time they offered no scientific material to support their opinionated speeches. They repeatedly said they believed evolution to be a better explanation of life than creation, but were utterly destitute of reasons they felt this way!

Dr. Schweitzer's part of the debate was spotted with funny stories and "cute" sayings, all of which were calculated to cloud the evidences presented by his opponents. He also made an emotional plea to the effect that evolutionists were being persecuted for their views much like Galileo and others were persecuted for saying the earth was round and revolved about the sun, all of which was completely off the subject.

28

Both evolutionists implied that only specialists had the right to voice opinions on evolution and that all others should simply "trust" their judgment — which concept leaves a lot to be desired!

And not only did the two U.T. professors fail to present affirmative arguments defending evolution, but they failed to respond to the arguments offered by their opponents, a fact evident to all present! It was clear to us that their knowledge of evolution was lacking or else they had failed to do their "homework!"

On the other side Drs. Gish and Morris, both widely recognized in their respective fields, did a masterful job in dealing with the scientific material. They presented argument after argument refuting the theory of evolution.

Among other things Dr. Morris pointed to the 2nd law of thermodynamics, explaining how the essential nature of evolution contradicts this law. Dr. Gish gave an in-depth discussion of the fossil record showing first that complex fossils appear abruptly at the Cambrian period denying the evolution time table, and second that there are absolutely no intermediate fossils linking the major groups of animals or plants. In responding to this Dr. Jones admitted that we have "not very much hope" of filling these gaps.

Dr. Gish made a comparison of the geological evidence with "models" of both the evolution and creation views. He candidly, showed that while the creation "model" paralleled the evidence, the evolution "model" stood in direct opposition to it!

Drs. Morris and Gish were very informative and appealed to the intelligence of the audience. As for the evolutionists, the same cannot be said. About all we learned from their remarks was how to avoid the issue! We felt that after having driven almost 200 miles, we deserved to hear something constructive on their part! Instead, their showmanship was an insult to one's intelligence. We felt we had been cheated! And to think — these are supposed to be leaders in their fields; men of science and open to serious investigation!

The debate (if it could truly be called a debate) was a one-sided affair. The creationists won hands down.

Creation vs. Evolution

By Demas Brubacher
Bible Baptist Reminder,
Clarksville, Tennessee
February, 1975

On January 14 four of the faculty members of Clarksville Baptist College had the privilege to attend a debate with its issue: "RESOLVED THAT EVOLUTION IS A MORE SATISFACTORY SCIENTIFIC EXPLANATION OF THE ORIGIN AND HISTORY OF LIFE THAN IS CREATION."

A crowd of 2,200 crowded into the Alumni Gym on the campus of the University of Tennessee, Knoxville. Over half were UT students. On the side of evolution were Drs. Schweitzer and Jones of the University while on the side of creation were Drs. Morris and Gish of the Institute of Creation Research, San Diego, California. All four men are highly recognized scientists and specialists in their fields.

It was exciting to see the creationists beat the evolutionists on their own territory without using one single Bible verse. This irritated the evolutionists and in the final rebuttal, Dr. Schweitzer played foul and violated the rules of the debate by accusing them of believing creationism only because of their religious convictions. Even the audience resented this tactic.

The irritation was further observed at the end of the debate when the voice of one of the scientists from the paleontology department was heard on the floor angrily calling out to Dr. Gish that he was "falsely misrepresenting the facts." He then challenged Dr. Gish for the written proof concerning the finding of a new problem for the evolutionists, namely, a highly complex fish fossilized with simple-celled animals. Dr. Gish calmly showed the written evidence for all to see but the hot-headed professor cried it was a forgery!

It was shocking to see the unscientific attitude of the evolutionists towards the problems of "gaps" and fossil frustrations. Their answer time and time again was that they didn't "worry" about them. Never was a serious attempt made to answer any charge that evolution was unscientific.

For the serious seeker in the crowd I must say he was exposed to more truth concerning creation than about the teachings of the theory of evolution. No doubt many went away wondering about the so-called facts they have been fed on evolution.

U.T. Geology Professor Ridicules Participant in Creation-Evolution Debate

Letter to the Editor
from R.E. McLaughlin
The News-Sentinel
January 26, 1975

These comments have been prompted by the review by Lois Thomas of the debate on evolution and creation theory held at UT on Tuesday night, Jan. 14. This writer is particularly concerned by the front page exposure in The News-Sentinel the following day given especially to the performance of Dr. Duane Gish from the Institute for Creation Research in California.

Even the most casual observer would have detected that the majority of the audience was an organized body selected by design to respond favorably to the presentation of Dr. Gish. The cheers, whistles, applause and other demonstrations of approval were registered at appropriate points as if rehearsed. Indeed, at least one member of the audience was observed to have memorized in advance parts of Dr. Gish's presumed extemporaneous remarks.

It is unfortunate that your reporter chose to judge the merits of the points made during the debate on the basis of audience response. Reporter Thomas apparently missed all of the irrelevant but crowd-pleasing asides and innuendoes interjected by Dr. Gish as part of his stagecraft. It is to be hoped that she does not share his view concerning the relationship between the length of a scientist's hair and his scientific credibility, to cite one example. She also failed to note that the loudest cheers and boos were for the Tennessee and Alabama football teams, respectively, when mentioned by that debater.

This writer's own characterization of most of the debate audience is that of a fundamentalist pep rally with Drs. Gish and Morris serving as cheerleaders. It was within such an atmosphere that Drs. George Schweitzer and Arthur Jones were asked to participate. This writer was embarrassed for them and for the University of Tennessee as the site of the event.

Quite properly, both Dr. Schweitzer and Dr. Jones directed their major efforts toward the more serious affront to both scientific and societal order represented by the expressed views and published writings of the Morris-Gish team. The peregrinations of these self-appointed experts have left a wake of discord and bitterness from coast to coast.

Very little space was given by your reporter to Dr. Jones' reply to some of Dr. Gish's alleged "evidence" used by him to discredit (your reporter's term) the fossil record of gradual and long-term evolution of life on earth. Dr. Gish repeated many times over the allegation that no transitional forms had ever been found. He then proceeded to illustrate with a lantern slide one of the best examples of such a form in the fossil record. This discrepancy was missed, ignored, or misunderstood by the majority of the audience and your reporter.

Another lantern slide alleged to show the sudden emergence of multicellular life in the Cambrian Period actually was a scene from the Silurian Period some 120 million years later. Again, this was missed by most of the audience. It was readily apparent from his remarks that Dr. Gish has little familiarity with the recent scientific literature on the subject wherein logical and documented explanations for gaps and bursts in the fossil record abound.

Dr. Gish glibly drops the names of eminent paleontologists whose writings he suggests support his point of view. On closer examination it can be shown that these references are variously out of date, out of context, misquoted, misunderstood or deliberately falsified. This writer intends to alert those paleontologists in the group cited by Dr. Gish, who are respected colleagues and personal acquaintances, to the use of their names in this manner. It can be anticipated that their reactions will be explosive.

It is clear to anyone knowledgeable in such matters that Dr. Gish's expertise in regard to the fossil record, evolutionary theory, or the operation of the evolutionary process is minimal. The most serious gaps in the fossil record constantly alluded to by this speaker were information or comprehension gaps in his own knowledge of the subject.

Only the large contrived portion of the audience at the Alumni Gym would have given him the enthusiastic reception noted by your reporter. Dr. Gish won no debate on the merits of his case. The organizers and directors of the debate chose to exclude any challenge to the examples of so-called fossil evidence presented by Dr. Gish in true demagogic style. Questions from the audience sent to Dr. Gish concerning his examples were either destroyed before they reached him or were ignored.

It should be pointed out that Dr. Gish's writings have been thoroughly discredited by the scientific community where he has no standing whatsoever, either by training or research, in the field of paleontology — the study of the fossil record on which he poses as an expert. An invitation (about which he boasts) to address an audience of geologists, including paleontologists, was a lampoon-type social affair in Washington and Dr. Gish's role was that of an invited clown.

Your readers should know also that, by accident or design, attempts to arrange a discussion of his views with knowledgeable students of paleontology and other geological subjects at UT were thwarted during the day of the debate. One can only conclude that it was feared that exposure to the lamp of knowledge might have some destructive effect upon the "evidence" which Dr. Gish disseminates unchallenged elsewhere.

Debate Critic Must Not Know Rules of Debate, Moderator Charges

Letter to the Editor
from Robert W. Glenn,
Dept. of Speech and Theatre
at the University of Tennessee
The News-Sentinel

Arthur Koestler says in his study of Dr. Paul Kammerer, the Austrian experimental biologist, that "In the heat of a controversy . . . scientists are apt to behave as if they were wearing blinkers, just as ordinary mortals." Kammerer was a Lamarckian, and was pursued to his suicide by William Bateson and other Neo-Darwinists who denied that acquired characteristics could be inherited. As the letter of a contemporary Neo-Darwinist, Professor R.E. McLaughlin (News-Sentinel, Jan. 26) shows, the subject of the development of life still produces heated controversy and limited vision.

My first impulse on reading Dr. McLaughlin's letter was to answer ironically, confirming his impression of a conspiracy that involved the UT Issues committee, the Usher Corps, New Life, several hundred members of the audience, the debate's moderator and at least two of the four debaters, and that controlled both audience responses and the treatment of issues and evidence during the debate. The notion of an evening that was thoroughly planned and coordinated would amuse Drs. Jones and Schweitzer and the students who organized the debate, but a more direct sort of education is needed here. For I am convinced that Professor McLaughlin does not know what he was listening to.

The Jan. 14 Issues presentation at UT was advertised as "A Formal Debate," that is, as a clash of evidence and arguments bearing upon a set topic, conducted by trained advocates within an agreed format. The theory in debate as in the law court is that through the combat of adversaries the truth will prevail. Dr. McLaughlin fails, in several respects, to comprehend this principle.

First, Dr. McLaughlin is distressed that a discrepancy in Dr. Gish's account of the fossil record "was missed, ignored or misunderstood by the majority of the audience and your reporter," and that the misdating of some slides "was missed by most of the audience." But it was the duty of the affirmative advocates, Drs. Schweitzer and Jones, to alert the audience to any discrepancies or inaccuracies in the negative presentations.

Second, Dr. McLaughlin commends the affirmative debaters for directing "their major efforts toward the more serious affront to both scientific and societal order represented by the expressed views and published writings of the Morris-Gish team." But is the commendation deserved? The agreed topic for the debate was whether evolution or creation provides the better scientific explanation of the origin and development of life. Even if Dr. McLaughlin is correct, and the negative debaters drew unwarranted conclusions from misrepresented evidence, it must be conceded that Drs. Morris and Gish did generally confine their remarks to the scientific evidence.

Third, Dr. McLaughlin reports that one listener "was observed" by someone "to have memorized in advance parts of Dr. Gish's presumed extemporaneous remarks." The implication is that the audience did not witness a spontaneous debate but a totally rehearsed performance. It is unthinkable, of course, that Drs. Jones and Schweitzer would be parties to such an arrangement, but more to the point Dr. McLaughlin misunderstands the nature of a debate. Each side was given 50 minutes of speaking time for prepared speeches and 20 minutes for replies to their opponents. The former were ex plicitly identified as "constructive" speeches, the latter as "rebuttal" speeches. All four of the constructive speeches were thoroughly prepared in advance; all four of the rebuttal speeches were spontaneous, extemporaneous, directed to issues raised by the constructive presentations.

Fourth, Dr. McLaughlin writes of "the large contrived portion of the audience," of "the majority of the audience" being "an organized body selected by design to respond favorably to the presentaton of Dr. Gish." To be sure, the audience was one-sided; Dr. Schweitzer said at the outset that he felt like a lion in a den of Daniels. But do we need a conspiracy to explain the fact? Must we invent contrivers, organizers, selectors, designers? Or can we not proceed, after the manner of science, to seek the most economical explanation? Is it not more likely that the debate topic was more salient for a special creationist listener, who would initially agree with Drs. Morris and Gish, than for an evolutionist listener, who would initially agree with Drs. Jones, Schweitzer, and McLaughlin, and that therefore more of the former chose to attend?

And fifth, Dr. McLaughlin impugns the motives of the "organizers and directors of the debate," who "chose to exclude any challenge to the examples of so-called fossil evidence presented by Dr. Gish in true demagogic style. Questions from the audience sent to Dr. Gish concerning his examples were either destroyed before they reached him or were ignored." As the moderator of the debate, I must take exception to each charge. No question was ignored; each card on which a question was written was read by me and by one of two students who assisted me. No card was destroyed; all were saved until the end of the debate for the four participants to examine. Obviously not all questions could be asked; of about 250 questions received, there was time to put only eight to the debaters. But of these eight at least two involved the very question that Dr. McLaughlin asserts we conspired to suppress, viz., the validity of Dr. Gish's account of the fossil record.

To write, as Dr. McLaughlin does, of an audience that is "contrived," "organized," "selected by design," of a debate being managed "in true demagogic style" because Dr. McLaughlin did not hear his question asked, of Drs. Morris and Gish being "cheerleaders," "self-appointed experts," of Dr. Gish being "an invited clown" — this is the language of passion, not of reason, of paranoia, not of understanding. If embarrassment is in order for Drs. Jones and Schweitzer and for the University of Tennessee, its cause must be the tone of something other than the Jan. 14 debate.

Dr. Gish Answers Charges by U.T. Professor Regarding Evolution-Creation Debate

Letter to the Editor
from Duane T. Gish,
Associate Director,
Institute for Creation Research
The News-Sentinel
March 4, 1975

Recently my attention has been called to the letter by Dr. R.E. McLaughlin of the University of Tennessee Department of Geological Sciences published in The News-Sentinel on Jan. 26. This was in reference to the debate at UT on Jan. 14 in which Dr. Henry Morris and I debated as creationists against Dr. George Schweitzer and Dr. Arthur Jones as evolutionists. Dr. Robert Glenn of the UT Department of Speech and Theatre, the moderator, in his letter published in The News-Sentinel, has already answered many of the intemperate charges by Dr. McLaughlin. I wish to address myself to errors in facts contained in Dr. McLaughlin's letter.

McLaughlin claimed that a slide I used to illustrate the nature of living things found in the so-called Cambrian Period (and thus the kind of very complex creatures that suddenly appear in the fossil record for which no evolutionary ancestors can be found) was actually a slide showing a scene from the Silurian Period, which is supposed to be 120 million years later. It is regrettable that a professor charged with teaching students at UT does not have a better knowledge of the fossil record than he displays. The slide I showed was from The American Museum of Natural History, New York City, and was their slide No. K-10273 (of their Earth History set) entitled Cambrian Diorama.

McLaughlin stated that he hoped your reporter did not share my view concerning "the relationship between the length of a scientist's hair and his scientific credibility." The only time I mentioned the length of hair was in reference to Neanderthal Man and the fact that he would not have to be given a haircut to conform to today's hair styles.

37

During the debate I mentioned that spores and fragments of vascular (woody) plants have been found in the Cambrian. McLaughlin shouted out from the audience, "That's a lie!" and after the debate he came upon the platform and demanded that I document that fact (he did apologize for his intemperate outburst). I immediately did so by referring him to articles by S. Leclerq ("Evidence of Vascular Plants in the Cambrian," "Evolution," Vol. 10, p. 109, June 1956) and by Daniel Axelrod ("Evolution of the Psilophyte Paleoflora," "Evolution," Vol. 13, p. 264, June, 1959). He was silent concerning Axelrod's article, but charged that Leclercq's article contained mistranslations of Russian to French to English, and this is the statement he is circulating at UT.

My statements were not based on a mistranslation, but can be abundantly documented. The significance of this evidence is that it is now known that complex plants existed in the Cambrian Period which, on the evolutionary time-scale, is 200 million years or so before even simple land plants are supposed to have evolved! The latter theory is apparently what McLaughlin still believes and is teaching his students, even though evidence invalidating it was published by other evolutionists 15 years ago.

The case for creation that Dr. Morris and I presented was based strictly on carefully documented scientific evidence. We neither misquoted, quoted out of context or distorted the facts in any way. The fact that we always quote facts published in articles by evolutionists to support the case for creation and to point out contradictions to evolution theory infuriates McLaughlin. But the fact that creationists can use articles published by evolutionists to establish the nature of the real factual evidence strengthens their case immensely. Creationists do not differ with evolutionists on the nature of the facts, but do differ as to the interpretation to be placed on those facts. As we creationists have repeatedly pointed out, evolutionists must attempt to somehow explain away the contradictions between predictions based on evolution theory and what we actually find in the fossil record. On the other hand, this evidence does not have to be explained by creationists, for it is remarkably in accord with predictions based on creation.

McLaughlin charges that attempts to arrange a discussion during the day of the debate of my views with knowledgeable students of paleontology and other geological subjects at UT were thwarted. McLaughlin charges that responsibility for this rests with creationists and was due to our fear of having our case exposed to the "lamp of knowledge." As a matter of fact, the UT students who attempted to arrange a meeting for us at UT on the day of the debate reported that McLaughlin refused to allow such a meeting to be held anywhere near the Department of Geological Sciences. These students felt that this was an attempt to suppress the meetings and discourage attendance by those students who needed to be reached. These students, on their own, then decided that nothing further could be accomplished by attempting to arrange such a meeting. The onus for the failure to arrange this meeting rests on McLaughlin, not the creationists.

The rational, scientific, well-documented case presented by Dr. Morris and myself during the debate which so powerfully strengthens the case for creation while exposing fatal weaknesses in evolution theory apparently left McLaughlin in a rage. The laws of thermodynamics, the laws of probability, the operation of natural processes and the facts of the fossil record all attest to the fact that not only did evolution not occur but that it could not have occurred. This highly ordered universe and the incredibly complex living things found on planet Earth demanded a Creator.

NOTE: In order to abbreviate Dr. Gish's letter, the reply by Dr. Gish concerning McLaughlin's allegation that Morris and Gish were merely invited as clowns by the Pick and Hammer Club of the U.S. Geological Survey Office of Menlo Park was deleted. This portion read as follows:

McLaughlin stated that I boasted about an address before a group of geologists, which he charged was actually a "lampoon-type social affair in Washington and Dr. Gish's role was that of an invited clown." As a matter of fact I do not boast of an address before an audience of any kind. In our conversation after the debate, McLaughlin asked me if Dr. Morris and I had ever spoken before a group of professional geologists, and it was only then that I mentioned that we had jointly addressed a regular meeting of the Pick and Hammer Club of the U.S. Geological Survey Office at Menlo Park, California (not Washington, D.C., as McLaughlin reports). McLaughlin then, with absolutely no knowledge whatsoever of the facts, interjected his "lampoon" and "clown" theory.

Since neither Dr. Morris nor I have a direct pipeline to the brain of Dr. Tor H. Nilsen, the U.S.G.S. geologist who invited us (as McLaughlin apparently has), we cannot know his motivation for inviting us. We do know that no one was smiling as we addressed this group of professional geologists and no one was joking or smiling during the discussion period that followed. To give the final lie to McLaughlin's allegation, Dr. Nilsen has recently sponsored Dr. Morris' membership in the Geological Society of America (Dr. Morris also holds membership in numerous other professional societies). Perhaps McLaughlin would like to charge that membership in the Geological Society of America is reserved for clowns!

He Challenges Professor to Face Dr. Gish in Evolution-Creation Debate

Letter to the Editor from John Waddey
The News-Sentinel
February 3, 1975

Last Sunday Dr. R.E. McLaughlin of UT wrote a lengthy tirade ridiculing Dr. Duane Gish and his part in the recent debate on Creation and Evolution. As one who attended the debate, I would like to make some observations on the learned scientist's very unscientific letter.

1. Does Dr. McLaughlin feel that his respected colleagues of the university did not do an adequate job of championing the evolutionary dogma? He tries hard in his letter to do what they seemed helpless to do. If they were as successful as he implies, there should have been no doubt as to their overwhelming victory.

2. Would the doctor have written so hotly if The News-Sentinel's front page story had, in a similar vein, declared the team of Schweitzer and Jones winners?

3. In paragraph two, he asserts without proof or evidence that " . . . the majority of the audience was an organized body selected by design to respond favorably to the presentation of Dr. Gish." Being present, I saw no evidence of this. The debate was held on campus, in a public building, was sponsored by a campus group, and was widely advertised and well attended. I challenge his assertion and call for proof.

4. I did not feel that reporter Thomas based her remarks about the debate on mere audience response. Remember, Doctor, that she gave most all of Dr. Schweitzer's first speech, namely his "Zap, ooze and Chitty Bang Bang analysis of origins." Also Dr. McLaughlin asserts that Dr. Gish offered mainly, "crowd-pleasing asides and innuendoes . . . as stagecraft." Would he be so kind as to give us another letter listing these?

5. The doctor accuses Gish of judging a scientist's credibility by the length of his hair. Sorry again, but Dr. Gish said that the only difference between Neanderthal man and modern man was the dirt on his face and the length of his hair. It was Dr. Schweitzer who made the joke about his own long hair.

6. Dr. McLaughlin was embarrassed for Drs. Schweitzer and Jones and for UT. I do not blame him for this. In fact if those two scientists with their multiple doctoral degrees are the best UT has to represent the case of evolution, then either the university or the theory is in serious trouble.

7. It was interesting to note that Dr. Schweitzer, who had both the first and last speeches in the debate, broke one of the basic rules of public controversy by introducing a host of new

41

material in his last speech, knowing full-well that his opponents would have no chance to reply.

8. In his fifth paragraph he accuses the creation scientists (who by the way hold earned doctorates from the University of Minnesota and the University of California at Berkeley) of leaving a wake of discord across the land. Both of those scientists showed a fine, pleasant attitude. It is Dr. McLaughlin who is bitter and is sowing discord by his caustic letter!

9. Would our writer do us a favor and bring forth the "documentary evidence" either from the fossil record or in present day life of the transitional forms that bridge the evolutionary gaps? Your fellow scientists from UT both agreed that the gaps were there and the transitional forms were missing.

10. Again he accuses Drs. Gish and Morris of misquoting, falsifying and taking out of context the statements of evolutionary scientists that admit the flaws and failures of their theory of origins. If one will review the tape recordings of the debate, it will be most obvious just who has misquoted, falsified and taken out of context.

11. It is regretted that the professor even accuses the organizers and directors of the debate and the moderator of "excluding any challenge" to the creation contentions. But the height of his folly was daring to suggest that questions directed to Dr. Gish were "either destroyed or ignored." Strangely my question to Dr. Schweitzer was not answered either. However, I do not accuse him of dishonesty or cowardice because the moderator did not read my question out of the hundreds received.

12. He labels Dr. Gish as a "clown," rather than a competent scientist. Are Berkeley PhD's of no value these days? Really, sir, the clown of the night was the distinguished Dr. George Schweitzer with his "Chitty Chitty Bang Bang" song and dance and his vaudeville show in his first speech. Do you not remember all those jokes and the audience laughter in his speech?

13. Dr. McLaughlin closes his letter by suggesting "That by accident or design" Dr. Gish refused to discuss the subject of

evolution "with knowledgeable students of paleontology . . ." on the day of the debate, thus he surmises that Gish must be afraid that the lamp of knowledge "might prove destructive to his position." Sir: He confronted two notable scientists, professors and authors of your institution; were these two not able to give an adequate apology for your view? Could you have done better?

I believe that Dr. Gish could be prevailed upon to return to Knoxville to meet Dr. McLaughlin in a debate on the merits of evolution if the respected geology professor will agree to represent his side of the question. After your powerful letter, we would expect your ready acceptance of an opportunity to refute Dr. Gish face to face and to chasten all of those who hold the creation point of view. I personally will contact Dr. Gish for you.

The readership may want to hear the debate for themselves. A copy is on file in the Undergraduate Library. They may secure copies of the tapes from Robert Glenn of UT. His phone is 974-4186.

Professor Rejected 'Lamp of Knowledge' Ten Years Ago, He Says

Letter to the Editor from M.H. Tucker
The News-Sentinel
February 2, 1975

I attended the recent debate on evolution and creation at UT. I also read Lois Thomas' review. Furthermore, I read Dr. McLaughlin's letter of criticism of the review. I offer the following observations on his letter.

First, I did not find the review slanted as suggested by Professor McLaughlin. In fact, I detected a studied effort on her part to remain neutral in her reporting.

Second, though I was among the majority which favored the creationists' view, I was not aware of "an organized body selected by design to respond favorably" to Dr. Gish. I assumed the audience was made up of those who, like myself, had an interest in this subject and had read announcements on the debate. Unless the professor has proof of an audience "selected by design," it seems out of keeping with the high standards of UT for one to make such a charge. Science is not the only field where facts and proof are desirable.

My third observation is that Dr. McLaughlin was not pleased with Drs. Jones and Schweitzer's defense of evolution. I also noted their weak defense. Perhaps one weakness was revealed when Dr. Jones said, "We are following a game plan." Being restricted to their game plan, they could not be expected to respond to their opponents with any force. Perhaps Dr. McLaughlin could have succeeded where his colleagues failed. Perhaps arrangements can be made for him to demonstrate his expertise in paleontology. I am sure the professor has not forgotten his encounter with a creationist by the name of Basil Overton in 1965 at Tyson Jr. High to arrange a discussion with his "knowledgeable students of paleontology." This offer was made to him in a conversation on the parking lot of Tyson Junior High in my presence. He said, "No!" To use Dr. McLaughlin's words, "One can only conclude that it was feared that exposure to the lamp of knowledge might have some destructive effect upon" the evolutionary evidence which Dr. McLaughlin disseminates from his classroom.

Finally, Tennessee taxpayers should raise their voices against the practice of using their tax dollars to pay salaries and buy textbooks which present the view of evolution but refuse to present to the student the view of creation. Yet, Dr. Jones stated during the debate evolutionists "make no effort to withhold information."

Charges Fly After Texas Tech Debate

On the afternoon of February 9, 1975, on the campus of Texas Tech, Lubbock, Texas, Drs. Morris and Gish debated Drs. Rae L. Harris and R.J. Baker, evolutionists and members of the faculty. The debate was witnessed by almost 2,700 in an audience composed mainly of students.

During the debate Dr. Gish called attention to the fact that fossil cuttlefish had been discovered in so-called Early Cambrian strata. Cuttlefish are highly complex invertebrate predators which, previous to this, had been reported from strata no earlier than Jurassic, which, according to evolutionary geologists, are 400 million years younger than Early Cambrian strata. Dr. Gish pointed out that this find had added another highly complex animal to the already diverse and complex Cambrian fauna for which no ancestors can be found. He also suggested that since no fossils of cuttlefish had as yet been found in strata allegedly laid down between the Cambrian and the Jurassic, perhaps there was no real time span between these two geological "periods," but that the difference between the fossil record of each could be attributed to differences in ecological zonation and other effects of the Flood.

Although the scientific article and the numerous newspaper articles describing this important find had been published in November, 1974, Dr. Harris, although a geologist, was unaware of this report. This apparently was as embarrassing to Dr. Harris personally as the facts were embarrassing to the case for evolution. Dr. Harris tried to detract from the importance of the find and to conceal the damage to evolution theory by publishing a series of false charges against Dr. Gish in local newspapers. The articles by Dr. Harris and Dr. Gish's published defense are presented here in their entirety.

Debater Cites Wrong Fact

Letter to the Editor
from Rae L. Harris, Jr.,
Prof. of Geoscience,
Texas Tech University
The University Daily, Lubbock Texas
February 12, 1975

I was extremely disappointed to learn upon reading the article in the Journal of Paleontology referred to by Dr. Gish during the debate, that a man in his position connected with theology and "science," would misquote by error or design the report and conclusions of another so that an apparent "win" might be achieved in a scholarly debate.

During his presentation, Dr. Gish made the statement that a recent investigator had found "fossil cuttlefish" in the Cambrian rocks. Dr. Gish then expounded along the line that because fossil cuttlefish had only previously been known from Jurassic and younger rocks, this find was proof that the geological fossil record was in error. The argument being, if cuttlefish lived in Cambrian time, and no fossils of this animal were found in intervening rocks nor had been assigned to the geological time units between Cambrian and Jurassic (nearly 300 million years), geologists were ignoring the record and had falsely and capriciously built up an incorrect order in the record of life to support the theory of Evolution.

I now find, having had to check the cited reference because I do not carry such journals with me, that the article cited does not report the data claimed by Dr. Gish, and the article's conclusions are not the conclusions attributed to it by Dr. Gish. The authors of the paper conclude "If correctly assigned to the Class, this find extends the range of the Cephalopoda from the Late into very Early Cambrian." To outline what his paper reports, it will be necessary to break down the groupings of the Mollusca type animals into their paleontological classifications Phylum-Mollusca, Class-Cephalopoda (plus 4 others) Subclass-Coleoidea (plus 2 others), Order-Sepeoidea (plus 2 others). Squid and cuttlefish belong to the Sepeoidea Order and are still only reported from Jurassic and younger rocks, as of today.

The animal written up in the cited article was not claimed by the authors to be a cuttlefish. On the contrary, the statement was even made that the find "does not necessarily signify an ancestor-descendant relationship but alternatively may indicate that the radular denticles of the Sepia as well as those of Campitius (the new find) are little evolved from those of the ancestral mollusc and that Campitius may represent a previously unrecognized group of molluscs."

The conclusion and data of the article are thus completely different from that reported and cited by Dr. Gish. The authors did not even suggest (they actually state it might be a new group of molluscs) they had found a "fossil cuttlefish" in

Cambrian rocks. Perhaps in the future some investigator might find fossil cuttlefish in earlier rocks than now known, and if they did the record of life will be improved, but, the geological record is based on what is known, not on what we would like it to be. I cannot help but resent on a personal and moral basis being made to publicly say that I have never heard of such an important peleontological find, when in fact the find had not occurred. The above statements were checked with one of the authors.

Gish Answers Alleged Wrong Facts

By Duane T. Gish,
Institute for Creation Research
The University Daily
February 26, 1975

I wish to reply to the letter by Dr. Rae L. Harris which appeared in The University Daily on Feb. 12 concerning the debate on creation vs. evolution between Dr. Henry Morris and myself, representing the creationists, and Drs. Harris and Baker as the evolutionists.

As we have occasion to debate this subject, it is always our hope that such a debate will be conducted in the spirit of "Come, let us reason together." However we may differ with our opponents in philosophy or in the interpretation of the scientific evidence related to origins, Dr. Morris and I always assume that our opponents are honest men of goodwill, and we have never publicly charged an opponent with lack of integrity or of deliberately misinterpreting important evidence. Furthermore, Dr. Harris failed to have the courtesy of sending me a copy of his letter, and I would not have had the opportunity to answer his charges had not a copy of the letter been sent to me by a resident of Lubbock. Regrettably, Dr. Harris has thus tried to accomplish in this manner what he could not accomplish in our debate where each party was present to hear all the arguments and to offer rebuttal. While Dr. Harris has pulled the shroud of self-righteousness comfortably about himself, may I suggest his halo may be slightly askew? His letter was actually an attempt to divert attention from the fact that he and his colleague had failed to defend evolution theory against its fatal weaknesses.

During the debate I stated that a paleontologist had recently found evidence for the existence of fossil cuttlefish in Early Cambrian strata. I stated that cuttlefish are highly complex invertebrate predators which had been previously found only in rocks of the Jurassic (or younger rocks). The Jurassic is dated by evolutionary geologists at about 150 million years, while they date Early Cambrian at about 600 my. I stated that this pushed the existence of cuttlefish back 400 my. in the geological column and that if the evolutionary time scale is really valid, evolutionists must then explain how the cuttlefish, could have been in existence for 400 my. (from Early Cambrian to the Jurassic) without leaving any fossils.

Dr. Harris quoted the article which I used for documentation (see Firby and Durham, J. of Paleontology, Nov., 1974, p. 1109) as stating that this find extended the range of Cephalopoda from the Late Cambrian to Early Cambrian. This is a difference of only about 80 my. at the most, in contrast to the 400 my. between the Jurassic and Early Cambrian. The significant point here, which Dr. Harris attempts to conceal, is that while some members of the class Cephalopoda had been found in Late Cambrian, the highly complex cuttlefish had not. Would Dr. Harris say that finding human skeletons in the Jurassic would not be a highly significant paleontological find simply because it extended the range of mammals from Cretaceous to the Jurassic? The discovery of such a creature as the cuttlefish in Early Cambrian rocks was so startling it was given prominent display in newspapers all over the U.S.

Dr. Harris further attempts to establish that I falsely represented this creature as a cuttlefish. If I have done so, then I am the victim of misrepresentation, as were the Associated Press and United Press International whose reports of this find represented it as undoubtedly that of a cuttlefish. For example, the UPI report (San Jose, California, Mercury, Nov. 29, 1974) stated "The ancient squid-like cuttlefish had teeth and used them to prey on other sea creatures . . ." Later in the article it was stated with reference to statements made by Firby and Durham, "Further studies concluded the teeth 'denticles' were from prehistoric cuttlefish, they said." There seems to be no doubt, then, that Firby and Durham, in talking to reporters, repeatedly referred to their find as a cuttlefish.

In the article referred to earlier, Firby and Durham state (p. 1109) "Bands of denticles morphologically similar to but larger than the medial teeth of the radula of the living cuttlefish (Sepia) occur in the lowest trilobite-bearing Lower Cambrian of California." Later on (p. 1118) they state "Morphologically the denticles compare closely, except for their larger size and slightly less expanded base, to the simple medial teeth of the radula of the Cuttlefish Sepia." There seems to be no doubt that this find could have been placed within the genus Sepia and that Firby and Durham, in designating the new genus Campitius, were merely following the tendency of most paleontologists to assign distinctive names to their finds. It is therefore altogether honest and correct, as Firby and Durham themselves have done, to refer to this creature as a cuttlefish.

Dr. Harris stated in his letter that "I cannot help but resent on a personal and moral basis being made to publicly say that I have never heard of such an important paleontological find, when in fact the find had not occurred," I regret Dr. Harris' embarrassment, but the fact remains that a very important paleontological find, just as I represented it, had been made of which he was not aware until it was called to his attention during the debate at Tech.

Dr. Harris' letter was an attempt to confuse and to divert attention from scientific evidence that provides such poweful support for creation and is so extremely damaging to evolution theory, namely, the abrupt appearance of highly complex animals in great variety — trilobites, brachiopods, jellyfish, worms, sponges, swimming crustaceans, etc. — in rocks designated as Cambrian, and failure to find a single, unquestionable multicellular fossil in earlier, or Precambrian rocks (see Cloud, Geology, Nov. 1973, p. 123). The discovery of cuttlefish (or Campitius if you wish) in the lowest Early Cambrian merely adds another complex creature to the record for which no evolutionary ancestor can be found. This abrupt appearance (on geological time-scale) of complex animals without ancestors, and the systematic absence of transitional forms between higher categories (phyla, classes, orders, families) revealed by the fossil record is exactly the evidence predicted on the basis of creation but contradicts predictions based on evolution theory. The laws of thermodynamics, the laws of probability, the operation of natural processes, and the fossil record thus all attest to the fact that not only did evolution (particles-to-people) not occur but it could not have occurred. This highly ordered universe and our planet earth with its population of incredibly complex living things demand a Creator.

Original Quote Correct

Letter to the Editor from Rae L. Harris
The University Daily
February 27, 1975

At this point, all I wish to do in reply to Dr. Gish's letter of Feb. 26 is to quote the authors of the paper in question, from both the article itself and from direct telephone conversation.

"Because of the morphological similarity of the denticles to those of Sepia AND OTHER CEPHALOPODS, the taxon is assigned to the Phylum Mollusca and PROVISIONALLY to the Class Cephalopoda."

"IF CORRECTLY assigned to the Class, this find extends the range of the Cephalopoda from the Late into very Early Cambrian."

Systematic Description "Phylum Mollusca, Class Cephalopoda?, Family Incertae Sedis, Campitius n. gen."

"The teeth of the GONIATITE Eoasianites, and the AMMONITE Arnioceras, but not those of the ammonite

Eoasianites are likewise GROSSLY SIMILAR to those of the Campitius."

"However, it should also be noted that the close similarity of the denticles of Campitius to those of Sepia does not necessarily signify an ANCESTOR-DESCENDANT relationship but alternatively may indicate that the radular denticles of Sepia as well as those of Campitius are little evolved from those of ancestral molluscs and that Campitius MAY REPRESENT A PREVIOUSLY UNRECOGNIZED GROUP OF MOLLUSCS."

From telephone conversation of Monday Feb. 10, Dr. Durham (co-author of the article in question) stated: "Yes, you can quote me that we did not write we had found fossil cuttlefish in the Cambrian rocks."

Further Dr. Durham said: "The importance of the find is that we looked for and found evidence of powerful predators in the Early Cambrian which we reasoned must have existed because of the abundance of other animals to feed upon."

Telephone call of Feb. 26: Dr. Durham again stated that he had not claimed to have found a fossil cuttlefish. He stated: "In detail, the denticle material found is not like that of cuttlefish in the absence of the lateral more specialized radulae. You can say that this was not a cuttlefish, but an ancient ancestor type that may or may not be on the cuttlefish's family tree."

In conclusion, my first letter appears to remain correct. Dr. Gish had, and has, a copy of Dr. Durham's article. He can not then quote newspaper accounts as source material.

Gish Offers Final Comments

Letter to the Editor
from Duane T. Gish
The University Daily
March, 1975

I think it would be most appropriate that I make a few final remarks in reply to Dr. Harris' original charges (The University Daily, Feb. 12) and to his rebuttal (The Daily, Feb. 27) to my reply (The Daily, Feb. 26).

In Harris' rebuttal he quotes Dr. Durham as saying "Yes, you can quote me that I did not write we had found fossil cuttlefish in the Cambrian rocks." It is true that in the journal article *(J. of Paleontology,* November, 1974) Firby and Durham did not write they had found cuttlefish in the Cambrian rocks. From the limited amount of fossil material they had recovered, they were commendably cautious in what they published in a scientific journal. On the other hand, as I conclusively documented in my letter of Feb. 26, in talking with reporters about their discovery, they repeatedly referred to it as a cuttlefish. That is why, in talking to Harris, they were merely able to authorize him to say that they did not "write" that they had found a cuttlefish, but *were not able to authorize him to say that they had not told reporters that they had found a cuttlefish.* The reference to the fact that one Los Angeles newspaper account reported that they had found fossil teeth of fish was merely a smokescreen designed to conceal the above facts. We received several newspaper clippings from around the country based on the Firby and Durham news conference, and none of them referred to a fossil fish, but each one of them correctly quoted Firby and Durham as referring to their find as a cuttlefish.

Finally, whether this was in fact a true cuttlefish or was more correctly a cuttlefish-like creature does not in any way alter the false nature of Harris' charges against me nor diminish in the slightest the significance of the finding of this fossil in Early Cambrian strata. In calling this creature a cuttlefish in the debate with Harris and Baker, I was applying exactly the same evaluation of this creature as was made by Firby and Durham in relating their findings to reporters and thus to the lay public. To accuse me of dishonesty or of distorting evidence is slanderously false.

I finally wish to emphasize again that the discovery of either a cuttlefish or a cuttlefish-like fossil in Early Cambrian strata was a highly significant, even astounding, paleontological discovery. Most evolutionary paleontologists would have denied the remotest possibility of finding such a highly complex predator in Early Cambrian rocks. According to evolutionists, the Early Cambrian supposedly represents a time before even corals and starfishes had evolved, let alone a very highly complex predator in Early Cambrian rocks. If fossils of Neanderthal Man were found in Cretaceous rocks, supposedly laid down more than 70 million years ago, it would be silly to deny that this was an astounding discovery on the basis of whether Neanderthal Man was true human, *Homo sapiens*, or whether he was merely a human-like creature, *Homo neanderthalensis* (he was in fact, *Homo sapiens*). In fact, as one geologist stated, if something like this ever did come to pass, all historical geologists would give up their profession and take up truck driving.

University Debates Feature
New Orleans Seminar

Two creation-evolution debates, one with the Acting Head of the Geology Department, the other with a renowned physicist, were the key features of a Creation Seminar at the University of New Orleans, February 3-5, 1975. Meetings were held in the University Student Center, with the two debates held in the large ballroom. A student organization, Iktheus, arranged the Seminar and debates and Joel Robertson, President of Iktheus, served as moderator. In spite of Mardi Gras activities and the fact that the University of New Orleans is primarily a commuter campus, over 400 attended the first debate and approximately 300 the second.

In the first debate, Dr. William Craig debated Dr. Henry Morris, I.C.R. Director, on the testimony of geology and the fossil record relative to origins. The next night, Dr. Max Herzberger, protege and colleague of Dr. Albert Einstein, as well as one the world's top optical physicists in his own right, debated Dr. Morris on the relevance of the second law of thermodynamics to creation or evolution. A spirited discussion from the audience followed each debate. In the first debate, Dr. Morris stressed the universal, systematic gaps between basic kinds in the fossil record as evidence confirming the creation model. Dr. Craig argued that, though the gaps were real, they could be explained in other ways than by creation.

In the second debate, Dr. Herzberger suggested that most physicists and other scientists had not defined and used the second law properly and that, if it were defined in accordance with the mathematical definition of "minimum action" it could be interpreted as allowing both positive and negative changes in entropy. Dr. Morris documented the case that the tendency toward randomness specified in the second law (as normally defined) was indeed universal and that there were no available mechanisms to enable an evolutionary increase in complexity ever to occur by natural processes.

Conversations with many students afterwards indicated that the creationist students had been greatly strengthened in their creationist convictions and that many of the evolutionist students recognized that creationism was a valid scientific model and should be taught in their classes along with evolution.

In addition to the debates, three other open lectures, one by Dr. Morris and two by Dr. Duane Gish, were held on the U.N.O. campus. A debate had originally been scheduled to include Dr. Gish, but the other participant withdrew and, as the students sponsoring the meetings put it, no biologists could be found in the city of New Orleans who were willing to defend evolution in a public debate, even among those who were teaching formal courses on the subject to their students in the city's various colleges and universities.

Many other meetings were held in New Orleans during this period. Dr. Morris spoke to a very responsive audience of 150 medical students and faculty at a noon meeting at the L.S.U. School of Medicine and Dr. Gish spoke the next day to a similar audience at the Tulane University Medical School. In addition, Dr. Gish spoke to the students at a Baptist high school and a Jewish high school, while Dr. Morris spoke to students at a Catholic high school, a public high school, and a Christian junior high school. Dr. Morris also spoke at both Sunday services of the Carrolton Avenue Presbyterian Church on February 2.

54

Overflow Audience Hears
University of Manitoba Debate

About 400 students and faculty crowded into an auditorium at the University of Manitoba, Winnipeg, which was designed to hold only 300, for the debate during the evening of February 6, 1974.

Participants in the debate, which was held as part of the week-long Life and Learning Experience of the University, were I.C.R. staff scientist Dr. Duane Gish, and University of Manitoba professors Dr. Kenneth Stuart and Dr. Martin Samoiloff, both of the Department of Zoology. The moderator was Steve Wuerz, graduate student in biochemistry. The question debated was "Resolved that special creation offers a more satisfactory explanation of the scientific evidence related to origins than does evolution." Dr. Gish, of course, argued for the affirmative.

Dr. Gish, as the first speaker, began by presenting evidence that evolution theory is no more scientific than the concept of special creation, and that each requires a faith commitment to a particular view of the universe and its origin. He then emphasized the evidence based on the laws of thermodynamics and the laws of probability that seems to exclude even the remotest possibility of evolution. Using slides, he then presented evidence that highly complex forms of life abruptly appeared in the fossil record without ancestors and that transitional forms between the basic types of plants and animals are systematically absent. He concluded that basic laws of science, known natural processes, and the historical record inscribed by the fossils demonstrate that the special creation model is superior to the evolution model for correlating and explaining scientific data on origins.

Dr. Samoiloff, while conceding that theories concerning unique, historical, events of the past are not subject to scientific test and that evolution in the present world would be too slow to produce the kind of change required to verify the general theory of evolution, maintained that this theory is supported by a reasonable extrapolation, through postulated geological time, of the small changes that are observable. He cited the

55

derivation of a new variety of grain at the University of Manitoba that was not interfertile with the strains from which it had derived.

Dr. Stuart spent about half of his time explaining why evolutionists could expect difficulties in interpreting the fossil record. He maintained that fossilization is so rare that the fossil record would be very sparse to begin with, and that periods of erosion along with periods during which no sedimentation was occurring would further impoverish the record. He further claimed that most fossils were those deposited on continental shelves, and that older deposits had suffered longer periods of erosion and had been buried deeper. Sampling of the fossil record should, therefore, give a very biased account according to Stuart.

Dr. Stuart maintained that the sudden appearance of a variety of complex animals at the Precambrian-Cambrian boundary was due to the fact that some change in geological conditions had permitted hard parts to evolve abruptly and that little or no record of Precambrian animals is found because these animals were all soft-bodied creatures. He further maintained that while transitional forms leading up to major kinds are usually missing, the first to appear are relatively few in number.

In rebuttal, Dr. Gish pointed out that Dr. Stuart had spent about half of his time explaining why the fossil record presents so many difficulties for evolutionists in spite of evolution being true, but that creationists do not have to explain the fossil record because it is just as predicted on the basis of creation. He pointed out that Stuart's explanation for the sudden appearance of complex animals in Cambrian rocks without apparent ancestors has no scientific support. He emphasized again the vast discrepancy between the actual facts of the fossil record and predictions based on evolution. He pointed out further that the evidence for minor changes cited by Stuart and Samoiloff as evidence for evolution in no way provides proof for evolution since these changes not only are insignificant compared to the changes postulated by the general theory of evolution but also result in no increase in complexity. They are predicted on the basis of the creation model as well as the evolution model.

Stuart, in his rebuttal, used Dr. Gish's slide of the alleged fish-to-amphibia transition to outline several reasons why evolutionists believe the Crossopterygian fish was ancestral to amphibia, even though a large gap not bridged by transitional forms exist between the two. He also claimed that the fossil of Archaeopteryx, though Archaeopteryx was a bird, would have been mistaken for a reptile if it did not have feathers. He further claimed that the change from a non-flying reptile to the flying reptile, although no transitional forms exist, was not really such a big change because it only involved change in length of the fourth finger(!)

In his rebuttal, Samoiloff claimed that although biochemical data could be explained by both the evolution and creation models, the biochemical similarities between animals, especially those between man and his evolutionary nearest of kin, the chimpanzee, were more easily understandable on the basis of evolution.

In Dr. Gish's final rebuttal he emphasized a statement by an evolutionist admitting that there was no fossil evidence for the reptile-to-bird transition. He expressed his doubt about the "feathered-reptile" description of Archaeopteryx and stated that he has yet to see a reptile that just needed some feathers stuck into it to enable it to fly! He concluded by re-emphasizing that gaps in the fossil record between major types are systematic, just as predicted on the basis of creation but contradicting evolution.

Dr. Gish's presentation was well-received by the audience. It is believed that this debate will have a definite positive effect on this campus in behalf of Biblical, scientific creationism.

Gish Debates
Anthropology Chairman

On October 20, 1974, a crowd of 1500 witnessed a debate at the University of Missouri-Columbia between ICR scientist

Dr. Duane Gish and UMC's Dr. James Gavan. Gavan, chairman of the Anthropology Department, presented the affirmative position on the resolution: "That the theory of evolution is superior to the theory of special creation as a scientific explanation for the evidence relevant to the present biological world." Gish presented the negative side.

The large crowd included not only students and professors from UMC, but many laymen, students and pastors who travelled hundreds of miles to be on hand for this unique event. Twelve church buses were counted as the auditorium began to fill.

Gavan presented virtually no scientific evidence to support evolution, choosing instead to attack creation as being unscientific. Claiming that because creation is a "sacred" concept while evolution is "secular," he concluded that evolution is therefore scientific while creation is not. Gavan also referred to the criteria of falsifiability and the scientific method in creation's failure to qualify as a scientific theory.

Gish countered by stating that if Gavan had read creationist literature more carefully, he would have known that ICR scientists do not claim that creation is scientific. Quoting from evolutionists, Gish proceeded to show that evolution also fails to pass the test of a scientific theory: observation, repeatability, experimentation, and falsifiability.

With reference to the second law of thermodynamics, Gavan attempted to show that creationists misused the law in its application to evolution. He maintained that the second law applied only to closed systems and that the sun's influx of energy to the earth was sufficient to account for biological evolution. Gish, however, stressed the all-pervasive nature of the second law and the tendency of all spontaneous processes to proceed with an increase in entropy. In addition, Gish showed that the sun's energy alone was not sufficient. An energy conversion mechanism as well as system for directing, maintaing, and replicating these energy conversion mechanisms would be required in addition to an open system and an adequate source of energy.

During the remainder of his first presentation, Gish presented the evidence for creation from the fossil record. Emphasis was placed on the abrupt appearance of complex invertebrates in the Cambrian and the absence of transitional forms, especially with reference to flight. Gish's well-illustrated lecture was frequently interrupted by applause from the audience. It was estimated that two-thirds of those attending supported the creationist position.

There was much confusion with respect to the discussion on transitional forms. Gavan repeatedly used the term "intermediate" and when questioned later, admitted that his use of the word intermediate did not necessarily imply ancestral. Gavan repeatedly challenged Gish to define what he meant by an intermediate form. Gish's use of the term "intermediate" clearly implied that of an ancestral relationship. This point seemed to be an evasive issue with Gavan while Gish proceeded to present his case from the evolutionists' usual reference to ancestral intermediates.

As in previous debates, it was once again the evolutionist who brought religion into the discussion. Using a projected slide, Gavan showed a letter signed "Yours in Christ" by Dr. Henry Morris of ICR. In a further attempt to characterize creation as a religious effort under the facade of science, Gavan referred to the Creation Research Society's belief in a literal interpretation of the Bible.

Gish countered by pointing out the fact that the religious beliefs (evolutionary humanism) of men such as Julian Huxley had never prevented evolutionists from being given a hearing for scientific evidence. "We make no denial that we are Christians," said Gish as the audience broke into the most enthusiastic applause of the evening. However, moans and catcalls from Gavan supporters erupted when Gish said, "I'm a little confused — does Dr. Gavan want to suppress Christianity? Then why bring out the point of the Institute for Creation Research being a Christian organization?" Gish was applauded when he said that we should all be given a hearing for scientific evidence regardless of whether we are Christians or atheists.

At one point in the debate, Gavan stated that there had never been an inquisition in the name of evolution. But Gish disagreed, saying that he knew of graduate students who have been prevented from obtaining Ph.D.'s because they were creationists, and professors who have been dismissed and have not been given tenure because they expressed creationist convictions. "Yes," Gish affirmed, "there is an inquisition in the name of evolution."

As on other occasions, Gavan questioned Gish's reference to an article by Dr. Daniel Axelrod which Gish cited as evidence for woody plants in the Cambrian. Gavan said he had a letter from Axelrod indicating that Gish had misquoted from the article. However, Gish produced a copy of Axelrod's paper, which provided irrefutable evidence that Axelrod had reported that fragments of woody plants had indeed been found in the Cambrian Period of the geological column.

It was interesting to note that although Gavan had edited a book on primate evolution and has recently authored a book on the same subject, he made no effort to present documented evidence from his field. Gavan said he had contacted all of Gish's previous debate opponents, yet he offered little in refutation of the creationist position. Gavan has had access to *Acts and Facts* and has attended two creation seminars held in Columbia. In fact, the debate was a direct result of Gavan's attendance at the 1974 Missouri Creation Seminar during which he was given fifteen minutes to read a prepared paper critical of the creationist position.

The debate was jointly sponsored by the UMC Department of Anthropology and the Missouri Association for Creation (MAC), Inc. **Cassette tapes of the debate are available from MAC, 101 N. Anderson, Columbia, MO. 65201.**

SAN DIEGO NEWSPAPER
FEATURES CREATION DEBATE

A public debate in print, between Dr. Henry Morris, Director of the Institute for Creation Research, and Dr. Russell Doolittle, Professor of Biochemistry at the University of California at San Diego, highlighted the editorial pages of the

San Diego UNION on September 19, 1975, giving the many readers of the area's largest newspaper an opportunity to read at first hand the main arguments of the two sides of the creation-evolution issue.

The dialogue reproduced below was at the special invitation of UNION editors. Neither Dr. Morris nor Dr. Doolittle was permitted to read the other's paper prior to publication, and each side was limited to 800 words.

It is noteworthy that Dr. Doolittle did not attempt to discuss any SCIENTIFIC evidence for evolution, relying on philosophical and religious argumentation exclusively, yet criticizing creationists for believing in creation for religious reasons. Dr. Morris showed briefly that the limited changes in the present and the absence of fossil intermediates in the past precisely correspond to predictions from the creation model, also noting that evolutionists commonly use only non-scientific arguments which, in fact, Dr. Doolittle, as it turned out, had used.

Evolution is a Natural Theory   Dr. Russell Doolittle

The natural evolution of all the earth's creatures was postulated well in advance of Charles Darwin's famous theory.

Darwin's own grandfather, Erasmus Darwin, had boldly proposed that all living things had been generated from one original parent type during the course of millions of years because of a natural tendency for "improvement."

What Charles Darwin showed, in his classic "The Origin of The Species," was how genuinely natural this result had to be.

Briefly put, the principles of Darwinian evolution hold that inherited traits are continuously subjected to a slight but significant random variation, and as a result of their shuffling during passage from generation to generation give rise to a procreative lottery whereby those creatures possessing hereditary talents best suited for reproduction under a prevailing set of circumstances come to outnumber their less successful kinfolk.

Since the resources available for a given kind of lifestyle are limited, eventually one generational line of a family predominates.

This Theory of Natural Selection was put forth by Darwin more than a century ago, and at the time it provoked a violent reaction among scientists and laymen alike, to say nothing of the clergy.

Darwin went on to produce another great treatise entitled "The Descent of Man," in which he detailed the evidence for the common ancestry of man and apes. The essential correctness of all he proposed is borne out by the fact that a century later his theory and general conclusions are universally accepted among biologists.

Indeed, overwhelming evidence in support of evolution by natural selection has been amassed in the fields of anatomy, palentology, physiology, pathology, embryology, genetics, cell biology, biochemistry and molecular biology.

It is the latter, mostly developed during the last two or three decades, which has given us a completely mechanistic understanding of the natural variation of genes and a decipherable step-by-step reading of the relationship of all living things — animals, plants and microbes.

The question arises, does the average person understand and appreciate the conclusion that all organisms — including human beings — have evolved as a result of natural selection? Clearly some self-proclaimed Fundamentalists (I would protest that natural selection is very fundamental) do not. But what of the middle-of-the-road, average, not overly zealous lay person?

I suspect that a curious kind of dualism exists and that many people accept evolution—without quite understanding it—becase of popular references to it in this Space Age by the popular press and the respect paid it in television spectaculars from the British Broadcasting Corp.

At the same time, and on equally tenuous grounds, many of these same people feel the need for some sort of divine creation somewhere in the process. Whenever there is a contest between blind faith and analytical thought, faith is usually the path of least resistance.

For example, some people seem to accept the principles of evolution as they relate to all the creatures on earth except human beings, somehow finding the notion that people are akin to monkeys distasteful.

Others find everything about organic evolution consistent with their religious beliefs, the entire ecologic concert being harmoniously guided by some divine spirit who has a disproportionate interest in mankind. The genuine evolutionist, on the other hand, contends that man's existence is entirely attributable to natural phenomena.

There is no claim here to know everything about the universe — indeed, there are a plethora of unanswered questions about spacetime relationships and the origin of the cosmos which boggle the present-day human mind, as well as many fine points about biological evolution itself which remain mysterious or controversial. But there is not reason for supposing that—given more study and reflection—reasonable explanations will not be forthcoming.

Men and women, in forms not too different from the present-day varieties, have frequented the earth for well over a million years, and for the last few thousands of these they have been writing down some of their musings. It is only natural that as their contemplative powers grew they should ponder their own origins and the question of "how it all came to be."

Because the real answers to these extraordinarily difficult questions were not apparent when the questions were first raised, "reasonable explanations" evolved, lots of them, in many different cultures.

As though anticipating the bank advertisements of our own times, which urge the debt-ridden to consolidate all their bills into one "easy-to-handle super loan," these ancient questioners came to put all those things which they were unable to explain into one super inexplicable and untestable phenomenon.

In short, they created gods in man's image.

Organized religions flourished in pre-science days for a variety of reasons apart from the fact that people were usually born into them and carefully indoctrinated.Religions gave (and still give) people a sense of identity, and they gave them hope of something better than the miserable lot so many of them knew.

And last, but not necessarily least, most of the great religions offered pre-packaged explanations of all the wonders of the world. All one needed was faith (a frequent companion of hope).

Naturally, science and the scientific method for asking and answering questions tended to run counter to these long-standing doctrines, and the initial encounters between Creationists and Scientists were frequently fiery.

In 1633, for example, Galileo was forced to appear before the Inquisition and renounce the Copernican notion that the earth moved around the sun and not vice-versa. And in the 1860's, Darwin was castigated—even by the most renowned biologists of the day—as a "vicious atheist" and "the most dangerous man in England!"

Today there are about as many legitimate biologists who don't accept the natural evolution of man from an ape-like progenitor as there are astronomers who think the sun goes around the earth. There is a small band of fervent anti-evolutionists, some of whom purport to be "scientists" who preach an unassaultable doctrine based on faith and who continue to raise specious and fallacious arguments against evolution.

These arguments are not really directed at scientists, of course, but are aimed instead at those dualistic types mentioned above who never have been quite sure what natural selection is anyway. And faith is so much less confining than reason.

Creationism Provides The Answers   **Dr. Henry M. Morris**

When creationist parents object to the exclusive teaching of evolution in the public schools, they are usually informed that all scientists are evolutionists and that their belief in creation is based solely on religious faith in the book of Genesis.

Both statements are wrong. There are today thousands of qualified scientists who do not believe in evolution (over 500 in the Creation Research Society alone) and the number is increasing rapidly.

As far as religious faith is concerned, evolution requires a higher degree of faith in events which are unobservable, unprovable, and unreasonable than does creation.

When asked to defend evolution scientifically, evolutionists often demonstrate the "religious" nature of their commitment to evolution by becoming emotional, attacking "fundamentalists," rather than calmly setting forth objective proofs that evolution is really a fact of science as they claim.

A better way would be to recognize that the entire subject of origins is beyond the scope of the scientific method. Neither creation nor evolution can be proved scientifically, since neither can be either observed or repeated. Nevertheless, the two can be compared scientifically in terms of comparable, but opposite, "models" of origins.

The "evolution model" is an attempt to explain the origin and development of all things in terms of naturalistic, random processes, operating over essentially unlimited ages of time. Whether or not there is a god behind the process ("theistic evolution") is irrelevant as far as scientific analysis of the process is concerned.

The "creation model" is the concept that there was at least one period of special creation sometime in the past, in which period the Creator (an omniscient, omnipotent, eternal, personal being) brought into existence the whole universe in completed functioning form.

Each of the basic "kinds" of organisms was specially created, with the ability to reproduce its own kind, and with the genetic ability for wide variation within its kind, but not for changing from one kind into another kind. In particular, man was created as man, not produced by evolution from some population of apelike primates.

Similarities in anatomy, in embryology, in blood chemistry, are often cited as evidence of naturalistic descent from a common ancestor, but the extreme complexity of such organic systems is better evidence of creative planning by a common designer.

Furthermore, the differences between kinds are more significant than their similarities. How did cats and dogs ever get to be so different from each other, for example, if they evolved from the same ancestor in the same environment by the same process?

Neither evolution nor creation can be observed in operation today. The small changes in organisms that do take place today (e.g., the shift in dominant coloration of the "peppered moth," mutations in fruit flies, the different "races" of men, etc.) fit both the evolution and creation models and so cannot "prove" either one.

However, they do fit the creation model better, since all such changes are horizontal (variation within kinds, at the same level of order and complexity), as one would expect from the creation model, not vertical (variation leading toward higher kinds and greater complexity), as must be true in the long run if the evolution model is correct.

The evolutionist may say, however, that these small changes are really unlimited and vertical, but that they are so slow as to be unobservable, requiring millions of years to accomplish significant evolutionary advances, (thus admitting that evolution is outside the realm of real science).

If it is true that such changes have taken place over millions of years in the past, then there ought to be evidence of intermediate evolutionary forms in the fossil record. Such transitional forms are completely missing, however, if they ever existed.

Dr. David Kitts, one of the nation's leading evolutionary paleontologists, in the September 1974, issue of the journal Evolution, has admitted that evolution faces some "nasty difficulties—the most notorious of which is the presence of 'gaps' in the fossil record. Evolution requires intermediate forms between species and paleontology does not provide them."

There are only variations within kinds in the fossil record, with systematic gaps between the kinds (just as there are in the present world) exactly as creationists would predict from the creation model!

It is not possible to discuss here all the scientific evidences (from thermodynamics, probability, genetics, physics, geology, and other sciences) that support the creation model. At Christian Heritage College, the subject of "Scientific Creationism" is taught in a formal six semester-hour course, and is the basic framework of interpretation in all other courses.

There is definitely no scientific proof of evolution, and all the available scientific data fit at least as well (and usually better) in the creation model. Consquently, by all standards of academic freedom, civil rights, and scientific objectivity, the creation model ought to be accepted on at least an equal basis with the evolutionary philosophy in all our public schools and other tax-supported institutions.

If the evolutionist objects that the concept of a Creator is itself "religious," he should be reminded that the concept of no creator is equally religious. Atheism requires a much higher degree of faith than creationism, since it negates the fundamental scientific law of cause-and-effect.

Naturalistic evolutionism requires its followers to believe that randomly moving particles of primeval matter had the ability and knowledge to develop a complex universe of living organisms, and even to evolve intelligent creatures who could exercise faith in evolution! Creationism at least postulates a first cause which is competent to explain such effects.

chapter II

CREATION GOES TO COLLEGE

Creation on the Campus!

One of the most exciting developments of the past few years has been the re-introduction of creationism to the nation's college and university campuses. Less than a decade ago, a formal lecture or debate defending creationism as a scientific concept would have been impossible on a university campus. The doors were shut and, with rare exceptions, there were no creationist scientists who were willing and able to give such lectures anyhow. The situation today is altogether different.

Most of this change can justifiably be attributed to the Institute for Creation Research. Without in any way minimizing the essential research and publications work of the Creation Research Society or the promotional activities of other creationist organizations, it is the I.C.R. scientists who have been doing most of the actual speaking and debating on the campuses across the nation and who have thereby opened the university community to a serious re-evaluation of the creation-evolution question.

During 1975 alone, for example, Dr. Duane Gish and Dr. Henry Morris have spoken or debated on over 60 college and university campuses, not to mention numerous public schools, scientific organizations, and teachers' associations. It is estimated that over 30,000 college students have heard one or more of these creationist messages during 1975. The majority of these students, of course, were non-Christians.

Some of the nation's leading universities — University of California (Berkeley, Los Angeles, San Diego, etc.), Louisiana State University, University of Kansas, University of Wisconsin, (Madison, Milwaukee, Oshkosh), University of North Carolina, Tulane University, Oregon University, Texas Tech, University of Missouri, Kansas State, University of Minnesota, Virginia Tech, Colorado State, University of Texas, University of Tennessee, Auburn University, University of Florida, Penn State, and many others — have been reached through lectures of this sort in the past three years, not to mention numerous colleges and universities in Canada, Australia and New Zealand.

In addition to those campuses visited personally by Dr. Gish and Dr. Morris, at least some students on nearly every campus have been reached through the I.C.R. books, the CAP program, I.C.R. radio broadcasts, *Acts and Facts*, or other means.

The Institute for Creation Research believes this campus-related ministry to call students back to serious recognition of God as Creator could be one of the most strategic missions of our time. It is hoped that readers of *Acts and Facts* will continue to judge it worthy of support.

The Case for Creation
Reaches Fullerton Campuses

Rather unique circumstances were provided for Dr. Gish's recent visits to the campuses of Fullerton State College and Fullerton Community College near Los Angeles.

Dr. Gish, through Campus Crusade, had been invited to speak to several classes on these campuses. A Christian student on the State College campus, although a creationist, had enrolled in a course on evolution. When he heard that Dr. Gish was visiting the campus, he prayed that God would open the way for Dr. Gish to speak to this class.

The student was astounded when, during the first class session, the professor attacked the creationist position, singling out Dr. Gish. He claimed that Dr. Gish was once an evolutionist, had submerged somehow and then had re-emerged as a creationist (Dr. Gish has always been a creationist). He further stated that he would gladly invite Dr. Gish to speak to his class, but could not afford to pay the fees demanded by Dr. Gish! No member of the Institute, of course, solicits fees from any educational institution and, as a matter of fact, the Institute is usually not reimbursed for expenses by schools. Furthermore, no member of the Institute receives any honoraria given for his lectures.

These remarks did, however, provide the opportunity the student had prayed for. When he asked the professor, "If we can get Dr. Gish here at no expense, will you invite him to speak?" The professor could hardly refuse! Arrangements were accordingly made for Dr. Gish to speak to the class.

The class provided an ideal opportunity to present the scientific case for creation. The professor unwittingly, of course, had done a beautiful job of setting the stage! Furthermore, this was a three-hour evening class, allowing time to present all of Dr. Gish's material. Visiting students and professors swelled the attendance to about 150.

Dr. Gish was able to demonstrate that evolution theory was no more scientific than creation, that evolution theory contradicted well-established natural laws, and that the fossil record was much more in accord with creation than evolution.

Following the lecture, the professor teaching the class neither made a single comment nor asked a single question! Others did, of course, and one was a professor of botany who prefaced his questions with comments complimenting Dr. Gish on the case for creation he had presented. All questioners were cordial and respectful. Dr. Gish was much encouraged by this response.

The next day Dr. Gish had opportunities to speak to other classes and a general audience on the State College campus. Again, the responses were encouraging. Later, Dr. Gish spoke at a 2½-hour session at Fullerton Community College where several rabid evolutionists were eager to challenge him. The session was barely under way when Dr. Gish was given challenging questions. However, as the case for creation was presented, the atmosphere began to quiet. We believe that even the most committed evolutionist, when presented a well-documented case, must admit that there *is* a case for creation.

Dr. Gish has also had similar excellent opportunities at Wartburg College, Waverly, Iowa, and at Grossmont College in San Diego.

Morris Lectures At L.S.U., Shreveport

After a month at home base in San Diego during the Christmas holidays, Dr. Henry Morris, ICR Director, began again an intensive lecture ministry during the last half of January, 1974, with particular interest in the secular campus ministry.

The first university meeting of the New Year was held on January 14 at the Shreveport campus of Louisiana State University, in the Science Lecture Auditorium. Although it was the first day of the second semester and there had been no opportunity to advertise the meeting, over 100 students and faculty members attended. Interest was high, and an excellent writeup of the meeting appeared next day in the *Shreveport Times*. The meeting was arranged by the Baptist Student Union at L.S.U. Dr. Morris was in the Shreveport area at the invitation of the First Baptist Church of Bossier City, where he brought six messages on the theme "Science and Salvation through the Book of Colossians", on January 13 and 14. This church is the second largest Baptist church in Louisiana, with about 1500 in attendance at the Sunday morning service.

University of Florida Hosts
Creation Lecture

Jointly sponsored by the University's cooperative biology curriculum faculty and Campus Crusade for Christ, Dr. Henry Morris gave a special lecture on scientific creationism on the University of Florida campus in Gainesville on February 27, to an interested audience of about 150 students and faculty. Presiding at the meeting was Dr. Tom Immel, Associate Professor of Zoology at the University and author of several books in the field of environmental biology.

Prior to the lecture, Dr. Morris held an informal discussion at Dr. Immel's home with a number of Christian faculty members, mostly in departments related to the biology curricular program.

ICR Staff Scientist at Peoria

Dr. Gish presented two lectures at the adult session of the Vacation Bible School of Grace Presbyterian Church of Peoria, Illinois, on June 13. While in Peoria, he appeared briefly on two television programs and participated in an hour-long radio talk show.

Dr. Gish also participated in a panel discussion on creation versus evolution at Bradley University. Other participants were Dr. Richard Hoffman, a chemist at Illinois Central College, and Dr. Merrill Foster, Professor of Geology at Bradley University, Dr. Foster is a theistic evolutionist and presented the case for evolution, while Dr. Hoffman, although not a professing Christian, presented powerful arguments against evolution on the basis of probability, drawing upon his knowledge of chemistry, probability theory, thermodynamics, and the structure of biologically active molecules, such as proteins. Dr. Gish presented the case for creation based on thermodynamics and the fossil record.

While in the Peoria area, Dr. Gish also had an opportunity to visit with Stanley Taylor, Director of Films for Christ. The very popular and informative film, *Footprints in Stone*, was filmed and produced by Films for Christ. This film documents evidence showing the co-existence of dinosaur and human footprints in the Paluxy River bed near Glen Rose, Texas. Dr. Gish toured the studios of Films for Christ with Mr. & Mrs. Taylor, and discussed with Mr. Taylor their plans for future films.

Creationist Interest Continues
On Oklahoma Campuses

A year and a half after the debate at the University of Oklahoma between I.C.R. creationists and faculty evolutionary leaders, interest among students and teachers continues to grow. A return visit by Dr. Henry Morris to both Oklahoma University and Oklahoma State University, on September 30 and October 1, respectively, was marked by well-attended meetings and keen audience interest in the subject of scientific creationism.

At the Oklahoma campus, numerous students told Dr. Morris of having been converted to creationism and to full acceptance of Christ largely as a result of the 1973 debate (see *Acts and Facts*, March, 1973, Vol. 2, No. 2). A diligent effort had been made by Christian students and faculty members to arrange another debate on each campus for this occasion, but they were unable to find evolutionist professors who were willing either to debate or to participate in a panel discussion with Dr. Morris.

Approximately 500 University of Oklahoma students attended the evening lecture on "Scientific Creationism" and approximately 300 attended the lecture on "The Man-Monkey Controversy" next evening at Oklahoma State University. In each case a lively discussion period followed.

In addition to the main evening meetings, Dr. Morris spoke to a special faculty luncheon at each university, with about 25 professors present at each. He was also guest teacher in a paleontology class and in a geology class on the Oklahoma campus and spoke to a Campus Crusade gathering at Oklahoma State. Advertising and arrangements for the meetings on both campuses were handled by students and staff of Campus Crusade for Christ, and by key Christian faculty members.

University of Oregon Seminar
Draws Record Attendance

What is believed to be the largest registered and paid attendance at a formal Creation Seminar observed to date was a noteworthy feature of meetings held on the campus of the University of Oregon in Eugene on January 10, and 11, 1975. Dr. Duane Gish and Dr. Henry Morris were the lecturers for the nine-hour series of sessions, with a consistent attendance of approximately 750 participants at all sessions.

The Seminar was sponsored by the University's official "Search" program, with the arrangements and promotion handled by a number of student organizations under the leadership of John Hail and Ron Woodruff. Lecture topics by Dr. Gish included "Human Origins," "The Fossil Record" and "The Origin of Life." Dr. Morris spoke on "The Evolution-Creation Controversy," "Entropy versus Evolution" and "Uniformitarianism or Catastrophism." The large majority of registrants of the Seminar were students, most of them at the University of Oregon.

Minnesota Colleges
Hear Dr. Morris

Two more college campuses, one secular and one Christian, both in the State of Minnesota, have recently hosted creationism lectures. Approximately 200 interested students and faculty members at the Southwest Minnesota State College in Marshall, Minnesota, heard Dr. Henry Morris speak on "Creation, Evolution and Science," on January 31, 1975. The meeting was arranged by Dr. Kurt Qagner, Associate Professor of Physics there, who had become a Christian only a year ago, and who has an activie and fruitful testimony on the campus now.

The previous day, January 29, Dr. Morris spoke to the 200 college and seminary students at the Schools of the Associated Lutheran Brethren in Plymouth, Minnesota on the theme of "The Scientific Integrity of the Literal Genesis Record."

Astronomy — Geology
Lectures given in
Colorado

Professor Harold Slusher lectured on astronomy and geology as related to creationism versus evolutionism to classes and at an evening symposium sponsored by Fort Lewis College on February 3 in Durango, Colorado. The evangelical ministers' association sponsored an evening lecture at a local high school on February 4. The meetings were well attended by students and interested individuals. The discussion periods that followed the lectures were filled with many questions and vigorous debate.

Morris Speaks at Fairleigh-Dickinson

"The Scientific Impossibilities of Darwinism" was the provocative title of a special lecture by Dr. Henry M. Morris, I.C.R. Director, at Fairleigh-Dickinson University on May 1. The one-hour lecture, showing that: (1) evolution does not occur at present; (2) did not occur in the past, and; (3) could never occur at all; was followed by another hour of lively questions and discussion from the audience, but with no refutation of the scientific evidence presented, and with an excellent response from most of those present. Approximately 250 were in the audience, composed entirely of students and faculty.

Fairleigh-Dickinson is a large private university in Teaneck, New Jersey, especially characterized by its large Jewish enrollment and its very "liberal" program. The meeting was sponsored jointly by the University Student Activities Office and the Campus Bible Fellowship. One student in the latter organization said that this was the first time, to his knowledge, that creation had ever been defended in any organized session at the University.

New Mexico Seminar Reaches
Students and Scientists

An intensive advertising campaign designed to make the entire community aware of the existence of a strong case for creationism preceded the Albuquerque Creation Seminar on April 26-27. Billboard and bus-side advertisements, bulletin inserts in 130 churches, bumper stickers, posters and mailings to University of New Mexico students and faculty,

75

and announcements to the large scientific community at the Sandia laboratories on the Kirtland Air Force Base resulted in community-wide awareness of the issue. The complex of meetings and promotion was organized and sponsored by the Albuquerque Christian Fellowship, under the chairmanship of David Lewis, supported by the University of New Mexico Campus Crusade for Christ. Faculty Adviser for both groups as well as moderator of the Seminar meetings was Dr. John Oller, Chairman of the University's Department of Linguistics.

The Seminar began on Friday night in the beautiful Woodward Auditorium on the New Mexico University Campus with a lecture on "Fossils and the Flood" by Dr. Henry Morris, followed by the film *Footprints in Stone*. On Saturday, Dr. Duane Gish gave three lectures, "The Fossils Say No," "Human Evolution," and "The Origin of Life." Dr. Morris spoke on "The Evolution-Creation Controversy," "Evolution versus Entropy," and "The Young Earth."

A public meeting followed on Saturday night, at Albuquerque's new downtown Convention Center, with Dr. Gish and Dr. Morris both speaking in a scientific-evangelistic vein. Cards turned in after the meeting indicated a good number of decisions for Christ.

ICR Scientist Speaks
At U.C. Berkeley

An overflow audience of at least 600 students and professors heard Dr. Duane Gish present the scientific case for creation on the campus of the University of California at Berkeley on the evening of Friday, May 23. The large audience, especially since the lecture was on a holiday weekend and conflicted with several other events on campus, indicates the intense interest in this subject on university campuses today.

Collegians for Christ, most of whom are members of the Oakland Chinese Bible Church, distributed thousands of fliers on the campus and placed posters in all of the twelve science departments. Much credit for the large turnout must be given to Collegians for Christ.

Dr. Gish also spoke in several area public and private high schools, and participated with Dr. Michael Stark, a biochemist with the U.C. Medical School, in a creation seminar on Saturday at Merritt College which was sponsored by the Chinese Bible Church (Rev. Louis Lightfoot, Pastor), where Dr. Gish spoke at all services on Sunday.

University Meetings In
Kansas Make Impact

A week-long emphasis on scientific creationism at the leading universities of Kansas featured Dr. Henry Morris, I.C.R. Director, as speaker at numerous meetings, and attracted wide interest from students and faculty. The meetings promoted by various student organizations, were held during the period October 9-17, 1975.

At the University of Kansas, in Lawrence, a crowd of 750 heard Dr. Morris speak on "Creation, Evolution, and Modern Science," followed by an hour of intense discussion and questioning. The student organizations had made extensive efforts with university faculty members to set up a creation-evolution debate, but none on the faculty were willing. Many of those who had been reluctant to participate in a formal, structured debate, did attend the meeting and then attempted to criticize the creationist position during the question period, primarily on philosophical grounds. The moderator, a leading scientist on the chemistry faculty, and a creationist, chided the evolutionist scientists for being unwilling to defend evolutionism in a formal, structured debate. Dr. Morris also was guest lecturer at three university classes (an advanced class on organic evolution, a class in ancient history, and a class in Biblical literature), and to a large Saturday morning gathering of Christian students. It is significant that the University of Kansas is the headquarters publication office for the Society for the Study of Evolution and the important journal *Evolution*.

At Kansas State University, in Manhattan, capacity crowds filled the 600-seat chapel for two evening lectures, one on "Scientific Evidence for Special Creation," the other on

"Scientific Evidence for Recent Creation." In addition, Dr. Morris spoke to a faculty luncheon on the theme "The Religion of Evolution" and to two area high school assemblies. On Sunday, October 12, he was speaker at all services of Manhattan's Grace Baptist Church (Rev. Horace Brelsford, pastor), which had initiated the K.S.U. meetings. At this church, Dr. David Mugler, Associate Dean of Agriculture at Kansas State, teaches an outstanding class of university students. Approximately 250 attended the class as Dr. Morris spoke on the theme "What is Man?"

At the large private school, Washburn University, in Topeka, Dr. Morris spoke to students and faculty on "Scientific Evidence for Creation," with 260 over-crowding the only available auditorium. In addition, he lectured in a day-long seminar on creationism, to about 350 students and staff from eight area Christian schools, as well as the midweek service at South Knollwood Baptist Church, sponsor of the Topeka meetings.

Many reports of lively discussion sessions at dorms and fraternity houses following the meetings, letters-to-the-editor, etc., have come in. A number of conversions and of Christians being strengthened and freed from doubts have been reported. It is believed a significant and permanent impact for the truth of creation has been made on these key educational centers in Kansas.

Wisconsin University
Students Hear Gish, Morris

Students from three campuses (Madison, Oshkosh, and Milwaukee) of the University of Wisconsin heard the evidences for special creation in a series of special meetings with Dr. Duane Gish and Dr. Henry Morris on October 24-27. The largest attendance was at the Milwaukee campus on Monday night, October 27, where Dr. Morris spoke to an audience of 560, on the subject "Evolution, Creation, and Modern Science." On that afternoon, Dr. Morris participated in a video-taped panel analysis of "The Creation Model," at Racine.

On Friday, October 24, Dr. Gish had given three lectures to students from the main campus in Madison, while Dr. Morris spoke for four sessions at the Oshkosh campus. One of these sessions was at a large class on invertebrate zoology whose professor had first agreed, then later declined, to participate in a debate with Dr. Morris. Lively question sessions followed all the lectures. On the next day, Dr. Gish spoke four times at Oshkosh and Dr. Morris three times at Madison. The largest crowds (approximately 250 for several sessions) were at Oshkosh.

In addition to the regular seminar sessions, the two I.C.R. scientists spoke at the various Sunday services of the Bethel Baptist Church and the First Assembly of God, the two churches which co-sponsored the seminar. The Milwaukee meeting was sponsored by the Midwestern Association for Creation Research, the same group that had sponsored two national creationist conventions in 1972 and 1974.

Another campus of the University of Wisconsin was reached indirectly, as two evolutionist professors from the Parkside campus, Dr. Wayne Johnson and Dr. Dennis Dean, participated in the one-hour video-taped panel on "The Creation Model." A third evolutionist participant, Charles Harmon, was Chairman of the Science Department at Racine's largest public high school. Moderator was Richard Bliss, Science Coordinator for the Racine Unified School District, and I.C.R.'s North Central Extension Scientist. The panel consisted of a 10-minute presentation of the scientific case for creationism by Dr. Morris, followed by critical questioning of Dr. Morris (with his answers) by the other panel members. The tape was sponsored by the Racine school system, and will be used in the schools of Racine and Milwaukee, as well as in classes at the University of Wisconsin (Parkside).

EVOLUTION IN CHRISTIAN COLLEGES
Henry M. Morris

The evolutionary philosophy thoroughly dominates the curricula and faculties of secular colleges and universities today, as most people are well aware. It is not so well known, however, that this philosophy has also had considerable effect on many Christian colleges. When this fact is pointed out, the reaction of many Christians seems to be one of surprise or even doubt. "How could ——— College, so well known for academic leadership in the Christian world, possibly be teaching evolution, especially when its faculty members all assent to a statement of faith? Surely there must be some mistake."

There is no mistake, however. Although there are still many Christian schools whose faculties are strongly Biblical and strictly creationist, many of the most highly respected schools have compromised with evolutionism to an alarming degree. A recent article entitled "Creationism and Evolutionism as Viewed in Consortium Colleges" (*Universitas*, Vol 2, No. 1, March 1974) documents this fact quite thoroughly. Written by Dr. Albert J. Smith, a biology teacher at Wheaton College, this paper gives the views of 38 teachers in science and math from the Christian College Consortium, a group of about 10 or 12 of the leading Christian colleges.

Dr. Smith points out that, in the opinion of their own science faculties, these institutions have *no well-defined position* on creation or evolution. Nevertheless, these people also say that their institutions must "maintain a conservative stance for promotional purposes." Interesting!

As far as the faculty members themselves were concerned, Dr. Smith says: "Efforts to characterize and identify with the departmental positions results in all respondents calling themselves 'theistic evolutionists,' 'progressive creationists,' or infrequently 'fiat creationists.' "

It is good to know there are still a few "fiat creationists" in the Consortium, but it is evident they constitute a small minority. "Progressive creationism," of course, is a semantic variant of "theistic evolutionism," both systems adopting the geologic-age framework which is essentially synonymous with naturalistic uniformitarianism and rejecting the straightforward Biblical teaching of a completed recent creation and worldwide flood.

None of the colleges in the Consortium openly teach

evolutionism in the manner of secular colleges, of course. Some teachers do try to present both creation and evolution, and the evidences for and against each, to their students. The predominant attitude, however, is apparently that the question of origins is unimportant and irrelevant. "Relatively few colleges emphasize the creationist-evolutionist dialogue at all. The students are encouraged to make up their own minds regarding personal position."

Quotations given in the article from the individual responses of faculty members show that many of them use the standard cliches in trying to avoid this question. "—creationism (a Biblical statement) and evolutionism (a scientific statement) are not considered to be antagonistic but rather at different levels; creationism considers the *who* and the *why* while evolution considers the *how*, the *when*, and the *how much*." " . . . the important thing is not *how* but *Who*."

The reason why true creationists object to such views, of course, is because the Bible *does* say how, when, and how much, as well as who and why! Furthermore as the scientists of the Creation Research Society and the Institute for Creation Research have shown, the true facts of science do correlate much better with these Biblical statements on creation than with evolution. Such facts, however, seem always to be overlooked by "Christian evolutionists" and "progressive creationists."

Saying that the evolution/creation question is "not a significant problem," "not basic to the Christian faith," "unimportant," "a dead issue," and the like (all these judgments are quoted from respondents of the Consortium) is, I believe, merely a devious way of saying: "Well, acceptance in the academic world requires me to believe in evolution, and I don't want to face up to the Biblical and scientific reasons for rejecting evolution, so I would prefer to bypass the problems."

On one occasion several years ago, I spent several hours discussing this problem with a professor of geology at one of the Consortium colleges. He insisted that Christians *must* accept the geological-age system as taught by evolutionary geologists. When I asked him then as to how he, as professedly a Bible-believing Christian, reconciled the Genesis record of creation and the flood with this system, his reply was that he didn't know of any way they *could* be reconciled (he agreed that neither the gap theory nor the day-age theory were acceptable). When I also asked him how he reconciled Jesus Christ's acceptance of the literal Genesis record of creation and the flood with the geological ages, he replied that he didn't know how to reconcile that either. His final conclusion was that all of this was unimportant anyway. Only one thing apparently *was* important — namely, to accept the geological ages!

More recently, I had two opportunities to talk at some length to the present Head of the Geology Department at this same college on the same subject. He took much the same position, also adding that we would never be able to understand the meaning of the Genesis record of creation and the flood until we get to heaven! It is not necessary that we understand it now!

I must confess a certain lack of patience with this type of logic. How can one say the doctrine of special creation is unimportant when it is foundational to every other doctrine in Scripture? How can one say the evolutionary philosophy is not significant, when it has been made the basis of fascism, communism, animalism, racism, modernism, atheism, and practically every other harmful philosophy known to man? How can *Christian* college professors teach their students that evolution is an optional question when the Scriptures plainly teach otherwise?

"How long halt ye between two opinions? If the Lord be God, follow him: but if Baal, then follow him." (I Kings 18:21).

chapter III

CREATIONISM AND THE PUBLIC SCHOOLS

THE CHRISTIAN CREATIONIST
IN THE CLASSROOM

Henry M. Morris

How should a student who is a Christian and a creationist behave in a class taught by a teacher who is a strong and opinionated evolutionist? This is one of the most common and urgent questions asked by creationist parents. If the student is silent about his convictions and pretends to go along with the classroom teachings, is this a hypocritical compromise for the sake of expediency? On the other hand, if he challenges the teacher, arguing and taking an open stand against the evolutionary philosophy, will this not result in a failing grade in the course, ridicule by the teacher and other students, and possibly even shut the door to the career he has chosen?

This is a very real problem, with no easy answer. Essentially the same question is asked also by college students and even by graduate students working on their Ph.D. degrees. I have known students who have failed courses, and some who have been denied admission to graduate school or have been hindered from obtaining their degrees, largely for this very reason. When I was on the faculty at Virginia Tech, a professor who was on the graduate faculty there in the Biology Department told me that he would never approve a Ph.D. degree for any student known to be a creationist in his department, even if that student made straight A's in all his courses, turned in an outstanding research dissertation for his Ph.D., and was thoroughly familiar with all the evidences and arguments for evolution.

On the other hand, I have also known many other students who have received excellent grades even while taking a strong stand against evolution, as well as many who have earned graduate degrees, in spite of being known as Christians with solid creationist convictions.

What makes the difference? There is certainly no simplistic solution, applicable always and everywhere. Individual teachers are different, schools are different, and students are different, and these differences all make a difference! However, there are certain general principles that should always be at least considered:

(1) Wherever possible, one should bypass the problem by enrolling in a Christian school, or at least in a class with a Christian teacher. Whenever such vital questions as origins or basic meanings are to be discussed in courses or textbooks, the happiest situation is for both student and teacher to have the same ultimate motives and goals. Unfortunately, this solution is often impossible or impracticable.

(2) As long as a student is enrolled in a given class or program, he is under the authority of the teacher and is supposed to be there for the primary purpose of learning, rather than witnessing. He should, therefore, at all times be respectful and appreciative, doing his best to learn the material presented, whether he agrees with the teacher's personal philosophy or not. This is the Biblical admonition (Titus 2:9,10); Colossians 3:22-24; Ephesians 6:5-8) concerning masters and servants, and this would apply in principle at least to the relation between (school)-masters and those in their charge. Also, especially in the case of minor children, the teacher is *in loco parentis*, and the obedience of children as to parents is commanded (Galatians 4:1,2). If this situation becomes intolerable, due to gross irresponsibility or abuse of authority on the teacher's part, then probably the

proper course is to withdraw from the class, giving a careful and objective explanation, in writing and with documentation, of the reasons for withdrawal, to both the teacher and administrator concerned.

(3) Differences in attitudes and beliefs between teachers and students can often be resolved, or at least ameliorated, by a sincere attempt to maintain an attitude of objectiveness and good humor relative to their differences. Emotional arguments, especially when defensively oriented around religious or anti-religious convictions, will alienate, rather than attract (Proverbs 15:1; 25:11- Colossians 4:6).

(4) The student should be well-informed on both sides of the evolution-creation question, so that such objections as he may have opportunity to raise (whether in class, on term papers, in formal debates, or by other means) will be based on sound evidence, not on hearsay or misunderstanding. Most teachers (not all, unfortunately, but most) will respond with interest and fairness to a well-prepared and soundly reasoned argument for creationism, especially if presented objectively and scientifically, in an attitude of respect and good will (II Timothy 2:15; I Peter 3:15).

(5) Other things being equal, a person should be able to do a better job in any course or at any task if he is a Christian than he could have before becoming a Christian, since he now has greater resources and higher motives than before. The subject matter of any course has value to him as a Christian witness, even if for nothing else than to make him better informed concerning what others believe. Therefore, he should study diligently and do the best job of which he is capable (I Corinthians 10:31; Colossians 3:23). Any teacher is more likely to respond favorably to the suggestions of a good student than of a poor, lazy, belligerent student.

(6) There is no substitute for a consistent and winsome Christian walk in public and a life based on prayer and the study of Scripture in private, in meeting this particular problem as well as other problems involving similar tensions and confrontations in life (Proverbs 16:7).

Creation Workshop Sponsored
By School District

At the invitation of the Del Norte County (Calif.) School Board and the Citizens Committee for Scientific Creationism, Dr. Henry Morris and Dr. Duane Gish conducted a workshop for teachers and laymen in Crescent City, January 31 - February 2, 1974. This workshop, the first of its kind, will serve as a model for others to be sponsored by school districts. Mr. Louis Goodgame, a local science teacher, served as chairman and was the prime motivator in setting up the eventful meeting.

In 1973, Mr. Goodgame organized a survey of the county residents relative to the teaching of evolution and creation in the public schools. The results of the poll, which covered 1,346 homes, showed that 89% favored teaching creation in the public schools; 8% opposed; 8% were undecided. These figures show that though many favor a balanced teaching of creation and evolution, an over-whelming majority (89%) favor teaching creation. Comparable statistics would probably be found in most school districts in the U.S., providing the basis for re-establishment of balanced teaching concerning man's origins in our educational system.

Following the publication of the results of the survey, a Citizens Committee for Scientific Creation, with Mr. Goodgame as Chairman, was formed. This was followed by the formation of a Teachers' Committee on Scientific Creation, with Mr. Vern Babcock, Assistant Superintendent of Education, as Chairman.

Late in the year, a survey of the teachers of Del Norte County indicated sufficient interest for the school district to proceed with plans for a workshop on scientific creation. The Citizens Committee on Scientific Creation offered to pay half the costs of such a workshop. An invitation to conduct the workshop was extended by the School Board of Del Norte County to the Institute for Creation Research. Arrangements were made with Azusa Pacific College to grant one unit of graduate credit for the 15 hours of instruction given, while undergraduate credit, where requested, was granted by Christian Heritage College.

The response to the workshop was exceedingly gratifying. Those attending came not only from Del Norte County but also from Humboldt County in California, as well as from three counties in Oregon. A total of 153 registered for full-time attendance, and an additional 98 registered for part-time attendance, for a total of 251.

Was the workshop effective? The following statistics reflect the answers of a Student Questionnaire:

No. of
Replies

(111) Before the workshop what was your belief in Evolution?
  56% Opposed
  21% A philosophy
  11% A scientific theory
  06% A weak scientific theory
  04% Undecided
  02% A law, proven fact

(99) **Since the workshop what is your belief in Evolution?**
  38% No change
  30% More faith in Creation
  28% Less confidence in Evolution
  04% Need to re-study
   0% More faith in Evolution

(97) **Before the workshop what was your belief in Creation?**
  55% A law, proven fact
  20 A philsophy
  13% Based on faith
  06% A scientific theory
  04% Undecided
  02% A weak scientific theory

(99) **Since the workshop what is your belief in Creation?**
  65% Believe more fully

28% No change
04% Creation over Evolution
03% Need to re-study
0 Less confidence in Creation

(85) **Should both Creation and Evolution be taught in the public schools on a scientific basis?**

88% Yes
07% Undecided
05% No

These statistics, as well as many written comments submitted by those attending, reflect an overwhelmingly favorable response to the worskhop. This workshop represents another step in the campaign to re-establish a balance in public education throughout the county.

Poll Strongly Favors Creation
in California School District

The teaching of scientific creationism in public schools received overwhelming support in a recent poll conducted in the Cupertino Union School District, adjacent to San Jose, California. Over 84% of the citizens polled answered, "Yes," to the question: "In your opinion, should scientific evidence for creation be presented in the schools along with evolution?"

The poll was planned and conducted on a sound statistical sampling basis. Of the 2,000 citizens polled, 84.3% replied, "Yes"; 7.8% replied, "No"; 6.3% were uncertain; and 1.6% thought neither should be taught. The poll also ascertained the personal beliefs concerning origins of those interviewed, with 44.3% indicating their belief in creation, 23.3% in evolution, 3.5% in "both" evolution and creation, 10.6% in "neither," and 18.3% uncertain. It was noteworthy that, even among those who said they were evolutionists, 75.4% favored the teaching of scientific evidence for creation along with evolution, while only 20.1% expressed opposition. The Cupertino district is the largest elementary school district in the state and is quite cosmopolitan in makeup. It seems likely that the opinions of its citizenry would be representative of the state, and probably of the nation, as a whole. A similar poll conducted in the Del Norte District, a more rural area in Northern California, had given similar results (see *Acts and Facts,* April 1974).

The Cupertino Board of Education considered the results of the poll at two meetings, on May 14 and June 11, 1974. At the first meeting, Dr. Duane Gish of I.C.R. was invited to give a 30-minute presentation of the scientific evidence for creation, and the general reaction of the Board seemed favorable, though non-committal.

In the intervening month, however, strong opposition developed. The Superintendent of Education, Dr. Donald Todd (a professed humanist) and his administrative staff, the American Civil Liberties Union, liberal pastors in the area, and others led the opposition. The A.C.L.U. filed a letter stating that action permitting creation in the schools would amount to an unconstitutional teaching of religion.

The June 11 meeeting was planned with a long agenda, with the creation question near the bottom. Consequently, it was well after 10:30 P.M. before it came to the floor, and the Board chairman would permit only minimal discussion from the floor. Several spoke briefly on both sides, including Dr. Henry Morris of I.C.R., who stressed that creationism was at least as scientific as evolutionism and was the belief of thousands of scientists today.

The Board finally voted to go on record as favoring the inclusion in instruction of "several theories of the origins of life" (refusing, however, to denote them as *scientific* theories), but to leave its implementation up to a committee to be organized by Dr. Todd and his staff.

The poll was organized and conducted by an informal organization called the Citizens for Scientific Creation, under the leadership of Mrs. Nancy Stake. Over 200 people assisted in the poll, including a number of outstanding professional and community leaders, and these will no doubt continue to be in contact with the Board of Education and its committee to insist that creationism not be distorted in the implementation of the Board's policy.

The poll-taking approach seems to be an excellent means of demonstrating community concern over the creation/evolution question and of at least gaining the attention of local school officials. Those interested in organizing similar efforts in their own communities may obtain further information and advice by writing either Mrs. Stake (18970 Fernbrook Court, Saratoga, California 95070) or Mr. Louis Goodgame (organizer of the Del Norte poll), P.O. Box 992, Crescent City, California 95531.

THE BOOK OF GENESIS
Henry M. Morris

When creationists propose that creation be taught in the schools along with evolution, most people seem to think this means studying the Genesis record of the creation and other events in early earth history. A number of proposed laws have actually been introduced in various legislative bodies proposing that this Bible account of creation be taught in the public schools.

We believe this approach is wrong for two main reasons. First, it will appear to give substance to evolutionists' claims that religion and Bible teaching are being introduced into the schools and, in the present climate of political and judicial opinion, such an approach will very likely be declared unconstitutional by the courts and have the effect of barring the teaching of creation altogether. Second, teaching the account in Genesis *would* involve the teaching of the Bible and religion in the schools and, in view of the wide variety of religious interpretations of Genesis and the Bible that exist, such teaching, if handled by a non-Christian or "liberal" Christian, might well be as objectionable to conservative Christians as it would be to atheists.

Therefore, we think a better approach is to teach *only* the *scientific* aspects of creationism in the public schools, keeping the Bible and religion out of it altogether, but nevertheless demonstrating to the student that the concept of a Creator and primeval special creation is at least as good a scientific model of origins as is the evolution model.

Lest anyone wonder whether, by advocating such a position, I no longer believe the Genesis record, let me say emphatically that it is only because I *do* believe Genesis and the Bible so strongly that I am confident a strictly scientific study of the physical world and the history of life is bound, in the long run, to conform precisely to what the Genesis record had said all along.

As a matter of fact, I am currently engaged in writing a textbook on the Book of Genesis, for use in my course on Genesis at Christian Heritage College. In researching and writing this commentary, I have been thrilled to see again and again, more clearly than ever before, how completely accurate, believable, and relevant each of the 50 chapters of Genesis is today. Genesis is the foundational book of the Bible and, therefore, of all meaningful human experience.

I heartily encourage everyone to study diligently (though not in the public schools!), and believe thoroughly, the Genesis record of early history.

Citizens Committee Holds Oregon Rally

Dr. Henry M. Morris, Director of the Institute for Creation Research, addressed a special meeting sponsored by the Ad Hoc Citizens Committee for Quality Education in Hillsboro, Oregon (a county seat and a suburb of Portland) on July 27, meeting in the auditorium of the J.W. Poynter Junior High School. Nearly 300 people were in attendance as Dr. Morris spoke on "Creation and Evolution in the Public Schools."

The Citizens Committee had been formed for the immediate purpose of opposing the installation of the controversial new social studies program, entitled "Man — A Course of Study" (MACOS) in their schools. This program, extremely evolutionistic and humanistic in its teachings on man, has been sharply criticized in many places because of its subtle techniques for encouraging children to question parental authority and even to justify senilicide and infanticide under certain conditions.

A pilot program had been approved by the school board and was to be given to all children in the grades and schools affected except those whose parents requested their exemption. As a result of careful research on the course and objections by a number of concerned parents and publicity in the local newspapers, the school board changed its directive so that only students whose parents specifically requested it would be enrolled in the course. However, certain teachers were reported actively pressuring students to enroll. MACOS has been criticized by many leading educators because of its deceptive teaching techniques, in addition to creationists' objections to its overt evolutionism and humanism.

The one-hour lecture by Dr. Morris at the rally emphasized the superiority of the scientific creation model over the evolution model in its ability to explain the known scientific data concerning man and the physical world. A question period followed, and the general response of the audience was enthusiastic.

EVOLUTIONARY SMOG

Henry M. Morris

As everyone knows, the term "smog" is a word invented to describe the baleful combination of smoke and fog which has come to characterize modern urban complexes. It is also an excellent description of the type of arguments offered by evolutionists alarmed at the thought of having to teach creationism. The fog of irrelevancies and the smokescreen of bombast which emanates from evolutionary spokesmen provide in themselves full evidence that the evolutionary system is without scientific foundation.

The most common of these obfuscatory arguments is that the teaching of creationism is "religious," and hence unconstitutional. This was the main thrust of the case presented by attorneys for the National Association of Biology Teachers to both the Tennessee State Supreme Court and the U.S. District Court, in attempting to strike down the 1973 Tennessee law requiring equal treatment of Biblical creationism in textbooks used in the state.

Unfortunately, this argument convinced both courts, and the law was indeed ruled unconstitutional just this August. U.S. District Judge Frank Gray Jr. included the following irrelevancy in his written decision: "Every religious sect, from the worshippers of Apollo to the followers of Zoroaster, has its belief or theory. It is beyond the comprehension of this court how the legislature, if indeed it did, expected that all such theories could be included in any textbook of reasonable size."

This is pure buncombe, and it is difficult to believe that intelligent men (biologists, attorneys, judges, etc.) are not well aware of that fact.

There are *not many* different concepts of origins, but *only two* — creation and evolution. No creationist has proposed that textbooks should discuss all the cosmogonic myths of the various ancient and modern tribes, and this is not the issue. All of these are evolutionary systems, anyway, not creationist, postulating a closed-system universe and eternal matter, with the gods and goddesses (personifying the forces of nature) operating on this primordial material to bring it into its present variety of forms.

There is only one alternative to these many ancient and modern evolutionary explanations; namely, the special creation of all things by a transcendent personal Creator. This concept does not have to be expressed in terms of the Genesis revelation, but only as a scientific model of origins, without explicit reference to the Biblical terminology. It is true, nevertheless, that *only* in the Bible can one find this concept of special creation. All others, whether ancient or modern, are merely variations of the fundamental evolutionary cosmogony.

If the intellectual establishment is really disturbed about the danger of teaching religion in the schools, then it ought forthwith to urge the banishment of evolutionary teaching from the classrooms. The creation model correlates all the real *facts* of science far more directly and effectively than the evolution model. Evolution is unproved, unproveable, untestable, unreasonable and impossible! One must exercise a very high degree of credulous faith in a process which is contrary to all scientific observation and experience if he is to be an evolutionist.

93

Nevertheless, the creationist recognizes that belief in creation also requires faith, though it is a reasonable faith rather than a faith contrary to reason as in the case of evolution. Consequently, he does not propose that evolution be outlawed, but rather that *both* creation and evolution be taught, strictly as scientific models, allowing students to read and hear the evidences for and against each, and then to make up their own minds what to believe.

What is unfair or unreasonable or unscientific about that? And why are evolutionists so anxious to smog up this simple issue?

INTRODUCING CREATIONISM INTO THE PUBLIC SCHOOLS*

By Henry M. Morris, Ph.D.

More people today than ever are objecting to the exclusive teaching of evolution in the public schools. Strong pressures are developing aimed at opening the schools to the teaching of special creation as a viable alternative to evolution.

Resistance to teaching creationism is still very strong, however. Opposition usually centers around two related arguments. First, evolution is widely claimed to be the only acceptable *scientific* theory of origins. Second, creation is assumed to be strictly a *religious* concept, which on that account has no place in a public school curriculum.

Both of these arguments are wrong and invalid. Creation can be shown to be a more effective scientific model of origins than evolution, and evolution can be shown to require a higher degree of credulous faith than creation. It is the purpose of this paper, however, to encourage a careful and objective study of *both* concepts of origins, on a scientific level only, in the public schools.

Creationists Need to Become Informed

If this effort is to succeed, creationists must first of all be able to support their claim that creation is as scientific as evolution and that evolution is as religious as creation. Political or legislative efforts to require creationist teaching

* Impact Series #20, (December 1974)

will be futile otherwise. Even if a favorable statute or court decision is obtained, it will probably be declared unconstitutional, especially if the legislation or injunction refers to the *Bible* account of creation. Furthermore, a teacher forced to teach creationism with no knowledge of how to do it and with a built-in prejudice against it is not very likely to give the students a fair exposure to it, probably doing more damage than if it were ignored altogether.

The only effective way to get creationism taught properly is to have it taught by teachers who are both willing to do it and adequately prepared to do it. Since most teachers now are neither willing nor able, they must first be both persuaded and instructed themselves.

This means that someone must do the persuading and someone do the instructing. This burden must ultimately fall on the concerned creationists of each particular community. However, although a community-wide census would almost certainly show a large majority favoring the teaching of both creation and evolution, only a remnant will be found willing to work to accomplish that end.

In any case, the concerned creationist minority, whether large or small, will need first of all to become informed on the issue and its various implications. Each individual needs to be aware of the significance of evolutionary teaching and of the scientific evidence favoring creation. He does not have to be a scientist to understand the latter, but he does need to take the time for a careful reading of some of the modern treatments of the subject by creationist scientists.

For example, he should read the two I.C.R. books, *The Troubled Waters of Evolution* and *Scientific Creationism*, or other books of comparable scope and treatment. The former shows the historical background and modern influence of evolutionary thought, and the latter shows the scientific superiority of creationism in every phase of the problem of origins.

He should then do his best to help others become informed. There are many ways to do this — Sunday School classes, letters-to-the-editor, gifts of books to libraries and key individuals, promoting creation seminars, etc. Perhaps the best way is by personal, friendly discussions with school officials and other people of influence.

In the following sections appear additional specific suggestions for creationists (or open-minded evolutionists) who are in various positions of key responsibility.

School Administrators

Members of state and local school boards, school superintendents, curriculum specialists and school principals are, of course, in the most important positions of all with regard to this problem. Some of these officials are creationists themselves and many others are sufficiently dedicated to true education and service to the community as to be willing to provide the young people in their schools an opportunity to hear both sides of this all-important question.

There are many ways in which this can be done. First, each teacher should be provided with a good reference handbook on scientific creationism and asked to study it. The Public School Edition of *Scientific Creationism*, prepared by the Institute for Creation Research, is designed specifically for this purpose, providing conveniently-organized and well-documented scientific evidence for special creation on all aspects of the subject of origins.

The teacher should then be encouraged (not required) to use this information in his or her classes. As long as no *religious* instruction is given (for example, an exposition of the creation chapters in Genesis), there is no legal problem involved. For example, when treating such a subject as human origins, the teacher can balance the usual evolutionary discussion of Ramapithecus, Australopithecus, Neanderthal, etc., by citing the creationists' evidence that such fossils are invariably either of apes or of men, with no true and unquestioned intermediates between men and apes. Such a discussion need not deal with such theological topics as the divine purpose for man, but only with the factual evidence concerning the unique physical and mental characteristics of men.

If possible, arrangements should also be made to conduct Workshops on Scientific Creationism for the teachers of the district. These can even be offered on a graduate credit basis, so that the teachers can apply the time spent on the Workshop toward a graduate degree. There are now many creationist scientists and teachers who are qualified to instruct in such Workshops, the purpose of which is to provide basic scientific orientation in the creation model of origins and in the deficiencies of the evolution model.

For those teachers who, for personal reasons, are unwilling to teach creation along with evolution, substitutes can be provided who could come in, say, for a special three-week unit on scientific creationism. It might be feasible to have one or more specialists available for rotating assignments of this kind.

Creationist literature can also be provided for school and classroom libraries. This is especially needed as source material for student papers and special projects. If only evolutionary books are available, as is true now in most libraries, it is obviously impossible for any student to carry out a meaningful research study on any topic related to origins. There is a great deal of sound scientific creationist literature now available. See, for example, the Appendix in *Scientific Creationism* for an extensive bibliographical listing.

School administrators may have two serious reservations about taking any of the above steps, one political in nature and one financial. As long as the teaching of creationism is done strictly in a scientific context, however, without reference to the Bible or other religious literature, such teaching is perfectly constitutional, legal and proper. In fact, the exclusive teaching of evolution is *not* constitutional, legal or proper, since belief in evolution requires at least as much faith as belief in creation and is therefore a religious belief. Evolutionary philosophy is the foundation of atheism and humanism, which are nothing less than non-theistic religions. Exclusive teaching of evolution has the effect of establishing religious systems of this sort as state-endorsed and state-supported religions. The political reservation is, therefore, not only invalid but actually applies in reverse. This is the very reason why there is so much concern about this question around the country.

The financial reservation is understandable, as most schools supposedly do not have enough funds to adequately finance existing programs, let alone a new program such as this. However, it is a simple matter of priorities. New programs of other sorts are continually being introduced, and nothing can be more important than giving the students a fair opportunity to choose between two philosophies that will have profound influence on them, one way or another, all the rest of their lives. Furthermore, the cost is not really very much. Providing one book per teacher, plus perhaps a dozen books for library use, plus an annual workshop would altogether comprise only a miniscule percentage of the district's annual budget, and there are bound to be certain marginal items in other programs that could be postponed if necessary. In fact, most school districts actually have funds already budgeted for supplemental materials.

Teachers

Creationist teachers are in a unique position to play a critical role in this strategic conflict. First of all, they are better able than anyone else to win their fellow teachers over either to creationism or at least to acceptance of an equal-time approach. If they have first become adequately informed themselves, they are then able, over coffee in the faculty lounge, in the faculty lunchroom, or in the homes of their colleagues, to discuss the subject on a friendly, scientific basis, and hopefully to convince them of the viability and importance of the creation model. Books and other literature can be given or loaned, invitations to hear creationist speakers can be shared, and other opportunities for personal help utilized.

As far as the teacher's own classes are concerned, by all means creationism should be included, no matter what the course subject or grade level may be. This is perfectly legal as long as the teaching is factual and scientific, and in fact, such teaching is necessary to balance the evolutionist bias that is almost certain to be present in the textbook and supplementary material for the course.

In some courses — for example, biology, ancient history, etc. — it may well be feasible to incorporate a formal unit on scientific creationism into the course content. The topics in the book *Scientific Creationism* would provide an excellent outline for such a unit, adapted by the teacher to the particular grade level.

More commonly, perhaps, the teacher should merely introduce creation as an alternative whenever the textbook or course plan contains evolutionary teachings or implications. For example, when an earth science textbook discusses the geologic age system and the great age of the earth, the teacher should also discuss the geologic evidence for the catastrophic interpretation of the fossil record and some of the scientific evidences for a young earth.

Other possibilities include the use of creationist films and slides, assignment of student projects which incorporate both evolutionist and creationist interpretations, and invitations to local creationist scientists as guest lecturers. In the latter case, the teacher may also be able to arrange for such speakers to address a school assembly.

Pastors

Because of their wide influence, not only with their own congregations but in the community as a whole, creationist pastors can often play a vital part in getting creationism back into the schools of the community. They have knowledge of the Biblical teachings on creation and are already aware of the problem and concerned about it. Once they realize the importance of promoting *scientific* creationism in the public schools, leaving Biblical and theological aspects to be taught in their churches and in the homes, they can often serve as leaders of community-wide creationist emphases, especially if they will work in cooperation with pastors of other churches and denominations.

Pastors are especially capable at the arts of persuasion and instruction, and this is exactly what is needed. They should be able to arrange opportunities to talk with school administrators at such length as necessary to present the case for creation adequately to them on a personal basis.

In his own church, the pastor should see that his own communicants are well instructed in the scientific, as well as Biblical, aspects of creationism. It is especially important that the children and young people in his church be well equipped with factual evidence for creation.

He can accomplish such instruction through a series of special messages, through using creationist Sunday School literature, through having special speakers, by providing creationist literature in the church library and for his members, and by various other means.

Scientists

Scientists and other professionally trained people (engineers, lawyers, medical doctors, etc.) are often capable of special leadership in creationist efforts. Young people are often led to believe that all scientists and other educated specialists are evolutionists, and the best argument against this fallacious claim is the personal testimony of scientists who are *not* evolutionists. The fact is, of course, that today there are thousands of scientists who are creationists, and usually there are at least several in every community.

Scientists and other professionals who are Christians have a peculiar trust from the Lord. At the same time, the atmosphere of their professions, emphasizing intellect and prestige as they do, poses a real temptation and danger. People in these positions are especially sensitive to academic ridicule and ostracism and therefore especially vulnerable to intellectual compromise. Furthermore, Christian scientists who have themselves taken a compromising position toward evolution seem particularly antagonistic toward those Christian scientists who will *not* compromise. Somehow an attitude of sweet tolerance toward the unbelieving philosophies of anti-Christian scientists is often accompanied by a bitter intolerance toward creationist scientists, whose very existence is a condemnation of such unnecessary compromise.

Nevertheless, creationist scientists must not be swayed by the objections of their evolutionist Christian colleagues. The facts of science, as well as the teachings of Scripture, are squarely against the evolutionary system and there is no reason whatever (except the fear of men) for yielding to such compromise.

Informed creationist scientists are perhaps the best qualified people in the community to deal publicly with evolutionists' objections to creation in the school, to serve as special speakers and consultants on scientific creationism where needed, and to engage in other similar activities. They should be conversant with all the literature on creationism, be active members in the Creation Research Society and generally serve as the scientific spokesmen for the creationist movement in their own communities. They can also help other creationists in the community who are not scientists avoid making unscientific statements which could react negatively against their cause.

Parents and Other People

The majority of concerned Christians and other creationists do not come directly under any of the above categories. Nevertheless each person is very important. The larger the group of vocal creationists in the community, the more probable it is that they can get a sympathetic hearing from school officials.

Parents are especially important, if they have children in the public schools of the district. Through personal conversations with teachers, principals, and school board members, in an atmosphere of friendly helpfulness, but also one of well-informed confidence in the soundness of their arguments, parents often can exert a very significant influence on classroom teachings and attitudes.

If feasible under the particular local circumstances, such citizens should establish a formal community organization, with some appropriate name (Citizens for Scientific

Creationism, Parents Concerned for Educational Integrity, Civil Rights for Creationists, Committee for the Improvement of Education, etc.). Someone can be placed in charge of promotion and publicity, with a view to arousing community concern over the problem. Sympathetic news and television reports can be very valuable; on the other hand, a sarcastic news story on creationism can do a great deal of harm, so the search for publicity should proceed cautiously, and the Committee should be as certain as possible that the reporter really has an understanding of the whole issue.

One very worthwhile project which the organization might undertake would be a community census or poll, in which the feelings of the people in the school district on the subject at hand could be determined. Those that have been taken so far confirm that the large majority of citizens do want to see both creation and evolution (rather than either one exclusively) taught on a scientific level in their public schools.

Another project might well be to raise funds to provide creationist books for the classroom libraries in their schools. Another would be to underwrite and promote a Creationism Workshop for teachers, as well as a Creation Seminar for people in general. Debates between evolutionists and knowledgeable creationists might be arranged. Advertisements for creationism can be placed in campus and community newspapers. Many other such projects might well suggest themselves in the particular area.

Students

Finally, we come to those who are the most affected by this controversy, the students themselves. What can creationist students do to counteract the evolutionary teaching in their own classes and schools?

There are many things such students can do, but one thing they should *not* do is to react belligerently or sarcastically against the teacher. As students, their purpose is primarily that of learning rather than of teaching or witnessing. They are both legally and morally under the authority of the school and the teacher, and whatever witness they may be able to give will carry far more weight if done in the proper way and through the established chain of command.

Also, there is no doubt that a teacher will pay more attention to the suggestions and criticisms of a good conscientious student than to those of a lazy and indifferent student. In any kind of effective Christian witnessing, the witness must know what he is talking about, be winsome and tactful, kind and patient, and especially where someone of higher authority is involved, respectful and courteous. Cleanliness and neatness don't hurt, either.

Assuming the above conditions as prerequisites, then the opportunities available to such students might include: raising questions, or offering alternative suggestions, in class discussions; using a creationist approach in speeches and special papers and projects; talking to the teacher privately about available creationist literature and speakers; inviting the teacher and classmates to attend creation seminars or similar meetings; suggesting a classroom debate on the creation-evolution question; giving sound creationist periodical literature or tracts to the teacher; and other similar actions.

Even if the teacher does not respond favorably, the student can still consider it a profitable learning experience. If there is a problem relative to passing tests in the course, the student can usually handle it adequately be prefacing his answers by some such assertion as "Evolutionists believe that —."

In those few cases where the teacher seems intolerably and rigidly bigoted, insisting that the student not only know the arguments for evolution but also believe them himself, it may be necessary for the student to ask his parents or pastor for help in the situation. If this likewise fails, there may finally be no recourse except to withdraw from the course, giving a courteous written explanation as to reasons. Such a last resort, however, should seldom be necessary or desirable. Reports of student experiences around the country indicate, on the other hand, that one or two creationist students have often been able to make a tremendous impact on the class, and even on the teacher, through their careful, courteous, consistent Christian testimony.

RESOLUTION FOR EQUITABLE TREATMENT OF BOTH CREATION AND EVOLUTION*

A Resolution to encourage equitable treatment of alternate scientific concepts of origins in the public schools and other institutions of the state —

1. WHEREAS, it appears that most, if not all, state-supported educational institutions require students to take courses in which naturalistic concepts of evolution are taught as scientific explanations of origins of the universe, life and man; [1] and

II. WHEREAS evolution is not demonstrable as scientific fact or testable as a scientific hypothesis, and therefore must be accepted philosophically by faith; [2] and

III. WHEREAS there is another concept of origins — namely, that of special creation of the universe, life, and man by an omnipotent personal Creator — which is at least as satisfactory a *scientific explanation* of origins as is evolution, and is accepted as such by a large number of scientists and other well-informed people; [3] and

IV. WHEREAS many citizens of this State believe in the special creation concept of origins and are convinced that exclusive indoctrination of their children in the evolutionary concept (including so-called "theistic" evolution) is inimical to their religious faith and to their moral and civic teachings, as well as to scientific objectivity, academic freedom, and civil rights; [4] and

V. WHEREAS even most citizens who are not opposed to the evolution concept at least favor a balanced treatment of

---

1. See Appendix A for documentation
2. See Appendix B for documentation
3. See Appendix C for documentation
4. See Appendix D for documentation
* I.C.R. Impact Series # 26 (July 1975)

104

these two alternative views of origins in their schools, thus allowing students to consider all of the evidences favoring each concept before deciding which to believe.[1]

Now, therefore, Be it resolved by the House of Representatives, the Senate concurring:

That the State Higher Education Commission and the State Board of Public Education be, and hereby is, urged to recommend to all state-supported educational institutions that a balanced treatment of evolution and special creation be encouraged in all courses, textbooks, library materials and museum displays dealing in any way with the subject of origins, such treatment to be limited to the scientific, rather than religious, aspects of the two concepts.

Background and Explanation

The Institute for Creation Research is primarily an educational organization, with a three-fold ministry of research, writing, and teaching in the field of scientific and Biblical creationism. It does not seek to organize or promote political or legal action requiring the teaching of creation in the public schools or other tax-supported institutions, although it does recognize that it is fair and equitable that both evolution and creation should receive essentially impartial and equal treatment in such institutions.

The I.C.R. frequently receives requests from citizens' groups in various communities for advice or help in such political or legal actions, however, and is of course keenly interested in those developments. Each state and each district is different, and outside organizations such as I.C.R. are in no position to make decisions as to the proper course of action for the concerned citizens of each community to follow in their own regions. The citizens themselves should choose and implement the best procedures in their own circumstances.

Two general observations are in order, however. Where possible, an educational approach is probably more effective in the long run than a legalistic approach. It has proved impossible heretofore to get effective "creation laws" passed

---

1. See Appendix E for documentation

by legislative bodies or "creation decisions" rendered by courts.

Secondly, the false idea that evolution is "science" and creation is "religion" has been exceedingly difficult to dispel. This issue is nearly always used as the main excuse for the rejection of attempts to reintroduce creationism into schools and other institutions.

The suggestion seems in order, therefore, that creationists should normally work through persuasion rather than coercion and should emphatically stress the scientific (rather than religious) aspects of creationism, as well as the basically religious nature of evolutionism.[1] When a political approach is followed in a particular state or community, then I.C.R. suggests that a *resolution* be proposed, rather than a legislative bill or an administrative or judicial directive. A resolution *encourages*, rather than *compels*, the teaching of creation, and so should not encounter the usual bitter opposition of the educational and scientific establishments. Also, if the resolution stresses (with documentation) that creation and evolution are both *equally* scientific and/or religious, and that fairness and constitutionality warrant an equitable treatment of both, then hopefully responsible officials will support it.

Accordingly, I.C.R. has prepared the foregoing sample suggested resolution for consideration by state legislatures, with these considerations in mind. It should, of course, be adapted to the particular state. With appropriate changes, it could also be modified to a form suitable for submission to state or local school boards, or to other bodies (e.g., to church denominational meetings, parent-teacher associations, museum advisory boards, or to other groups concerned with this problem).

The resolution itself is brief, taking less than two minutes to read, and so would not be too demanding on the time of

---

1. For specific suggestions, see the booklet *Introducing Scientific Creationism into the Public Schools*. (San Diego, Institute for Creation Research, 1975).

busy legislators or administrators. Documentation on its particulars is then provided in several brief appendices for those who can take the time for a more thorough briefing.

If this resolution, modified as necessary to meet the particular situation, can be of help to any groups of interested citizens, they are more than welcome to use it without further permission. In fact it would be better not to mention I.C.R. at all in connection with it, so that the officials involved will realize that it is their own constituents who are concerned with the issue.

Appendix A. Prevalence of Evolutionist Indoctrination

That evolution is taught exclusively and dogmatically in the public schools and textbooks of the nation is so well known as to need no documentation, at least for anyone familiar with the situation. Nor is evolutionist teaching confined to biology, as many might think. According to leading evolutionary ecologist Rene Dubos:

"The great religions of the West have come to accept an historical view of creation. Evolutionary concepts are applied also to social institutions and to the arts. Indeed, most political parties, as well as schools of theology, sociology, history, or arts, teach these concepts and make them the basis of their doctrines." ("Humanistic Biology," *American Scientist*, Vo. 53, March 1965, p. 6).

If one is inclined to question the universal prevalence of evolutionary teaching in school textbooks, he is urged to examine all the textbooks used in the schools of his own district. Perhaps, to save time, he could merely ask the district curriculum supervisor to show him even *one* regularly used textbook in which creation is taught as a credible *scientific* alternative to evolution.

Appendix B. The Unscientific Character of Evolution

The one-sided indoctrination of evolutionary teaching in the minds of young people is usually defended on the basis of the common belief that evolution is a proved fact of science, or at least the only properly scientific approach to the study of origins. Such ideas are quite wrong, however, as is evident merely by the recognition of the real nature of *science* (that is "knowledge").

"A hypothesis is empirical or scientific only if it can be tested by experience . . . . A hypothesis or theory which cannot be, at least in principle, falsified by empirical observations and experiments does not belong to the realm of science." (Francisco J. Ayala, "Biological Evolution: Natural Selection or Random Walk?", *American Scientist*, Vol. 62, November-December 1974, p. 700).

That evolutionary speculation does not meet such criteria is evident from the obvious requirement that vast spans of time would be required to observe any significant evolutionary changes.

"Our theory of evolution . . . is thus 'outside of empirical science' . . . . No one can think of ways in which to test it. Ideas, either without basis or based on a few laboratory experiments carried out in extremely simplified systems have attained currency far beyond their validity. They have become part of an evolutionary dogma accepted by most of us as part of our training." (Paul Ehrlich and L.C. Birch. "Evolutionary History and Population Biology," *Nature*, Vol. 214, April 22, 1967, p. 352).

"Dogma" is a religious term, not a scientific term! Evolution cannot be either proved or disproved, and so must be accepted on faith.

Evolutionists sometimes claim that evolution can actually be seen functioning today. However, the small variations observable in the present order of things are quite trivial, "horizontal" changes within restricted kinds, rather than "vertical" changes from kinds of lower complexity to kinds of higher complexity, such as true evolution requires.

"Evolution, at least in the sense that Darwin speaks of it, cannot be detected within the lifetime of a single observer." (David G. Kitts, "Paleontology and Evolutionary Theory," *Evolution*, Vol. 28, September 1974, p. 466).

The actual evidence of true "vertical" evolution is claimed by evolutionists to be found in the fossil record, which is supposed to be the documented story of the evolutionary changes over the millions of years of the geological ages. As a matter of fact, however, there are no fossils of forms intermediate between kinds in the fossil record either.

"Despite the bright promise that paleontology provides a means of 'seeing' evolution, it has presented some nasty difficulties for evolutionists, the most notorious of which is the presence of 'gaps' in the fossil record. Evolution requires intermediate forms between species and paleontology does not provide them." (*Ibid*, p. 467).

Appendix C. The Scientific Case for Creation

Evolutionists commonly object to the idea of incorporating creationism into curricula because they believe it to be unscientific, not capable of being observed or tested in the laboratory. Creationists, of course, recognize this criticism as valid; by its very nature, creation took place during a period of special creation in the past, and so is not observable at present. However, as shown in Appendix B, evolution is subject to exactly the same criticism. The trivial organic changes that can actually be observed can be as well explained in terms of creationism as they can by evolution. That is, they fit perfectly into the concept of the special creation of original basic kinds with ability to vary horizontally within the kinds.

Thus, as far as empirical scientific evidence is concerned, creation is on exactly the same basis as evolution. Neither can be proved or disproved. The writer of the Foreword to the latest edition of Darwin's *Origin of Species*, a leading evolutionary biologist and Fellow of the Royal Society, has himself recognized this fact.

"Belief in the theory of evolution is thus exactly parallel to belief in special creation — both are concepts which believers know to be true but neither, up to the present, has been capable of proof." (L. Harrison Matthews, in

Origin of Species, by Charles Darwin, London, J.M. Dent and Sons, Ltd. 1971, p.x.).

Although neither evolution nor creation can be scientifically proved, the real facts of science are more easily understood in terms of an initial creation than of a continuing evolution. Even evolutionists acknowledge this in some cases.

For example the extreme complexity of even the simplest forms of life are far too complex to have arisen by any chance evolutionary process.

"But the most sweeping evolutionary questions at the level of biochemical genetics are still unanswered. How the genetic code first appeared and then evolved and, earlier even than that, how life itself originated on earth remain for the future to resolve. . . . Did the code and the means of translating it appear simultaneously in evolution? It seems almost incredible that any such coincidence could have occurred, given the extraordinary complexities of both sides and the requirement that they be coordinated accurately for survival. By a pre-Darwinian (or a skeptic of evolution after Darwin) this puzzle would surely have been interpreted as the most powerful sort of evidence for special creation." (Caryl P. Haskins, "Advances and Challenges in Science in 1970," *American Scientist*, Vol. 59, May-June, 1971, p. 305).

As a matter of fact, it can be shown that practically every possible type of scientific evidence that has any bearing on the subject of origins fits better into the creation model than the evolution model.[1] This fact is entirely independent of whatever religious inferences might be drawn from either model.

As a result of an increasing public awareness of this type of evidence, there are now thousands of scientists and other educated intellectuals who have become creationists in recent years. The frequent claim that all scientists are

---

1. *Scientific Creationism (Public School Ed)* San Diego, Calif., Creation Life Publishers, 1974, p. 18pp

evolutionists is simply false. For example, the 12-year-old Creation Research Society (headquarters in Ann Arbor, Michigan) now has a membership of over 500 scientists from all fields, each with a post-graduate degree in science and each committed to belief in special creation. Another organization, the Institute for Creation Research, San Diego, has a full-time program of scientific research, publication, and education in scientific creationism. The creationist minority among scientists and educators is rapidly growing in number and strength everywhere.

Appendix D. Harmful Effects of Evolutionist Indoctrination

The evolutionary explanation for origins, although impossible either to prove or to test scientifically, is nevertheless defended by its proponents on the basis that it is the only explanation which is *naturalistic*, not involving the "supernatural" element of a divine Creator. According to a leading British evolutionist:

"The theory of evolution (is) a theory universally accepted not because it can be proved by logically coherent evidence to be true but because the only alternative, special creation, is clearly incredible." (D.M.S. Watson, "Adaptation," *Nature*, Vol. 123 (1929), p. 233).

Special creation, of course, is a perfectly "credible" concept if God exists, so this statement is a tacit admission that the theory of evolution is fundamentally atheistic, an attempt to account for the universe and life without God.

Not all evolutionists are atheists, but the theory itself is basically naturalistic and atheistic. This fact does not in any way make it "scientific," however. If *theism* is a religious belief, so is *a-theism!*

Evolution is a "dogma," a "belief," and therefore is in every sense a religious philosophy, not a science. It is a complete cosmology, a world-view, and since students in public schools everywhere are being indoctrinated exclusively with this belief, it has become in effect the *established religion* of the state!

But it is clearly unconstitutional for our schools to teach such an established religion. At the very least, this emphasis should be balanced with an equal emphasis on the alternative belief, namely special creation.

"Government in our democracy . . . state and federal, must be neutral in matters of religious theory . . . . It may not aid, foster, or promote one religious theory as against another." (Justice Abe Fortas, comment in connection with U.S. Supreme Court ruling striking down Arkansas anti-evolution law).

The one-sided teaching of the belief that the universe is a product of random processes, and man himself merely an evolved animal, naturally has profound implications for human attitudes and behavior. Further, the implicit teaching that evolutionary changes are inevitable and that evolutionary progress involves a struggle-and-survive principle, has led to many harmful social theories and practices.

"In turn, biological evolutionism exerted ever-widening influences on the natural and social sciences, as well as on philosophy and even on politics. Not all of these extrabiological repercussions were either sound or commendable. Suffice it to mention the so-called Social Darwinism, which often sought to justify the inhumanity of man to man, and the biological racism which furnished a fraudulent scientific sanction for the atrocities committed in Hitler's Germany and elsewhere." (Theodosius Dobzhansky, "Evolution at Work," *Science*, Vol. 127, May 9, 1958, p. 1091).

It can be documented[1] that the evolutionary philosophy has served as the pseudo-scientific basis and justification for racism, modern imperialism, nazism, anarchism, communism, behaviorism, animalistic amoralism, humanism, and practically all the other anti-Christian and anti-theistic social philosophies and movements of the past century and more.

---

1. Henry M. Morris, The Troubled Waters of Evolution (San Diego, Creation Life Publishers, 1975), 224 pages.

There are millions of people in this country, Christians in all denominations as well as many Jews and people of other religions, who strongly object to such systems as those listed above and to the naturalistic evolutionary teaching on which they are based. They are convinced, with good reason, that this type of religious indoctrination is destructive of their own religious teachings and subverts the moral and civic training which they try to give their children, and therefore is illegally discriminatory against their own constitutional freedoms and civil rights.

Appendix E. Fairness of a Balanced-Treatment Approach

In view of the fact that evolution and creation are the only two possible concepts of origins, that evolution requires at least as much of a "religious" faith as does creation, and that creation fits all the "scientific" data at least as well as does evolution, it is clear that *both* should be taught in the schools and other public institutions of our country, and that this should be done on an equal-time, equal-emphasis basis, insofar as possible.

This is obviously the only equitable and fair approach to take, the only one consistent with traditional American principles of religious freedom, civil rights, freedom of information, scientific objectivity, academic freedom, and constitutionality. That American citizens, when given opportunity to express their opinions, fully support this idea has been proven conclusively in recent carefully conducted, scientifically organized community polls taken in two California school districts.

One of these was a semi-rural district, Del Norte County in northern California. Here, a poll of 1326 homes revealed 89 per cent to favor including creation along with evolution in school curricula (*Acts and Facts,* Vol. 3, April 1974, p.1). The other was a very cosmopolitan district in the San Jose-San Francisco metropolitan region, Cupertino, the largest elementary school district in the state. In this case, a poll of over 2000 homes showed 84 per cent to favor including creation (*Acts and Facts*, Vol. 3, August 1974, p. 3). In both cases, the emphasis in the questionnaire was on *scientific* creationism, rather than its religious aspects.

There is little doubt that similar majorities would be obtained in most other school districts across the country, if people were informed on the issue and given opportunity to express their preferences.

Two final points should be stressed. There are really only two scientific models of origins — continuing evolution by natural processes or completed creation by supernatural processes. The latter need not be formulated in terms of Biblical references at all, and is not comparable to the various cosmogonic myths of different tribes and nations, all of which are merely special forms of evolutionism, rather than creationism, rejecting as they do the vital creationist concept of a personal transcendent Creator of all things in the beginning. It is not the Genesis story of creation that should be taught in the schools, of course, but only creationism as a scientific model.

Secondly, the idea of theistic evolution (that is, evolution as God's method of creation) is not in any way a satisfactory compromise between evolution and creation. It is merely an alternate form of evolutionism with no *scientific* distinction from that of naturalistic evolutionism, and is vulnerable to all the scientific, religious and legal objections outlined previously for evolutionism in general.

We conclude, therefore, that *both* creation and evolution should be taught — as scientific models only — in all books and classes where *either* is taught or implied. Administrators should assume the responsibility of providing adequate training and materials to enable their teachers to accomplish this goal.

chapter IV

CONFRONTATION WITH SCIENTISTS

SCIENTIFIC ESTABLISHMENT ALARMED AT CREATIONISM RISE

As more and more people are exposed to scientific creationism, increasing alarm is being expressed by leaders of the evolutionary establishment. Creationists once were ignored or ridiculed by such men, but amusement has now been displaced by anger and hostility on the part of many, interest and surprise on the part of not a few.

In the most recent (April 1974) issue of the journal of the National Association of Biology Teachers, Dr. William Mayer, in a lengthy letter-to-the-editor, accuses creationist scientists of using science as a back-door method of bringing religion back into the schools. He quotes extensively from I.C.R.'s *Acts and Facts*, as well as other creationist writings, to argue that the motivation behind the creationist movement is religious rather than scientific. He does not point to any errors in the scientific case for creationism, however.

Readers of *Acts and Facts* will recall that Dr. Mayer, who is Director of the Biological Sciences Study Center at the University of Colorado, responsible for the famous B.S.C.S. high-school biology textbooks, refused last year to accept a challenge to debate Dr. Henry Morris, then President of The Creation Research Society. He also refused an invitation from the Louisiana Science Teachers Association to appear on a panel with Dr. Morris. In both cases he had been assured that the discussion would deal solely with science and that Dr. Morris would not discuss the Bible or religion in any way.

In the April, 1974, issue of *Natural History*, an attractive journal published by the American Museum of Natural History, famed paleontologist Norman D. Newell has written a feature article, "Evolution Under Attack." He especially focuses on the Creation Research Society for his counter-attack, calling it "the most vocal of the anti-evolutionist groups". However, he has apparently taken only a superficial look at the Society, since he says it is located in San Diego and that its "members were active in the 1972 California ruling," neither of which statements is correct. The Society's head-quarters office is in Michigan, and it has repeatedly reaffirmed its official stand against participating in any way in legalistic or political efforts on behalf of creationism.

Similarly, Nicholas Wade, in Vol. 181 (1973, p. 696) *Science* (the official publication of the American Association for the Advancement of Science) attacked the Society on the same grounds, accusing it of political lobbying. Dr. Thomas G. Barnes, president of the Society, has been trying un-successfully to get the *Science* editors to publish his letter correcting a number of mistatements of fact in this article, and is now considering legal action if they continue to refuse.

The state of Tennessee last year passed a law requiring creation to be taught in its public schools as well as evolution. The National Association of Biology Teachers is hastily try-ing to raise funds from its members to fight this law up to the U.S. Supreme Court if necessary, and two biology professors from the University of Tennessee have filed suit to have the law declared unconstitutional.

These and other recent developments reinforce the impres-sion that creationism is now at least being taken seriously.

Creationism Theme of Louisiana
Science Teachers Convention

For the first time since the Scopes trial, so far as known, creationism has been the theme of the main session of an an-nual convention of state science teachers. In New Orleans, on

Nov. 20, 1974, Dr. Henry Morris was the featured speaker at the main general session of the Louisiana Science Teachers Association annual convention, speaking on the topic "Scientific Creationism for Public Schools." Dr. Morris emphasized that the creation-evolution issue was not an argument between religion and science, as evolutionists allege, but that the scientific model of creationism fits the facts of science much better than evolution, and therefore should be taught on at least equal scientific footing with evolution in the public schools.

Following the hour-long lecture, a large part of the audience stayed for a second seminar and discussion conducted by Dr. Morris. Every teacher present received a complimentary copy of a special Institute for Creation Research paper and bibliography dealing with the theme of the session. Audience response seemed very favorable to the concept of equal scientific emphasis for creation and evolution in the schools.

Morris, Gish Speak to
Professional Geologists

In an unlikely setting for a creationist emphasis, I.C.R. scientists Henry Morris and Duane Gish spoke recently (January 30) for two hours to a significant gathering of professional geo-scientists in California. The occasion was the monthly meeting of the Pick-and-Hammer Club, a society composed mostly of the scientists employed by the U.S. Geological Survey at Menlo Park, California, one of the three regional centers of the USGS (the others are at Denver and Washington, D.C.). Approximately 150 of the geologists and their guests attended.

Dr. Morris gave an illustrated lecture stressing the superiority of the general creation model over that of evolution, especially as emphasized in the principles of thermodynamics. Dr. Gish followed with his slide lecture showing the fossil record to be more compatible with creation than evolution. A spirited discussion with the audience continued for an additional hour. Attempts from the floor to refute the creationist arguments were, even in the opinion of some of the geologists themselves, innocuous and peripheral.

For example, following Dr. Gish's lecture in which he emphasized, among other things, the explosive appearance of highly complex forms in the fossil record in what is known as Cambrian rocks, one geologist claimed that the slide Dr. Gish used to illustrate this fact was erroneous, in that it included corals. He asserted that corals are not found in Cambrian strata, but only in Ordovician and succeeding strata (evolutionary uniformitarian geologists assume that Cambrian sedimentary deposits were laid down over an 80 million-year period beginning about 600 million years ago, and this was followed by the Ordovician, a "geological period" said to span about 60 million years).

While there may be some dispute among geologists on this point, the highly authoritative publication *The Fossil Record* (Geological Society of London, 1967) lists corals of the family Auloporidae among undoubted Cambrian forms and corals of the family Lichenariidae as at least possibly of Cambrian origin (pp. 354, 357). Thus, on this point, it is not a question of evolutionary geologists versus creationists, but of evolutionary geologists versus evolutionary geologists, and Dr. Gish was fully justified in placing corals in Cambrian strata.

Even more importantly, the presence or absence of corals in Cambrian rocks is simply irrelevant to the creation versus evolution question. Corals are members of the phylum Coelenterata, many species of which *are* found in Cambrian rocks. As a matter of fact, members of every one of the major invertebrate types, or phyla, are found in Cambrian rocks. Furthermore, if, as this geologist argued, corals are found in the Ordovician but not in the Cambrian, and the Ordovician deposits truly do represent a geological time span which followed an earlier geological time span, that is, the Cambrian, then *why aren't the evolutionary ancestors of the corals found in Cambrian rocks?* But the corals, just as do every one of the other major animal and plant types, appear in the fossil record abruptly with no known evolutionary ancestors.

Another geologist protested that Dr. Gish had restricted his discussion mainly to the vertebrates (actually Dr. Gish devoted a significant portion of his time to a discussion of the invertebrates and to the hypothetical transition of invertebrate to vertebrate), where evidence for evolutionary transitions might be less than desired, but that undoubted evidence for evolutionary transitions among invertebrates was demonstrable. He then cited his own work on fossil foraminiferans (tiny, mostly marine, organisms, with shells showing great diversity), among which he claimed he had good evidence for evolutionary change.

He apparently is unaware of the fact (as pointed out by Dr. Morris in *The Genesis Flood*, p. 282; see R.L. Langenheim, Jr., "Recent Developments in Paleontology", *Journal of Geological Education*, Vol. 7, p. 7, Spring 1959), that the work of Arnold with the living foraminifer *Allogramia laticollaris* showed that *great morphologic variation occurs within laboratory cultures* of these organisms. Now if one obtains great variation within a population of a single species in a laboratory culture, it is obvious that such variations among fossil collections of these organisms are absolutely meaningless as far as evolution is concerned. Thus Langenheim states, "Inasmuch as these forms mimic most of the basic plans of foraminiferan test morphology (the test is the hard part of the organism which is preserved as a fossil — Ed.), it may be deduced that specific and generic concepts based on shell shape — which includes all fossil foraminifera — are based on insecure biologic criteria . . . . Any given body form or chamber arrangement apparently must be potentially derivative from almost any ancestral type."

The foraminifers are wide-ranging organisms living under a great variety of environmental conditions. It is obvious, then, that alleged transitions between fossil species and genera of these organisms are meaningless. The exchange at Menlo Park, at least on this point, demonstrated that it was the evolutionary paleontologist who needed to do his homework, not the creationist.

Dr. Morris, in his lecture, pointed out one of the apparent insuperable barriers to a naturalistic evolutionary process from particles to people; the Second Law of Thermodynamics (the universal natural tendency of all organized systems or complex matter to be reduced to simpler or more random states). Dr. Morris carefully pointed out that simply having an open system with energy flowing in was a necessary *but not sufficient* condition for order and complexity to be built up. In addition to these conditions, Dr. Morris pointed out there must be energy-transforming mechanisms that can convert raw energy into a usuable form (photosynthesis in green plants and power tools in a carpenter shop), and there must be some system to control and direct specific applications of the energy conversion systems (the genetic system of the plant and the carpenter in the carpenter shop). Without these conditions, uncontrolled, undirected energy is destructive, not constructive. But because of the universal tendency of the complex to be reduced to the simple, of the organized to become disorganized, it would have been impossible for the required complex energy-conversion mechanisms and control systems to arise spontaneously from inanimate matter.

The morning following the lectures, Dr. Gish had an opportunity to visit the laboratory and office of one of the prominent geologists of the U.S. Geological Survey Office. During the conversation Dr. Gish had with this geologist, the geologist accused Dr. Morris of misusing the Second Law of Thermodynamics since, he said, Dr. Morris apparently did not understand that the Second Law of Thermodynamics applied only to closed systems, and that in order to build up the complex from the simple all that is needed is an open system and an adequate energy supply! This geologist either was not listening when Dr. Morris covered that point in detail in his lecture, or he failed to comprehend what Dr. Morris had said. Dr. Gish once more tried to explain to this geologist why there is an undoubted contradiction between the Second

Law of Thermodynamics and evolution. The only answer to this contradiction is — there is no answer! Evolution is impossible.

The I.C.R. speakers were reinforced in their own confidence, at least, in the scientific strength of the creationist case, as it seems to stand successfully even under attack by the leading scientific exponents of the evolutionary-uniformitarian position.

At the same time, it was again made apparent that creationist speakers should be careful in their presentations, avoiding ridicule of evolutionists and giving sound documentation for their arguments. The invitation to speak to the Pick-and-Hammer Club came originally as an after-effect of another meeting where one of the geologists happened to hear another creationist speaker (not a scientist, although advertised as such), speak sarcastically of geologists and their methods. Since he had given no time for questions, the geologists wanted to get him to their own meeting where they could expose him. However, instead of accepting their invitation, he referred them to I.C.R for a speaker. This background, of course, made for a tense situation for Dr. Gish and Dr. Morris, but it is believed the final outcome was a clear vindication of scientific creationism.

Stanford Research Institute
Hears ICR Director

Over 100 scientists and guests gathered in the Ness Auditorium of the Stanford Research Institute on May 8 to hear Dr. Henry Morris, Director of the Institute for Creation Research, speak on the theme "Science and History Versus Evolution." A high degree of audience interest was evident, even though most listeners obviously had been evolutionists. During the question period following the lecture, one scientist in the audience made the comment that he had been taught evolution all his life, that this was the first time he had ever heard the other side, and that he thought everyone should have a similar opportunity to hear the evidence for creation.

Stanford Research Institute, formerly associated with Stanford University, is one of the world's largest private scientific research organizations. It is located almost adjacent to the Menlo Park offices of the U.S. Geological Survey, where Dr. Morris and Dr. Duane Gish spoke recently to a large gathering of professional geologists.

Blick Brings Creation Message
To Engineering Educators

A unique opportunity to present scientific creationism to a strategic group of educators was given to Dr. Edward Blick, Professor of Aerospace, Mechanical and Nuclear Engineering at Oklahoma University, on June 18, 1974, at the annual convention of the American Society for Engineering Education in Troy, New York. Speaking on the subject, "Entropy and Living Systems," Dr. Blick stressed to a large audience of engineering professors that the available scientific evidence today, especially from the principles of engineering thermodynamics, showed creationism to be far superior to evolutionism, and urged them to point these facts out to their students.

Dr. Blick, who is a member of I.C.R's Technical Advisory Board, had been specifically asked to give this lecture, after presenting a similar paper at the 1973 A.S.E.E. convention. He reported interest to be very high and the response quite favorable.

Professional Engineers
Hear Creation Message

At a dinner meeting in the Christian Heritage College dining hall on January 23, 1975, the California Society of Professional Engineers (San Diego Chapter) heard Dr. Henry Morris, I.C.R. Director, speak on the subject "Engineering, Entropy, and Evolution." Many of the engineers present commented that this was the first time they had been exposed to a scientific case for creation, and that it clearly indicated the superiority of creationism to evolutionism.

The C.S.P.E. is a branch of the National Society of Professional Engineers, an organization requiring state registration as a licensed professional engineer for membership. Dr. Morris had been registered in four states prior to coming to California to found the I.C.R. and was a former officer in the Virginia Society of Professional Engineers.

Dr. Lester Speaks to National Science Teachers

On March 20, 1975, Dr. Lane Lester (Research Associate in Bio-Science at I.C.R. and Professor of Biology at Christian Heritage College) delivered a paper at the National Science Teachers Convention in Los Angeles. Attendance to hear the topic of "Assisting Teachers in Coping with the Evolution/Creation Issue" was excellent. Though 18 papers were being simultaneously presented, all 70 seats in the room were filled.

Dr. Lester stressed the importance of presenting both sides of controversial issues such as creation/evolution, mentioning that most students in public schools should be given the freedom to make up their own minds — emphasizing that freedom of choice should preferably be based on the following experiences:

1) Students should be taught the difference between facts and interpretations.

2) The facts involved in any issue should then be presented.

3) The students can then be led in a discussion to discover alternative interpretations of the facts. They would then be free to make up their own minds as to which interpretations are superior.

Throughout the paper, Dr. Lester used examples of biological facts that are used to support evolution, but which support creation as well or better. He also displayed various written materials available currently for students and teachers. The question and answer period following the paper's presentation was lively, with questions and opinions from both camps being expressed.

Gish, Morris Confront
University of Miami Geologists

On Thursday afternoon, April 3, 1975, Dr. Morris and Dr. Gish were invited lecturers at the weekly Geology Graduate Seminar at the University of Miami. The lecture room was packed to overflowing with geology graduate students and their teachers, as well as many students from other departments.

Dr. Morris gave a brief introduction on the general scientific superiority of the creation model over evolutionism, followed by a comprehensive slide lecture by Dr. Gish on the systematic gaps in the fossil record. A lengthy and lively question-and-answer session followed. The impact on the audience was so great that, toward the end, several of the geology faculty and graduate students tried desperately to overcome the evidence of the fossil gaps by stressing the "continuous record of evolution" which they claimed to have found in the microfossils dredged up in ocean-bottom sediment cores which they had been studying in their own laboratories, stating that the paleontological authorities whom Gish had cited (Simpson, Kitts, Langenheim, etc.) really were not up-to-date(!)

Dr. Cesare Emiliani, who is probably the nation's top authority in this special field of ocean-bottom cores and their relation to the supposed evolutionary changes during the Ice Age, although dogmatically maintaining that his microfossils showed continuous "evolutionary" changes, finally acknowledged that, from bottom to top, there was *no increase in complexity* of his fossils, and thus no real progressive evolution!

Reaction of most of the students was highly favorable. One Jewish woman graduate student, a recent convert to Christ, was heard to say that this session was exactly what she had needed to strengthen and stabilize her own new faith.

Hughes Scientists Hear
Evidence for Creation

Approximately 160 scientists, engineers and technicians on the staff of the giant Hughes Aircraft Co. in Los Angeles heard a special one-hour creationism lecture by I.C.R. Director Henry M. Morris on September 15 in a Hughes Co. auditorium. Dr. Morris spoke on the theme "Scientific Evidence for a Recent Creation," and the audience attention and response indicated keen interest. The meeting was sponsored by the Hughes Employees Bible Club.

chapter V

CREATION RESEARCH

CAREERS IN CREATIONISM
Henry M. Morris

One of the encouraging developments of recent years is the increasing number of talented young people who desire to dedicate their lives to the Lord's work in the specific work of promoting creationism. Quite a few young scientists have even applied for positions at I.C.R. or have asked us for help in finding positions where they could use their scientific training in creationist research or teaching. High school and college students frequently ask where they can get formal training, either at the undergraduate level or in graduate school, for a career in scientific creationism.

All of which is a most encouraging development. Fourteen years ago, when nearly everyone, even among evangelical Christians, thought creationism was dead, I expressed the following hope: "The writers hope, perhaps naively but sincerely, that this preliminary study will engage the attention of such potential workers and persuade them to undertake further, more extensive studies into these problems" (Whitcomb and Morris, *The Genesis Flood*, 1961, p. 217).

This hope is at least beginning to be realized. Within the past year, for example, I have met or heard from many young geologists and many students majoring in geology, who have become convinced that Biblical catastrophism is a much better scientific model than evolutionary uniformitarianism in explaining the data of historical geology. This shift in thinking is even more noticeable among young biologists and scientists in other fields.

Unfortunately, at least at this time, it is impracticable for such young scientists to anticipate actual careers in creationism as such. So far as I know, the Institute for Creation Research is the only scientific educational or research organization that maintains a staff of scientists whose specific responsibilities lie in this field, and its resources are insufficient for any significant enlargement in the near future at least. Of course, if any qualified scientists wishing to work with I.C.R. could somehow raise their own support, the picture would be different, but at present this is unlikely.

As far as teaching in Christian colleges is concerned, it is encouraging to note that more and more such colleges (as well as seminaries and Bible schools) are adding courses in creationism (or scientific apologetics) to their curriculum. Instructors for such courses, however, must also be able to teach other courses as well (e.g., biology, physics, etc.). There are no positions for anyone wishing to teach *only* creationism as such.

Neither are there any formal degree programs in creationism (for that matter, there are few, if any, formal degree programs in evolutionism!). To my knowledge, the most extensive actual course available in this specific field is the 6-semester-hour course in scientific creationism which we teach here at Christian Heritage College to all our sophomore students.

My advice, therefore, to young people seeking careers in creationism, is first to get a good education in a specific science major. The need is not so much for full-time scientific creationists (though we can hope that this may actually develop into a real career field in the future), but rather for good creationist scientists in every field. Creationist geologists, creationist astronomers, creationist anthropologists, etc., —this is the real need, not so much in Christian organizations, but in industry, in government, in secular universities, in every area of society, — perhaps most of all as teachers in public schools and state universities.

I would encourage each young creationist to get all the education of which he is capable, including a Ph.D. if possible. He will need this in order to do the best job of researching and communicating the data of his own field in terms of the creation concept of origins and history. He will also need it if he does hope eventually to work as a full-time "scientific creationist" in a Christian college or research organization.

To do this, he may well have to study his scientific discipline (particularly at the graduate level) in a secular university, since Christian colleges do not yet offer graduate training in science. He should, therefore, supplement such training by taking special seminars and short courses in scientific creationism and by keeping his reading up to date in this field. Also, he may have opportunity to carry out specific research projects in his own scientific field which can contribute to the over-all advance of scientific creationism as well.

This type of study and service can surely be as much of a divine calling as, say, a call to prepare for the Christian ministry or the mission field. In fact, in the present world intellectual climate, there is probably at least as great a need for dedicated Christian creationist geologists and other such scientists as for new recruits to the traditional full-time Christian vocations.

ICR Research Team
Studies "Overthrust" Areas

A survey of two mountain areas alleged to represent overthrusts of sedimentary strata was made in September, 1974, by a team sponsored and supported by the Institute for Creation Research. This study was one of the field expeditions that have been planned in an attempt to gain directly from the field evidence regarding the history of the earth. Overthrust areas are places where the fossil-bearing rocks are out of the order predicted by the evolutionist geologists. These areas are numerous and represent real evidence contradicting the evolutionist position if they are actually depositional features. The evolutionist maintains that the strata are out of order due to actual physical movement from gravitational sliding, thrusting, etc. The mathematical calculations stemming from physical mechanics argue strongly against thrusting of massive blocks of rock over large areas.

The team, made up of Clifford L. Burdick, Harold S. Slusher, Frank Baxter, and John Morris, arrived in Cody, Wyoming, on September 11 to investigate the Heart Mountain Thrust area. The aim of the expedition was to find and study the supposed thrust contact line between the thrust block and the underlying sedimentary strata. In the Heart Mountain area, Paleozoic rock lies on top of Eocene rock. Thus these rocks are out of the time order according to the evolutionary scheme by some 250 million years. A thorough search was made for contact exposures with very little success. One exposure showed Paleozoic limestone resting on a layer of brecciated limestone which in turn was overlying the Cenozoic sandstone. The sandstone showed no physical evidence of being overridden by the upper lying strata. However, it could not be decided whether the brecciation of the limestone was caused by actual displacement of the rock layer or superficial weathering of the outcrop. The results of the study were inconclusive since the contact planes were heavily covered by alluvium for most of the area of the alleged thrust at Heart Mountain and in the surrounding mountains.

Further study of another area, the Bannock thrust, in the Wasatch Mountains near Ogden, Utah, was made September 16. There the Cambrian strata are overlaid by the Precambrian rocks. Again great difficulties were encountered in finding good exposures of the contact plane where there should be physical evidence if thrusting occurred. There was no evidence of thrusting along the contact plane exposures that were studied. There was some evidence of local movement in some of the strata but this was very localized displacement. The observation of the general structure of the area gives the impression that there has been uplift of the strata with attendant local movement but no thrusting or sliding of the

Precambrian over the Cambrian. It would seem, therefore that the Bannock thrust is not really a thrusted area but is a simple depositional series that has had certain tectonic activity associated with it since that depositional action. It appears the Precambrian was deposited on the Cambrian, and thus the assumed order of evolution is invalid.

These studies were initial investigations. Both areas are quite complicated and further intensive examination of the structural geology in these two mountain ranges is needed to make a complete delineation of the events that caused these structures.

NOAH'S ARK: STATUS 1975*
By John Morris

Author John Morris, B.S., is Field Scientist of the Institute for Creation Research and has been in charge of the I.C.R. Ararat Project since 1972. The account of the 1972 expedition to Mt. Ararat is given in his book Adventure on Ararat *(San Diego, Institute for Creation Research, 1973, 116pp.).*

Rarely has any project associated with the creation movement so captivated the mind of the general public as has the continuing search for Noah's Ark. Newspapers everywhere have carried articles on the subject. Radio and television stations frequently desire interviews with those who are involved in the project. Newscasts detail the project and recent developments. The demand for lectures on the subject is constant.

The potential rediscovery of the Ark is of even greater importance than appears on the surface. It will not be merely another in the series of many archaeological discoveries brought to light in recent years. It is much more than mere supportive evidence for a children's Sunday School story. The anticipated rediscovery of Noah's Ark would produce major effects on all academic disciplines, the greatest impact being felt in the archaeological, geological and historical realms, with repercussions even in world politics.

---

*Impact Series #22, (March 1975)

Archaeological Significance

The Genesis account of the Flood of Noah is quite explicit. It describes the Flood as more than a local flood, more even than a regional catastrophe; suffice it to say that the Hebrew word used in the original text means "cataclysm" and is applied only to the Genesis flood. The New Testament equivalent is the very word from which we derive our English word "cataclysm."

Over and over again the Biblical writer proclaims the universality of the Flood. If there is any truth to the story at all, it is clear that this year-long flood was not only world-wide, but one which produced dramatic desolation. Indeed, it must have been a world-restructuring event. So great was its force, that in all likelihood even Noah would not have been able to recognize his former homeland. It is very unlikely that any vestiges of the pre-flood civilizations survived, at least in any recognizable form.

Noah's Ark, therefore, constitutes the one remaining archaeological link to the world before the Flood. No other major antediluvian artifact is ever likely to be found.

Furthermore, the very size and structure of the Ark would place it in the category of sensational finds, which would include the pyramids, Central American temples, and a few others. Mathematical calculations show conclusively that the size of the Ark was easily sufficient to house two of all kinds of land animals with quite a bit of room left over. Stability studies have shown that the length of 450' and cross section of 75' x 45' would have made the Ark virtually impossible to capsize. No doubt, such a structure could have been built only by men of an advanced civilization.

In short, no archaeological find could be of greater age or importance than the potential relocation of Noah's Ark.

Significance to Historical Geology

Popular concepts of origins would be greatly altered by the rediscovery of the Ark of Noah. Any model of earth history which uses as its basic assumption the doctrine of uniformitarianism would be found inadequate.

Uniformitarianism postulates that present natural processes have acted at approximately the same rates throughout long ages of geologic time and are responsible for the evolution of matter from non-matter, of life from non-life and higher forms of life from lower forms of life.

The direct opposite of the uniformitarian system is that of global catastrophism. The cataclysmic model states that present processes have not always acted as they do now, but at one or more times in the past were either greatly altered or else perhaps not operating at all, replaced by others, including creative processes which we do not observe today.

During the time of Noah's Flood in particular, many present processes would not have operated at present rates, and many others would have been greatly altered by changes in the make-up of the earth's surface and atmosphere.

These two assumptions, uniformitarianism and global catastrophism, are both all-encompassing and therefore mutually exclusive. Although uniformitarianism does not preclude local catastrophes, the concept of a worldwide hydraulic cataclysm is not compatible with the usual geological concept of evolutionary uniformitarianism.

Although neither can be absolutely proved, since they are out of the realm of scientific observation, if uniformitarianism can be shown incapable of explaining the facts, then catastrophism is necessary.

The remains of Noah's Ark have been reported to be at the 14,000' level on Mt. Ararat. Since a 14,000' high, year-long flood could not be either a local flood or a tranquil flood, the relocation of the Ark would provide overwhelming evidence in support of global catastrophism. Such a catastrophe is totally incompatible with uniformitarianism, and its evolutionary interpretation of the fossil record and geological ages.

Due to the fact that the anti-Biblical models of earth history known as theistic evolution and progressive creation

also rest to a large degree on the assumption of uniformitarianism, they would likewise be shown conclusively to be
invalid.

All of the various scientific disciplines, especially
historical geology, would be forced to undergo major
revisions, if the Ark were to be conclusively documented.
There would remain no further intellectual basis for the
theory of evolution.

Political Significance

Mt. Ararat, the resting place of Noah's Ark, lies in the
remote frontier of Eastern Turkey, overlooking both the Russian and Iranian borders. The remoteness is somewhat misleading, however, for there is no lack of military installations
and facilities in the area. The long-time rivalry between the
Turks and the Russians has resulted in the classification of
the area as a military zone. No one who resides out of the immediate area is allowed to approach the mountain without official permission from the Turkish government in the capital
city of Ankara. For the same reason, no air traffic is sanc-
tioned.

In the past few years the Russian image in Turkey has gained favor while the American image has suffered. Even in recent weeks, U.S. military aid to Turkey has been placed in
jeopardy and diplomatic relations have been partially
severed.

Any expedition allowed to search Mt. Ararat must do so
with permits granted in spite of the military sensitivity of the
area and reciprocal border agreements.

The Ararat area has seen almost constant war for
thousands of years. Two of the ethnic groups that have always
lived nearby have caused problems which affect the search
for the Ark. The remnant of the Armenian people, most of
whose members live in Russia within sight of Mt. Ararat, still
calls for retribution for the loss of their traditional homeland,
from which they were driven by the Turks in World War I.
The Kurdish tribes who now live on Mt. Ararat support, but
do not participate in the civil war in Iraq and Syria raging

over the issue of Kurdish independence, and Turkey is afraid that it will spread into their country. In both cases, the calling of attention to the Ararat area would favor the causes of the minorities.

Western tourism to Turkey has declined considerably since U.S. Turkish relationships have deteriorated. The discovery of Noah's Ark would see literally thousands of tourists flocking to see it if possible. This would partially alleviate Turkey's serious economic problems.

All of the implications are not yet known. It does seem obvious that Turkey would profit greatly from the discovery. To say the least, the Turkish international image and its sagging tourism industry would be enhanced, not to mention the better position at the bargaining and conference tables such a gesture of good-will and friendship would afford.

Previous Sightings

The search for Noah's Ark has been going on for at least thirty years on a major scale. Quite a few expeditions have studied the mountain with varying degrees of success but always with great degrees of hardship and danger.

While the Ark has not been rediscovered, researchers have turned up many earlier reported sightings, seemingly hundreds of reliable people who claim to have seen the Ark. The research has also shown that a major earthquake on Ararat in 1840 caused physical changes to the glacial patterns high on the slopes. Since 1840 many people claim to have seen the Ark. The following list contains most of the major reported sightings:

1853: Three Englishmen were shown the Ark by two Armenian natives.

1883: Turkish avalanche investigators discovered the Ark while studying the effects of a recent earthquake. The find was published in newspapers around the world.

1887: John Joseph, Prince of Nouri, of Malabar, India, discovered the vessel by design on his third attempt. He presented his claims to the World Parliament of Religions at the Chicago World's Fair a few years later, but was unable to raise financial support for proper documentation.

1902, 1904: "Georgie," an elderly Armenian immigrant, who escaped the turmoil following World War I and fled to the United States, saw the Ark twice as a teenager. He died in 1972 but his comments and interviews are available on tape.

1915, 1916: Two Russian flyers sighted the Ark from the air. The Czar dispatched 150 Russian soldiers and scientists to verify the claim. The ground investigations found the remains and succeeded in entering the three-storied structure and documenting it fully. However, when the Communists gained control, the documents were presumably destroyed, but many of the participants escaped and lived to tell the story.

1917: Six Turkish soldiers, returning home after service in Baghdad, decided to climb the mountain. They accidentally discovered the ship.

1936: Hardwicke Knight, a New Zealand archaeologist, accidentally discovered a field of timbers, very large and obviously handhewn, on the upper slopes of the mountain. Mr. Knight still lives in New Zealand.

1941-1944: During World War II Mount Ararat was flown over hundreds of times by planes from the United States air base in Tunisia and the Russian facility in Erivan. At least three sightings were reported: 1) Two Australian pilots, 2) One Russian pilot, 3) Two USAF pilots, but many more were rumored. The USAF flyers took pictures of the Ark which appeared in the Tunisia edition of "Stars and Stripes."

1948: A Kurdish farmer named Resit accidentally discovered the Ark. Under his insistence many of the villagers also observed it.

1952-1955: Fernand Navarra, wealthy French industrialist, found a great mass of hand-tooled lumber under the ice at the 13,000 foot level. He dug down to it, chopped off a portion about 9" x 9" x 5' and brought it back for analysis. The wood has been shown to be of great antiquity. Mr. Navarra is still alive.

1953: George Greene, mining engineer for an American oil company, spotted the Ark about 1/3 exposed from a helicopter. He photographed it from a distance of about 90 feet. Although at least thirty people alive today remember the pictures, they can no longer be seen, for Greene was murdered in 1962 and his belongings were destroyed.

1954, 1958: John Libi, of San Francisco, and Colonel Sehap Atalay of the Turkish army discovered wood in the same area as the previous sightings. Both men are still alive.

1962: Wilbur Bishop and Lawrence Hewitt, studying the summit of the 17,000-foot mountain from an airplane, were surprised to see a portion of a wooden structure at the 14,000 foot level. These two men are also still living.

1969: Fernand Navarra returned to Mount Ararat and guided explorers from SEARCH, Incorporated, to the spot of his discovery in 1955. Again fragments of wood were recovered.

Recent Expeditions

Just as the earthquake in 1840 signalled the beginning of the major sightings, so 1972 saw the beginning of major steps toward the eventual documented relocation. Many expeditions had searched for the Ark during the period 1946-71, without success. But early in 1972, Mrs. Violet Cummings, wife of long-time Ark research Eryl Cummings, published a fascinating book entitled *Noah's Ark: Fact or Fable?* detailing all of the research and results of the expeditions involved.

For the first time the general public was made aware of the intricacies of the search, and before long applications to the Turkish government for permits to climb Ararat were numerous. Almost all of them were rejected. This "Ark Fever" which so resembles the "Gold Fever" of 1849 has somewhat stabilized now with only five major American groups actively involved:

1) The Institute for Creation Research Ararat Probe led by John Morris (See the book *Adventure on Ararat*, published by I.C.R. in 1973).

2) A small private effort led by Eryl Cummings, Lawrence Hewitt, and Clifford Burdick.

3) SEARCH Foundation, Inc., President John Bradley.

4) A small private effort associated with John Warwick Montgomery.

5) The Holy Ground Mission Changing Center effort led by Tom Crotser.

The various expeditions of 1972 and 1973 are well-documented in various books and articles and need not be discussed here. In 1974 three separate summer efforts were launched, but published accounts of their work have been somewhat sketchy at best. More detailed factual information is still needed, but they will at least be mentioned briefly here.

Turkey's shaky political climate finally began to stabilize early in 1974 with the installation of a coalition government under the leadership of Prime Minister Ecevit. A somewhat favorable initial response to Ark efforts was received by the various groups, but when the Cyprus situation heightened to a crisis in early summer, all sensitive military areas were declared off-limits to foreigners.

Official permits were not issued to any of the groups, as far as is known. Although never giving up hope until late in the summer, both the I.C.R. group and the Cummings group wisely decided to stay home, only to be shocked later to hear that the three other groups had succeeded in climbing the mountain.

A group called National Association for Media Evangelism (NAME) based in Los Angeles recognized the value of the Ark toward their goal of evangelism and laid the groundwork for a documentary movie designed for television release, and contracted with John Warwick Montgomery who was to be responsible for acquisition of permits and logistics for the expedition. They spent portions of two days at the Navarra site on the northwest side, filming the area on 16mm movie film. No discovery was made. The following quotes were taken from a radio broadcast made by a commentator who was a member of the expedition shortly after returning (this same man contracted hyperthernia on the mountain and nearly died).

"Because of political difficulties, we had to ascend the mountain to the base camp at night."

" . . . we photographically mapped the area so it can be found again when the Turkish government hopefully allows the full scientific expedition it has been refusing for years."

The movie will not be released until June, 1975 at the earliest and will be in all likelihood top-quality work.

Another Hollywood producer caught Ark Fever last summer and also climbed to the Navarra site to make a movie, this time for theater release. Bart LaRue, whose primary goal was to produce a money-making film, returned from Turkey bragging (according to newspaper accounts) about how he had bribed numerous Turkish officials, and had also climbed at night to avoid detection. LaRue openly charged the Turks with such corruption among government officials as to make Watergate look like child's play.

In order to produce his film covering all the past work on the mountain, LaRue contracted with SEARCH, Inc. for all of their archival material. SEARCH was not directly involved with his 1974 expedition, but much of their movie footage and resource material will be in his film.

The third group of explorers represented a Texas cult known as the Holy Ground Mission of Palestine, Texas. Led by Tom Crotser, this cult feels that it has been appointed by God to write the last chapters of the Bible, and its members have been assigned the duty of restoring all meaningful and ancient remnants of Biblical days.

The Mission returned from Ararat claiming to have found the Ark. They are currently lecturing around the country showing pictures of their "discoveries." The photographs, however, seem highly questionable. They are out of focus, and of uncertain origin. Many previous explorers have been to the area in question on Mt. Ararat (including the author) and have not seen the Ark. Many who have seen the pictures and heard the lecture have left dissatisfied and unconvinced, feeling instead that the Mission may be using the Ark search in order to promote their own peculiar brand of theology.

Future Ark Research

It may be noted that the Institute for Creation Research effort is the only one backed by a serious scientific organization capable of properly interpreting the scientific data. The I.C.R. has applied for permission to take a 13-member team into Turkey complete with professional scientists, photographers and climbers. Without making any unreasonable claims, the I.C.R. plans to systematically search the mountain for any remains of the Ark, carefully study it, as well as other archaeological sites in the area, carry out geological and microbiological studies and document all findings photographically.

Whether or not the Turkish government will sanction such work is still open to question. Unfortunately, the methods of the three 1974 expeditions discussed above have made it unlikely that Turkey will be favorably disposed to allowing the search to continue. Add such officially non-sanctioned climbs and filming to the tense local military and ethnic situation, as well as the breakdown of Turkish-American relations and the chances for any further work on Mt. Ararat seems, humanly speaking, virtually impossible.

Those who have supported the Institute for Creation Research in its Ararat project may be confident that it neither has nor will become involved with any of these other groups. Our purpose is neither that of financial gain nor personal glory, but solely one of scientific inquiry and Biblical creationist confirmation. We will rejoice at the discovery if it is made and adequately documented, regardless of who does it, recognizing the spiritual significance as well.

In the meantime, we are trying to make the best possible preparations for an effective scientific expedition, Christian in both purpose and personnel, and conforming to high standards of industry, intelligence and integrity in all efforts relative to obtaining proper authorization for the search. The Ark will be revealed only in God's timing and according to His will, and it is essential that concerned Christians everywhere pray to that end.

New Flood Tradition Discovered

One of the many evidences for the historicity of the Biblical Flood is the widespread incidence of flood traditions. According to the Bible, all nations are descended from the three sons of Noah and so it would be expected that through stories passed down from generation to generation many of them would retain distorted memories of the great flood. It is significant that such flood stories have been found in tribes all over the world.

Among the tribes most remote from Ararat and Babel, and therefore least likely to have obtained the flood story from some other source, are those in the interior jungles and highlands of New Guinea. Many of these tribes have only been "discovered" in recent decades, and yet many of them do have records of an ancient world-destroying flood.

One of these tribes is the Alamblak tribe, along the Karawari and Wagupmeri Rivers in northern Papua-New Guinea. Les and Kathy Bruce (son-in-law and daughter of I.C.R Director Henry Morris) are missionary linguists with the Wycliffe Bible Translators and have been working with this tribe for four years, reducing its language to writing and studying the structure and history of its culture, as well as translating the Bible for them and trying to lead them to Christ.

They have found that Alamblak mythology varies in content and emphasis from lineage to lineage among the four clan groups. The following account of the Alamblak flood tradition combines stories from different lineage groups about the same event or preludes to it.

"There was a time when the sky was very close to the earth. Then people on earth could see up into heaven and the Yimtim lineage group had a ladder set up between the sky and the ground. For a long time the people of the Yimtim lineage ventured freely between the sky and the earth. Finally an ancestral hero became disgusted with the corruptness of most people on the earth so he climbed up into the sky and pulled the ladder up with him thus severing man's access to the sky.

Soon the warning came that the sky would descend to the earth and crush anything that got in its way; stealers, liars, adulterers, and stingy people particularly would be doomed as the sky was to crush mountain-top hamlets. This was a threat to all Alamblaks since each lineage hamlet was perched atop their own hill, so the people began making preparations for doomsday. Some people threw up temporary shelters in the valley areas. Others prepared special dances and ceremonies which included the installation of spears and posts to support the sky and the ridge pole of the houses when the sky descended.

Finally the sky began its descent and the people began their dancing and ceremony. It was a time of unprecendented danger from the soul-eating spirits lurking near the houses. Everyone had to remain inside their houses. The animals of the rain forest gathered together also and remained underneath the houses which were, as they are now, elevated on posts.

The sky split open during its descent and the people of the sky were seen dancing back and forth. When the sky reached the earth. the ceremonial posts and spears held it up. At this point the earth cracked open in many places and volumes of water began gushing up. The water rose until it covered the whole earth excepting the peak of one mountain."

From this point different traditions present their own hero who distributed the ground from the mountain peak and re-established mankind on the earth. Most lineages agree, however, that it was the crocodile who began to push the water back to its present limits exposing the earth again. The crocodile then began the repopulation of the earth by giving birth to human children, a startling example of the 'hopeful monster' theory of evolution!

Turkey Closed to
1975 Ararat Expedition

Although potential for future work remains, it appears that the Turkish government will not issue permits for a 1975 expedition to Mt. Ararat, either to ICR or any other group. John Morris, Field Director of the ICR Ararat Project since 1972, returned from Turkey on May 24 after spending a month there attempting to gain sanction for the proposed 1975 ICR Ararat Probe.

In meetings and private sessions with various Turkish leaders, Mr. Morris showed reasons why the project would constitute valuable scientific research dealing with the general subject of origins, would be a stimulus to Turkish tourism, would possibly yield the greatest archaeological find of all time, and would be a substantial good-will gesture coming at a time when international relationships are strained.

Most of these influential Turkish leaders did agree that the evidence indicates that the remains of Noah's Ark still exist on Mt. Ararat on their Eastern frontier. They realize that the documented relocation of the Ark would produce many positive results from their point of view. However, they did not feel that such a search was urgent or practical at this time.

Several of the Turkish officials indicated that, perhaps in three to five years, their own government would itself launch exploratory efforts to search for Noah's Ark. ICR would, of course, be delighted to have a part in the discovery, but the more important consideration is that the Ark be located and properly documented, regardless of who makes the initial find. Correspondingly, Mr. Morris willingly made the results of the ICR research available to Turkish authorities, and possible locations of the vessel were discussed with them in detail. It may be that these discussions will produce results faster than an American expedition could.

During January of 1975, when the official prospectus of the ICR probe reached Turkey applying for permission, a special Turkish Cabinet-level session decided to deny all such requests for the summer of 1975. In April, the ICR project leader spent two weeks in Washington, D.C. conferring with key legislators and administrative officials on the project and had hoped that his conferences in Turkey during May might encourage a reversal of this decision.

Several factors influenced this ruling. First, the recent termination of the Kurdish civil war to the south of Turkey has fostered growing unrest among the Kurds in the Ararat area. Secondly, Greek and Armenian influence have produced considerable anti-Turkish sentiment in America, Europe and the United Nations. Furthermore, due to Turkish reaction to the 1974 Greek involvement on the island of Cyprus, the American Congress has not only stopped sending military aid to Turkey, but has imposed an arms embargo, refusing even to sell defense equipment to Turkey. Furthermore, American officials have (according to Turkish reports) refused to ship equipment previously purchased and have even seized items that Turkey had sent here for repair. Unless normal relations are soon restored with this long-time NATO ally, America stands to lose more than merely a chance to explore Mt. Ararat.

A further problem is that, during July and August of 1974, three American Ark expeditions climbed Mt. Ararat without official approval. In the eyes of the Turkish government these expeditions are quite illegal, and all participants are subject to arrest upon their return. Abrasive and misleading publicity resulting from these expeditions has generated a strong anti-search sentiment among Turkish officials. Several times, particularly in the vicinity of the mountain itself, Mr. Morris was detained and nearly arrested merely for talking about this sensitive subject to local officials.

Because of ICR's strictly legal and ethical approach to the project, Mr. Morris and his traveling companions were released each time after their names were checked against the list of known Ararat offenders. These detainments provided an excellent opportunity to establish good relationships with the governmental officials of the Ararat area. Extensive photographs of the upper reaches of the mountain were displayed, and probable sites were discussed. The significant other archaeological findings around the base of the mountain surprised even the most knowledgeable of these officials. For the first time many began to see the overwhelming importance and implications of a serious scientific study of the area and the relocation of the remains of Noah's Ark. Each local official pledged his support of the ICR team in the future, as soon as governmental permission to explore can be acquired.

While in Turkey, Morris lectured five times to various U.S. Air Force and private groups and found interest in the project high. One of these meetings turned up striking new data concerning the existence of the Ark that is now being checked out. According to John Morris and the ICR team, there remains little doubt that Noah's Ark does exist, and its relocation is near.

Oil Seepage Rates Indicate Young Age for Earth's Crust

Some very interesting data contained in a 1972 article by Max Blumer in *Science*, "Submarine Seeps: Are They a Major Source of Open Ocean Oil Pollution." Vol. 176, p. 1257, offers strong evidence that the crust of the earth is not as old as it is held to be by evolutionary geologists. The author of the above article is forced to conclude that submarine seepage cannot be a major source of oceanic oil pollution for one reason and one reason only — if it were, the entire supply of offshore oil that is a likely source of submarine seeps could have been exhausted in as little time as 20,000 years.

The world's ultimate resources of offshore oil available by primary recovery (after deducting the fraction that represents natural gas liquids) is about 630 billion barrels, or 100 billion metric tons. An additional 300 billion barrels accessible by secondary recovery do not contribute to seepage. Estimates of the amount of oil now reaching the ocean from all sources, including natural seepage and that due to man's activity range up to 11 million metric tons per year. If pollution from natural seepage were as serious as that due to man's activity, this source of pollution would amount to as much as 5 million tons per year. If this were true, it would require only 20,000 years to deplete the entire source (100×10^9 tons/5×10^6 tons per year equals 20×10^3 years).

According to Blumer, petroleum ranges in age from 2 million years to as great as 600 million years. If 50 million years is taken as a typical average, and 5 million tons per year as the natural seepage rate, the total amount of oil available by primary recovery would have been lost to the oceans by seepage 2500 times. Blumer declares that these figures are geologically and geochemically untenable. Untenable, of course, only because of the assumption that the earth's crust and its entrapped oil pools are many millions of years old.

If, on the other hand, it is assumed that this oil were formed from the innumerable marine organisms that would have been buried by the vast cataclysmic action of the Flood about 5000 years ago (more or less) only one-fourth of the total would have been lost to seepage since that time at a rate of 5 million tons per year. This chronology is far more reasonable, based on seepage rates, than is evolutionary chronology, unless one is willing to accept a ridiculously low figure for the seepage rate.

Thus, if the seepage rate were as low as 2 thousand tons per year (a mere trace), it would still require only 50 million years for the entire present offshore oil supply to leak into the ocean. A figure as low as 2 thousand tons per year, is, of course, far, far below any acceptable figure. Seeps occur on land as well as under water, and have been used as guides in oil exploration. Even if oil reservoirs were generally well-sealed, the seepage rate must be significant, very much in excess of 2 thousand tons per year. Accepting a natural seepage rate as low as 1% of the quantity of oil that now reaches the oceans from all sources (a mere 50,000 tons, still only a trace considering the 140 million square miles of ocean floor), the present entire offshore oil supply would be lost in only 2 million years. Even that figure surely is far below the actual rate.

We must conclude that a chronology that demands an age of many tens of millions of years for these oil reservoirs is untenable. We remind our readers that it has been demonstrated that petroleum can be produced from garbage or similar material in as little time as 20 minutes under appropriate conditions (see *Acts, Facts and Impacts*, Creation-Life Publishers, 1974, p. 15). Furthermore, there are many excellent chronometers that indicate that the earth

145

must be much younger than estimated by evolutionary geologists (see *Scientific Creationism*, H.M. Morris, ed., Creation-Life Publishers, 1974, pp. 149-169).

chapter VI

CREATION INTERNATIONAL

ICR Staff Scientist
Tours Canada

Dr. Duane Gish, under the auspices of the Bible-Science Association of Canada and accompanied by its National Director, Dr. Earl Hallonquist, participated in a Canadian university debate and lecture tour, October 28-November 7, 1974. Dr. Gish lectured or debated on the campuses of 13 universities, from Victoria on the west coast to Halifax on the east coast. It is estimated that he spoke to nearly 5,000 students and faculty on the college campuses; to about 3,000 people at Sunday services at Metropolitan Bible Church, Ottawa, and the People's Church, Toronto; and that he reached over half a million people by television, including the popular Norm Perry Show in Toronto.

Dr. Gish presented the scientific evidence for creation in lectures at the University of Victoria, Victoria, B.C.; The University of British Columbia, Vancouver, B.C.; University of Manitoba, Winnipeg, Manitoba; Scarborough College, Toronto, Ontario; University of Windsor, Windsor, Ontario; Queen's University, Kingston, Ontario; John Abbott College, St. Anne de Bellevue, Quebec; University of Ottawa, Ottawa, Ontario, and Mt. Allison University, Sackville, New

Brunswick. Generally, the reception to these lectures was quite friendly, and in some cases could even be termed enthusiastic.

The reception to Dr. Gish's lecture on the Queen's University campus was especially gratifying. The professor on this campus who had been challenged to debate Dr. Gish refused, characterizing his published material as dishonest and even diabolical (there was a strong suspicion that his refusal to debate was due to his inability to refute the facts presented in this material, since otherwise he should have been eager to expose error and dishonesty). Every available square foot of the lecture hall was crammed with students and faculty, with many sitting on the floor, standing along the walls, and overflowing into the hallways. The prolonged applause and friendly questions which followed the lecture indicated an enthusiastic reception for the material presented. The professor who had been so critical of Dr. Gish failed to challenge him in any way or even to ask a single question.

Dr. Gish debated a panel of three evolutionists before a large audience on the campus of Althouse College, London, Ontario. He also debated a Dr. Sadleir at Simon Fraser University, Burnaby, B.C.; Dr. Thomas Leith of York University on the Richmond College campus of the University of Toronto; and Mark Ragan, a Ph.D. candidate, at Dalhousie University, Halifax, Nova Scotia. On the Norm Perry TV show, he participated in a 30-minute debate with a Dr. Nichols of York University. Although the "winner" of such a debate could only be decided by a determination of the shift in audience opinion toward creation or evolution, the results, in the (necessarily subjective) opinion of both Dr. Hallonquist and Dr. Gish, were most satisfactory.

The ICR staff and Dr. Hallonquist and his colleagues in the Bible-Science Association of Canada are convinced that the battle to restore creation as a viable alternative to the theory of evolution in educational and scientific circles can only be accomplished, with God's blessing, through a long educational process. This tour of Canadian universities was one step in that process.

Creation Literature Society
Formed in New Zealand

As one of the follow-up projects after Dr. Henry Morris' lecture tour of New Zealand, in the summer of 1973, the newly-formed Creation Literature Society of New Zealand, has been actively promoting the distribution of creationist literature throughout the two islands. Under the leadership of William Turkington and F.L. Horton, the C.L.S. has sponsored the free distribution of the book *The Remarkable Birth of Planet Earth* to all members of the Plymouth Brethren Assemblies requesting one. Other creationist books are being advertised and sold by the C.L.S. throughout the country.

During the time of Dr. Morris' lecture tour last summer, a well-known theistic evolutionist from England, Professor Robert Boyd, also lectured in many of the same universities and churches where Dr. Morris spoke. Since that time, a lively interchange in the Christian journals of New Zealand has been taking place between the creationists and evolutionists in the churches there. Interest and awareness concerning the issue is continuing to increase.

Newton Scientific Association
Active In England

Chairman Edgar Powell (a geologist-geographer of Great Britain) reports that the creationist Newton Scientific Association continues to be active in the scientific study of creationism in the British Isles. In addition to holding a number of meetings, the N.S.A. is undertaking to reproduce and distribute the I.C.R. Technical Monographs and other scientific creationist literature in England.

The Newton Scientific Association was organized in the fall of 1973, on the occasion of Dr. Henry Morris' visit to England, when he spoke at a dinner meeting held in the famous Spurgeon's Tabernacle in London. The meeting was called by Powell and other creationist scientists in England for the purpose of considering the form such a creationist scientific society should take in order to meet the special needs in the British Isles.

University of Toronto Hears
Creation Lectures

For the first time in a generation, the University of Toronto campus was the locale of lectures on creationism, on October 23-25, 1974, as Dr. Henry Morris spoke to students of Canada's largest and most prestigious university. Attendance at the five lectures increased from 200 to over 900, with the final meeting held in the University's Convocation Hall. Hour-long question periods followed each lecture.

While in Toronto, Dr. Morris also spoke to a special breakfast for pastors and Christian leaders, with 150 present, on the theme "Creation and the Gospel." Two lectures were given to students and faculty at the Toronto Baptist Seminary, as well as lectures at the Sheridan Community College and three area high schools. On Sunday, he spoke at the Benton Street Baptist Church in Kitchener and at Toronto's historic Jarvis Street Baptist Church.

Creation Scholarships
Established in Taiwan

Mr. Timothy Ho, through the Chinese Christian Mission, has announced the establishment of ten scholarships each year to be awarded to deserving students of Chung Yuan Christian College of Science and Engineering in Taiwan, Republic of China. The annual scholarships are for $30 each and are named the "Henry M. Morris Scholarships" in recognition of the contributions of the I.C.R. Director in the field of scientific Christian apologetics. The College has a student body of over 5,000, 10% of whom are professing Christians.

Dr. Paul Han, President of the College, recently completed the translation and publication of Dr. Morris' book, *Evolution and the Modern Christian*, into the Chinese language.

Scientific Creation Group
Established in Brazil

An organization of Brazilian scientists has recently been established to promote creationism in Brazil. Named the *Instituto "Linnaeus" de Pesquisa da Creacao*, the purpose of the organization is to translate and distribute creationist literature and to conduct creation seminars in schools, colleges and churches in Brazil.

The Director of I.L.P.C. is Dr. Antonio Pessoa Leite. A current project is the translation of the C.R.S. textbook, *Biology: A Search for Order in Complexity*, into Portuguese. Speakers from I.L.P.C. have already conducted creation seminars in two state colleges and several churches. Plans are being made for a presentation at the Federal University in Recife.

ICR Speakers Featured At
Muskoka Baptist Conference

The first week of the summer conference season at the Muskoka Baptist Conference, June 29-July 4, 1975, featured a "Conference on Biblical Authority and Modern Science," with three ICR speakers rotating through the week with morning and evening lectures. Dr. Henry Morris spoke on Sunday and Monday, with approximately 500 campers attending each of the two Sunday services, Dr. Haold Slusher on Tuesday and Wednesday, and Dr. Lane Lester on Thursday and Friday.

All sessions were color video-taped by Brian Robinson, President of "Educational Television," of London, Ontario, for possible use in high schools, universities, and cable television across Canada.

The Muskoka Baptist Conference is located on beautiful Mary Lake about 150 miles north of Toronto, and is sponsored by the Fellowship of Evangelical Baptist Church of Canada. Rev. R.D. Holliday is Managing Director.

Summer Institute Held in Toronto

The first of ICR's Summer Institutes on Scientific Creationism to be held in eastern Canada was co-sponsored by the Toronto Baptist Seminary, located in Toronto's historic Jarvis Street Baptist Church, on June 30-July 4, with 40 registered for the two-credit course. Faculty members were Professors Harold Slusher, Lane Lester, and Henry Morris. An unusual feature was the scheduling of evening class sessions which were open to the public. The three ICR scientists also gave messages in a number of Toronto churches on the Sundays preceding and following the Institute.

ICR Scientists Tours New Zealand
And Australia in Summer of 1975

Dr. Duane Gish, Associate Director of ICR, has just completed a six-week lecture tour of New Zealand and Australia. Dr. Morris, Director of ICR, had participated in a five-week lecture tour of New Zealand in 1973 (*Acts and Facts, Vol. 2, September, 1973*). Dr. Gish spoke in numerous high schools, teachers' colleges, universities, churches, and in many general public meetings in nine cities in New Zealand and in eight cities in Australia, including Auckland, Paeroa, Hamilton, Palmerston North, Wanganui, Wellington, Dunedin, Nelson, and Christchurch in New Zealand, and Sydney, Canberra, Brisbane, Adelaide, Melbourne, Geelong, Hobart, and Launceston in Australia. The total attending these lectures was estimated to be approximately 25,000 including 7,700 high school students, 4,200 university students, 400 teachers college students, 400 Bible college students, 3,000 at church services, and 9,200 at general public meetings. Uncounted tens of thousands of others heard Dr. Gish at least briefly via six television and twelve radio interviews or programs. Dr. Gish and the case for creation were featured in numerous newspaper articles throughout these two countries. Mrs. Gish, who accompanied Dr. Gish at the invitation of the sponsors of the tour, spoke to ladies' groups in eight cities in New Zealand and Australia. She spoke on the importance and the implementation of teaching the evidence for creation in public schools. Mrs. Gish was impressed by the interest that was shown in the subject of creation by the ladies, and their concern with the humanistic teaching their children are getting in the schools.

TV 2, privately operated television network in New Zealand, helped to give the tour an initial boost by sending a television crew to Auckland from Wellington to interview with a few shots of Dr. Gish lecturing at Auckland University and with a few shots of this campus, and used the interview as part of their nation-wide evening news program. In the Auckland area, New Zealand's largest city, Dr. Gish spoke in six high schools, four churches, and gave four lectures at Auckland University. Attempts to arrange a debate at the university failed. He also spoke at three public meetings, and at the New Zealand Bible College, New Zealand's largest evangelical Bible college.

At Hamilton, Dr. Gish lectured in seven of the nine area high schools and gave four lectures at Waikato University during a three-day period. After the fourth lecture at the University, Dr. Gish responded to challenges and questions from a panel consisting of five faculty members. The four lectures and the interchange with the panel offered an ideal opportunity to present an extensively documented case for creation, with what appeared to be highly effective results.

At Palmerston North, in addition to lecturing in several high schools, Dr. Gish gave three lectures at Massey University. After the first of these lectures, Dr. Gish responded to challenges and questions from a panel consisting of two faculty members. Again, the combination of several lectures with debate and extensive question-and-answer periods offered a unique opportunity to present a powerful case for creation and to establish rapport with students and faculty. At all meetings Dr. Gish repeatedly stressed the spiritual significance of this evidence, that is, that we are more than just mechanistic products of a mindless universe, and that there is indeed a God who is our Creator and Lord, a God to whom we are responsible.

An audience estimated at 1,300, the largest of the tour, heard Dr. Gish at a Sunday afternoon lecture in Wellington. This lecture followed three other public lectures in the

Wellington area, five lectures in area high schools, and two lectures at Victoria University. The second lecture at Victoria University was followed by challenges and questions from a panel of two faculty members and interchange with the audience, offering a good opportunity to present the scientific case for creation.

While in Wellington, Dr. Gish participated in the popular Paddy O'Donnell radio talk-show for a total of three hours, returning a second day at Mr. O'Donnell's request. During the first program, Dr. Lloyd Geering, Professor of Religion at Victoria University, was brought in by telephone. He had left his position as head of Knox Presbyterian Seminary in Dunedin after an unsuccessful attempt to oust him on heresy charges. After he had identified himself as an evolutionist, he was asked by Dr. Gish to summarize the scientific evidence that convinced him of the validity of evolution theory. Geering could not, at least he did not, offer a shred of scientific evidence to support his position. Several weeks later, Dr. Geering had an article in the Auckland *Star* about Dr. Gish's lecture tour. Although pointing out that Dr. Gish was basing his case for creation during this tour primarily on the scientific evidence, Geering suggested that perhaps Gish's science was pseudoscience rather than science. Again, he made no effort to refute the evidence that Dr. Gish had presented, but appealed to readers to accept evolution as a fact because evolutionists say it is so. The *Star* published Dr. Gish's rebuttal a week later, offering one more opportunity to present the case for creation to many thousands.

After lecturing at schools and universities in several cities of New Zealand's South Island, Dr. Gish spent two weeks lecturing in the major cities of Australia. This was the first real exposure of this rapidly growing nation to the scientific case for creation., Dr. Morris having given a single lecture in Brisbane during his 1973 tour.

Highlights of the Australian tour were lectures at Sydney and Melbourne Universities, and lectures before large public audiences in Brisbane and Adelaide. At Sydney University, Dr. Gish addressed a lunch-hour audience that overflowed a

400-seat auditorium. They listened in rapt attention, according to a newspaper article published the following day. During his lecture, Dr. Gish quoted an article published several years ago by Professor L.C. Birch, a biologist and evolutionist at Sydney University, which states that evolution is outside the limits of empirical science because it cannot be tested. Dr. Birch was in the audience.

After speaking in several public meetings and churches in Sydney and Canberra, Australia's beautiful capital city, Dr. Gish was met at the Brisbane airport by newspaper reporters, and television crews from two networks, reflecting the interest that had been stimulated in this city by the local organizer, Mr. Gordon Jones, Assistant Principal of Kelvin Grove Teachers College. In addition to the Teachers College and several high schools, Dr. Gish spoke to a public audience of 700. He also addressed a special evening meeting attended by 110 science teachers from the Brisbane area.

In Adelaide Dr. Gish spoke to 200 students and staff at a lunch-hour meeting at Flinders University and to audiences of 500 and 700 on successive evenings at a town hall. Dr. and Mrs. Gish, along with Dr. Harold Steward, a Christian physician, had a 30-minute audience with Sir Mark Oliphant, famous nuclear physicist and governor of the state of South Australia. Sir Mark, although concerned with the moral decay of his nation, is more interested in the social aspects of the gospel of Christ, exhibiting skepticism concerning its spiritual aspects.

At Melbourne, Dr. Gish spoke to 400 students, staff and others at Melbourne University. According to a report received later from a member of the faculty, the staff members present were very much impressed by the scientific evidence for creation. In addition to this lecture, lectures were also given at Latrobe University, the Royal Melbourne Institute of Technology, in several churches, a high school and at a general meeting.

At Hobart, Tasmania, Dr. Gish debated Dr. Richard W. Haines of Tasmania University before an audience of 400 in the town hall. After other lectures at a teachers college and at the WEC Missionary Training College at Launceston, Dr. and Mrs. Gish returned to Auckland to complete speaking engagements in that city, described earlier, before returning to the U.S.

The sponsor of the New Zealand portion of the tour was the Evangelical Alliance, Dr. Tony Hanne of Capernwray Lodge, Auckland, Director, and the sponsors of the Australian portion of the tour were the Bible Union of Australia and the Australian branch of the Evolution Protest Movement. The Bible Union has already requested the ICR staff to consider a more extensive lecture tour of Australia in the near future, possibly in 1976.

chapter VII

CREATION IN THE CITY

600 Attend Canton-Akron Seminar

Approximately 600 people attended the first Creation Seminar conducted by I.C.R. in the Northern Ohio region, on January 18-19, 1974, including an unusually large proportion of high school and college students. Sponsored by the Northern Ohio Sunday School Association, the Seminar was held in the large auditorium of the Canton Temple Church of God in Canton. Lee Belleman, President of the Sunday School Association and Christian Education Director of the Goss Memorial Church in Akron, was in charge of promotion and arrangements.

Speakers were Harold S. Slusher and Henry M. Morris. Professor Slusher conducted lectures and discussions on the topics: "Origin of the Universe"; "Evidence for a Young Earth"; and "Critique of Radiometric Dating." Dr. Morris spoke on "Evolution and Creation"; and "Geology and the Great Flood." In addition, the film "Footprints in Stone" was shown.

A great many Ohio pastors attended. One wrote, "I enjoyed the Seminar beyond description." One Kent State University student wrote: "I will soon be teaching in a public school. The Seminar has been extremely helpful."

Dr. Morris also spoke on Sunday, January 20, to the Goss Memorial Church, speaking to the college class on the subject

"Science, the Bible, and Man's Origin," and, at the morning worship service on "Creation and the Cross."

Seminar Reaches Winter Visitors in Florida

A three-day Creation Seminar in late February reached hundreds of winter visitors to the popular Florida Christian resort community of Bibletown in Boca Raton. An earlier seminar, in May, 1973, had been well received by the resident members and friends of the large Bible-town Community Church. Pastor of the church is Dr. Torrey Johnson, widely known as the founder of Youth for Christ.

Speakers at the Seminar were Dr. John Whitcomb, Dr. Duane Gish, and Dr. Henry Morris. In addition to the tourists and church members, a number of local Christian high schools and colleges sent large delegations to the Seminar.

Arrangements for both seminars were made by Dr. Robert Armstrong, an orthopedic surgeon in Boca Raton.

First New England Seminar
Held in Bridgeport

Over 400 registered in attendance at the first seminar on scientific creationism ever held in the New England states, so far as known, with Dr. Duane Gish and Dr. Henry Morris as speakers. The meetings were held in Central High School in Bridgeport, Connecticut, on April 26-27, 1974, and were sponsored by the Greater Bridgeport Fellowship of Evangelicals. Chairman of arrangements was Rev. Paul H. Anderson, pastor of the Calvary Evangelical Free Church in suburban Trumbull.

Interest was high in the meetings, and more creationist literature was purchased than at almost any previous seminar. However, one local science teacher walked out angrily during Dr. Gish's first lecture (on the origin of life), muttering that this sort of meeting should never be permitted. The sponsors, for weeks ahead, had tried to arrange a creation-evolution debate with Dr. Gish and Dr. Morris, but were unable to persuade faculty members at either Yale

University, Connecticut University or Bridgeport University to accept such an opportunity.

Seminar registrants came from New York, New Jersey, Massachusetts, Pennsylvania, and Rhode Island, as well as Connecticut. Dr. Gish and Dr. Morris also spoke in three of the Bridgeport churches on April 28.

Meetings Held in Georgia's
Top Southern Baptist Church

Dr. Henry Morris, Director of I.C.R., was one of three featured speakers at the first annual Bible Conference held at the large Roswell Street Baptist Church of Marietta, Georgia March 17-20. This church has the largest Sunday School among Southern Baptist Churches in the state of Georgia; and on March 17, when Dr. Morris spoke to the combined Sunday Schools, a record attendance of approximately 1650 was set.

The other two speakers were Dr. Herschel Hobbs, former president of the Southern Baptist Convention and currently the regular preacher on the nationwide Baptist Hour, and Dr. John Newport, Professor of Philosophy of Religion at the Southwestern Baptist Theological Seminary in Fort Worth, and a leading authority on occultism and demonology. All three spoke twice daily for the four days.

Response in the church to the creationist message was excellent. The pastor, Nelson L. Price, is also a member of the Board of Trustees at the New Orleans Baptist Theological Seminary. In his student days he had served as Louisiana state Baptist Student Union president at the same time that Dr. Morris (who at that time was Head of the Civil Engineering Department at Southwestern Louisiana University) was serving as state B.S.U. faculty adviser.

Creation-Evolution Institute
Held in Historic Church

The historic First Presbyterian Church of Augusta, Georgia, was the site for the first creationist Bible conference in Augusta on September 6-8. Dr. Henry Morris was the speaker, giving eight lectures and messages in the three days, on themes ranging from Scientific Creationism" to "The Many Infallible Proofs of Christianity". Attendance was from 400 to over 500 at each session.

Augusta's First Presbyterian Church was founded in 1809 and one of its present buildings completed in 1812. It was in this church that the Presbyterian Church in the United States (Southern Presbyterians) was founded in 1865. However, the church has recently separated from the denomination because of the increasingly liberal drift among the Southern Presbyterians. The church was the boyhood church of President Woodrow Wilson, whose father once served as pastor there. The present pastor is John W. Oliver, a graduate of Fuller Seminary, who has led the church from a neo-orthodox type of emphasis to a strong Biblical and evangelistic ministry in recent years, with attendance and giving greatly enlarged.

Response of the audiences, including many college students and professionals, to the creationist message was unusually enthusiastic. Many testified of strengthened faith and changed lives.

Lutheran Workers Study
Creationism at Minneapolis

With a 90-minute session each day for four days, approximately 400 pastors and other workers attending the annual Midwinter Conference of the Lutheran Evangelistic Movement were given a good introduction to the field of scientific creationism under the teaching of Dr. Henry Morris, I.C.R. Director, January 28-31. Meetings were held in Minneapolis at the historic Augustana Lutheran Church of that city.

The Lutheran Evangelistic Movement is an inter-Lutheran body with strong Biblical convictions and soul-winning ministries. This was its 39th Annual Convention. Many non-Lutherans also attended, including the complete geology class of Dr. John Cunningham at the Northwestern College.

In addition, Dr. Morris spoke to 4,000 Lutheran youth assembled in the Minneapolis Sports Arena on Feburary 1, for the 25th convention of the youth congress of the L.E.M., on the theme "Science and the Supernatural."

Miami Seminar Sets Records

Over 1000 people gathered in the auditorium of Coral Gables' beautiful Granada Presbyterian Church for the opening session of the first Greater Miami Creation Seminar on Thursday night, April 3, 1975, setting an all-time record for a regular creation seminar session, so far as known. The seminar continued all day Friday, Friday night and all day Saturday, with attendance holding up well at all sessions. Estimates indicated that at least 2000 different people came to at least one session during the seminar.

For the first time, all four ICR scientists — Lane Lester, Harold Slusher, Duane Gish and Henry Morris — participated in the same seminar, with three lectures each. In addition to the record attendance, ICR books were purchased in record numbers. All indications were that the creationist revival received a tremendous boost in the important southern Florida region, and that it will continue to grow there.

New York City has First
Creation Seminar

New York's famous Calvary Baptist Church was host to the first Creation Seminar ever held, so far as known, in the nation's largest city, on April 29 through May 2. Nearly 400 paid registrants were in attendance, as Dr. Henry Morris gave seven one-hour lectures on various aspects of scientific creationism. The film "Footprints in Stone" was also shown. The audience included many students from the different New York universities, as well as many scientists and teachers, so it is believed the influence of the seminar will be effectively felt throughout the area. Interest and enthusiasm were uniformly high.

The Calvary Baptist Church is the largest and most influential evangelical church in New York City, and is strategically located on 57th St. in midtown Manhattan, between Broadway and Fifth Avenue opposite Carnegie Hall. It has had a long succession of distinguished pastors, including Will Houghton,

William Ward Ayer, and Stephen Olford. Present pastor is Dr. J.C. Macauley, well-known author and Bible teacher. The church also sponsors an evening school, the New York School of the Bible, which also participated in the Creation Seminar.

First Creation Seminar Held in Las Vegas

For the first time, so far as known, a successful creation seminar has been held in what many believe to be the "sin capital" of the nation, Las Vegas, Nevada, where gambling, nudity, prostitution, etc., are both legal and brazen, and where crime, drugs, occultism, and dogmatic evolutionism abound in the schools and elsewhere.

The seminar, held on November 19-21, was sponsored by the West Oakey Southern Baptist Church, with Dr. Henry Morris as speaker. An open meeting, sponsored by the Baptist Student Union at the University of Nevada, attracted many students and faculty members, including the biology department head, who had been scheduled for a debate with Dr. Morris but withdrew prior to the meeting. The church was full for most of the eight sessions held there, and a two-hour, call-in radio broadcast on station KILA attracted much interest. Rev. Tom Popelka, pastor of the church, was in charge of arrangements.

Gish At Missouri Creation Seminar

The 3rd Annual Creation Seminar sponsored by the Missouri Association for Creation, Inc., was held in St. Louis, Missouri at Calvary Heights Baptist Temple (Rev. Carl Baugh, pastor) on Saturday, Oct. 18. Dr. Duane Gish of ICR was featured in two lectures, "Human Origins" and "The Fossil Record."

The past president of the Missouri Assn. for Creation, Glen W. Wolfrom, Ph.D. Candidate, Univ. of MO, began the seminar with the presentation "Science: A Perspective." He established that evolution is just as unscientific as creation, and that both creation and evolution may be evaluated as models for correlating and explaining scientific data.

162

Other speakers included David Rodabaugh, Ph.D., Univ. of Mo., Stephen Jones, Ph.D., Drury College, and John Lasley, Ph.D., Univ. of Mo. Dr. Rodabaugh spoke concerning "Mathematics: Evolution Illogical." Dr. Jones discussed "Biology: An Argument from Design — The Woodpecker." Dr. Lasley's topic was "Genetics: Variation Limited or Unlimited?" Other highlights of the day included showing of the film "Footprints in Stone" and a panel discussion with Jack Henry, Lt. Col. USAF (Ret.) presiding.

Nearly 200 persons from all parts of the state attended. Many scientists, teachers, and Christian laymen were present. The seminar is considered to have been the most successful ever in the state of Missouri. One of those attending commented, "The speakers presented useful information in an entertaining way. I've never seen anything like it before. . ."

Dallas-Ft. Worth Seminar Reaches 3000

A weekend creation seminar in Arlington, Texas, midway between Dallas and Fort Worth, reached a total of approximately 3,000 different people at the University of Texas at Arlington, Dallas Theological Seminary and the Pantego Bible Church, which sponsored the meetings, on October 3-5. Dr. Henry Morris, I.C.R. Director, and John Morris, I.C.R. South Central Extension Scientist, were the speakers. In addition, Dr. Morris answered call-in questions for an hour on Radio Station KPBC on a show hosted by writer Zola Levitt.

Over 250 students and faculty at the Arlington campus of the University of Texas attended a noon lecture on Friday, October 3, by Dr. Morris, sponsored by the Baptist Student Union. Just prior to that meeting, he had been the speaker at morning chapel services at Dallas Seminary, with a student body of over 800. Dr. Richard Seume, who was Dr. Morris's pastor in 1945-46, is Seminary Chaplain. Dr. Morris had been the Seminary's W.H. Griffith-Thomas lecturer in 1967, and his lectures were later published in his book *Biblical Cosmology and Modern Science.*

Audiences of up to 800 attended the various seminar sessions on Friday and Saturday. The weekend was climaxed with capacity crowds (1,200 each) in the Pantego Bible Church for Sunday services, Dr. Morris speaking in the morning on "Science and the Second Coming" and John Morris giving a slide lecture in the evening on "The Search for Noah's Ark." Interest and enthusiasm were high at all sessions in this strategic region of the country.

New England Seminar
Attracts Wide Interest

A two-day Creation Seminar held in Enfield, Connecticut (the town where Jonathan Edwards first preached his famous sermon "Sinners in the Hands of an Angry God") drew enthusiastic crowds of about 550 for the evening sessions and about 300 for the daytime sessions on Monday and Tuesday, November 4-5. Dr. Henry Morris was the speaker. The meetings were held in Enfield's Faith Baptist Church (Rev. B.W. Sanders, pastor) and were co-sponsored by the Northeastern Baptist Bible Fellowship. Pastors and members from about 25 churches in the New England states, as well as New York, New Jersey and Pennsylvania, attended.

Grand Rapids Seminar
Has Record Registration

Over 850 paid registrations were received at Grand Rapids' first Creation Seminar, held at Calvary Baptist Church of that city on October 31 - November 2. Although single meetings (debates, etc.) have occasionally attracted larger audiences, it is believed that this marks the largest actual paid attendance for a complete seminar. Faculty for the seminar consisted of Dr. Duane Gish and Dr. Henry Morris. The film "Footprints in Stone" supplemented the six two-hour, lecture-discussion sessions on Friday and Saturday. Dr. Morris also preached at the four worship services in Calvary Baptist Church on Sunday, November 2. Pastor of the church is Dr. John White and in charge of the seminar arrangements was Associate Pastor Dr. Howard Bixby. Calvary Baptist Church is affiliated with the General Association of Regular Baptist Churches and is one of the most rapidly growing churches in this association.

chapter VIII

I.C.R. AND THE MEDIA

ARARAT PROJECT FEATURED ON
N.B.C. TODAY SHOW

Before what is probably creationism's largest audience to date (estimated at 20 million!) a testimony to the validity of the Bible and scientific creationism was given by John Morris on N.B.C.'s "Today" show on the morning of April 15, 1974. The interviewers, Gene Shalott and the late Frank McGee, asked the young I.C.R. field scientist numerous questions about the search for Noah's Ark on Mount Ararat, as well as about creation and the Noahic deluge in general.

Mr. McGee identified the Institue for Creation Research as a "fundamentalist" organization located in San Diego. The N.B.C. news team seemed somewhat skeptical but nevertheless interested and impressed by the interview.

In addition to his appearance on the "Today" show, Mr. Morris also spoke to the Word of Life Bible Institute in up-state New York, as well as to churches in the New York, Philadelphia, and Baltimore areas while in the eastern states.

The ICR Ararat project has been featured in numerous newspaper and magazine articles around the world in recent months. John Morris has appeared on many radio and television broadcasts and is in much demand for speaking to churches and other groups. This is indicative of the tremendous interest in the search for Noah's Ark, and perhaps is a testimony of how God is preparing the world to understand the significance of the discovery when it finally comes.

Creation Receives National
T.V. Coverage

Dr. Duane T. Gish, Associate Director of I.C.R., was featured on nationwide CBS television news on May 15. The occasion was the monthly meeting of the Board of Education of the Cupertino Union School District, considering the proposal by the citizens for Scientific Creation to teach creation in the schools, as reported elsewhere in *Acts and Facts*. The meeting was also reported on national CBS radio news. Commentators noted that, as the largest elementary school district in California, action in Cupertino might set an important precedent.

At least one station, in Ohio, showed the entire 30-minute presentation by Dr. Gish. In the Tampa-St. Petersburg area the presentation followed by only a few days the video-tape rerun of the debate held in Tampa several weeks ago between two evolutionist professors at the University of South Florida and two creationists, Dr. Gish and Dr. Henry Morris. The combined effect of these two programs, according to reports, made a significant impact in the Tampa area.

ICR Ararat Project Featured
On Nationwide T.V. In Canada

The ICR Ararat Probe continues to be one of the most effective attention-getting activities within the creationist movement. The news media desire to feature worthwhile projects with an exciting flair, and the search for Noah's Ark certainly qualifies.

John Morris, the leader of the ICR expeditions, was interviewed September 19, on the Canada A.M. program, the nationwide morning talk show of CTV, by Helen Hutchinson. The reaction to the interview was extremely favorable. A few selected slides of Mount Ararat were shown as Mr. Morris detailed previous sightings of the ark as well as current work and plans for the future.

Church of Satan Opposes Creationism

The letter photographically reproduced below was received by the Cupertino School District Board of Education, following extensive efforts by concerned citizens to promote scientific creationism in the schools of the district. These efforts included testimonies by Dr. Gish and Dr. Morris, of I.C.R., to the School Board, and debates and lectures in the area by Dr. Gish.

the church of satan
post office box 4286 · san jose, california 95126

October 31, 1974

Board of Education
Cupertino School District
10301 Vista Drive
Cupertino, California 95014

Gentlemen:

As a formerly proud graduate of the Cupertino School District, I am dismayed and disgusted at your decision to teach the creation myth as science. A formerly excellent school district has suddenly become one of the worst in terms of constitutionality.

I realize that your decision is a "test case," to see if a religious doctrine will be accepted in the official teaching of a public school system, much as the furor over textbooks in West Virginia is a "test case" to see of non-Christian ideas can be ousted from the public schools of this nation.

In the end both of these "test cases" will be proven unconstitutional under the First Amendment. As long as there is one child attending school or one taxpayer supporting the school who does not believe in the creation myth, to teach this myth as science violates that child's and that taxpayer's rights. The only schools which should teach religion as science are parochial schools—where religion infiltrates every subject.

Despite so-called scientific evidence to the contrary, there is no evidence to support the Judeo-Christian concept of creation except the Judeo-Christian Bible. The evidence in this Bible was not recorded until centuries—perhaps thousands or tens of thousands of years—after the fact, during which time there was ample opportunity for errors to enter. Creation as you would teach it is a religious belief, not science, and this myth is being questioned, not only by evolutionists of the Darwin school, but by other theories based on scientific evidence. Are you also planning to teach Eric Von Daeniken's "chariots of the gods" theory, which is based on evidence which can be photographed and presented visually to the children? Are you planning to teach Richard Mooney's theory that man and most of the animals we know are vestiges of space exploration by other planets millenia ago, and which is based on the valid prospects of Man making similar explorations? Charles Darwin's theory of evolution—more properly called, I think, the survival of the fittest—can be easily demonstrated in the classroom; men and animals unable to survive wars and pollution are becoming extinct, as Darwin predicted they would

Where is there similar, produceable evidence for the theory of creation? Why is there no life being created today?

And there is the question if you must decide between a perhaps unpopular theory and religious myth, which is undoubtedly unconstitutional in public schools, why teach either? Why not leave "how we got here" as a question for parents to answer according to their conscience?

Sincerely,

Priestess Margaret Wendall

bubastis chapel

167

SCIENTIST BACKS HUMAN CREATION CLAIM
By MARK FLEMING

The issue Duane Gish addressed was familiar enough — creation or evolution, God or Darwin, Adam or ape. What seemed unusual was his line of argument.

Though Gish supported the Bible's side of the once-controversial question in a talk sponsored by Collegiates for Christ Friday, he didn't attack Darwinism as the work of the Devil.

Nor did he preach about a beast with seven heads or predict the end of the world. He didn't even quote the Bible.

Speaking before a packed house in 2000 LSB, Gish merely claimed the theory of special creation scientifically explains the origin of human beings better than the theory of evolution.

Scientific Creation

He appealed to fossil records, carbon-dating methods and Newton's Second Law of Thermo-dynamics. "If we compare both models to the evidence," he said, "creation makes more scientific sense than evolution."

Gish, a Christian with a PhD in biochemistry from Berkeley, set out to show that the human race was created fully developed and didn't evolve from lower life forms.

At first Gish sounded like any other Fundamentalist with a conscience to clear.

"Darwinism is absolutely, totally inadequate to explain our enormously complex universe," he said. "There is as much dogma and religion in evolutionary theory as in Christianity."

But there the harangue ended and a "scientifically valid discussion of alternative hypotheses" began.

Gish presented a slide-illustrated discussion of the fossil record, demonstrating the "systematic and regular absence of transitional forms between all the basic kinds of organisms in the fossils."

Abrupt Appearance

The absence of intermediary forms in the fossils, Gish said, is compelling evidence that humans and other complex life did not evolve step-by-step from lower life, but appeared suddenly, without ancestors.

"Monkeys appear, apes appear, men appear, all abruptly, with no links between them," Gish said.

He suggested, for example, that Peking and Java humanoids were giant apes and not human-like at all, and Neanderthal and Cro-Magnon beings "would go completely unnoticed if they were to walk down the street in a business suit today."

"Younger Parents?"

As additional evidence Gish cited anthropologist Richard Leaky's recent discovery of human bones 2.8 million years old. He said Leaky's find is more highly developed than some of our presumed human-like ancestors who lived much later.

"These can't be our true ancestors, for who ever heard of parents being younger than their children?" Gish remarked.

He also claimed that the theory of evolution contradicts Newton's Second Law.

He said that while the Second Law states that all things tend to go from the complex to the simple, evolution requires just the opposite — the continually building up from simple to complex forms.

"More Rational"

Gish often directed his comments to school textbooks that teach the theory of evolution as established fact. He protested this, saying that "evolution is no more scientifically valid than creation as a hypothesis for origins."

"I, as a scientist, simply don't find it rational to believe that living things have evolved from non-living things," Gish said. "I think it is more rational to believe that an omnipotent creator, independent of the universe, created human beings and other forms of life."

chapter IX

CREATION AND THE CHRISTIAN LIFE

A Collection of Director's Column Articles
Henry M. Morris

CREATION AND FAMILY LIFE

Many readers of *Acts and Facts* do not know that Dr. Tim LaHaye, whose Family Life Seminars have become so widely known around the country, is the president of Christian Heritage College and, therefore, also of the Institute for Creation Research. Although the Institute operates independently of the College to a large extent (with separate budget, separate staff, etc.), Dr. LaHaye is an enthusiastic supporter of I.C.R. and gives outstanding over-all direction to the combined ministries of both the College and the Institute.

I have discovered in speaking around the country in different communities that the people in those communities also are enthusiastic about Tim LaHaye and his Seminars, but did not realize that our Creation Seminars and the Family Life Seminars were associated indirectly in this way. In addition to his Seminars, Dr. LaHaye's books (*Spirit-Controlled Temperament, How To Be Happy Though Married, Transformed Temperaments, The Beginning of the End, The Message of the Book of Revelation* and *How To Win Over Depression*), have all been best-sellers and have been a blessing to thousands.

What might have seemed at first to be an unlikely partnership of ideas and emphases has thus, in God's providence, proved a most effective combination. After all, God's creation and man's family life are closely associated in the Bible! The institution of marriage was the first human institution established by God and the command to have children was God's first commandment to man (Genesis 1:27,28).

Because of the close relation of the home and family to God's creation, it is not surprising when we note today that a sound concept of marital and parental responsibilities goes hand-in-glove with a sound concept of Biblical creationism.

Similarly, it is no mere coincidence that the ascendancy of evolutionary philosophy in the past century was quickly followed by the decline of the sanctity of the home and marriage relationships. If man is not the special creation of God, then neither is the home. If man is an evolved animal, then the morals of the barnyard and the jungle are more "natural," and therefore more "healthy," than the artifically-imposed restrictions of pre-marital chastity and marital fidelity. Instead of monogamy, why not promiscuity and polygamy? Instead of training children in the nurture and admonition of the Lord, better to teach them how to struggle and survive in a cut-throat world, and then toss them out of the nest. Self-preservation is the first law of nature; only the fittest will survive. Be the cock-of-the-walk and the king-of-the-mountain! Eat, drink, and be merry, for life is short and that's the end. So says evolution!

Perhaps the greatest indictment of all against evolution is this assault against permanent, monogamous marriage and the sacred obligations of parents and children to each other. I believe that a strong emphasis on the full doctrine of Biblical creationism, in all its implications (including the proper Biblical roles of husband and wife) in both the home and church, is the best investment that can be made toward a happy home life, both in one's own home and in the future homes of their children, and ultimately toward a healthy society and preparation for eternal responsibilities.

Ecumenical Creationism

One of the most significant aspects of the study of creation is that men from every type of denominational background recognize its vital importance and are concerned about its relevance to their own denominational doctrines. For example, I have been invited at one time or another to speak on this subject in the churches and schools of over 65 different religious denominations. This has nothing to do, obviously, with the popularity of the speaker, but it does provide a striking testimony to the importance of the subject.

It seems that there are people and churches in practically every denomination that have been harmfully influenced by evolution and, at the same time, there are some in each denomination who are vitally concerned about the problem and are doing what they can to restore or to retain special creation as a basic doctrine in their system. Furthermore, although there are still large numbers in each group who are indifferent, it does seem clear that more and more people are getting involved all the time.

This common concern about creationism is drawing together from all these backgrounds people who have heretofore been kept apart by other theological differences. Special creationists, of course, no matter what their denomination, generally share certain other basic beliefs, such as belief in the God of the Bible and belief in the divine inspiration and authority of the Bible. Evolutionists in all denominations, on the other hand, also tend to share certain beliefs among themselves, including a rather loose concept of Biblical inspiration and even of the nature of God.

Lest anyone misunderstand, I am not in any way advocating ecumenicalism or church union, as the concept is usually promoted today. The church union movement is unrealistic when it proposes that Christians of strong, Bible-based convictions give them up for the sake of a superficial unity. Each church is to teach "the whole counsel of God" to its members, as it understands that counsel, and it must not reject that responsibility.

However, although there is no doctrine that is *not* important, surely there are some that are *more* important, and special creation is probably the most basic of all, save the doctrine of God Himself. It is amazing that so many churches, schools, and other institutions have very detailed and explicit "statements of faith," comprising what they believe to be their fundamental doctrines, but almost none of these include a specific statement regarding the special creation of all things in the beginning. This tragic oversight has resulted in the defection of great numbers of such institutions to the evolutionary world-view, and then inevitably later to liberalism and finally to humanism.

I would never suggest church unification on any basis short of spiritual unity on *all* the essential doctrines and practices taught in the Bible, and this ideal is probably impossible to attain before the Lord returns. In the meantime, however, it is quite practical to enjoy a genuine fellowship among believers in such truly *basic* doctrines as the fact of God, special creation of all things by God, the reality of Satanic and human rebellion against God, the necessity of salvation provided through God, the future consummation of all things in God, and authoritative Biblical revelation from God. In each case, of course, Christians understand by "God" the personal, omnipotent God of the Bible, manifest fully in Jesus Christ (Colossians 2:9).

At the practical level, all such believers can work effectively together in public movements and institutions to revive recognition of God as Creator, the doctrine which is the foundation of all other truth. All believers ultimately are in a warfare not *against* each other, but *with* each other, against Satan and his purposes (Ephesians 6:12). The creation-evolution issue is at the very center of this warfare. Is God really the sovereign Creator of this universe, or is He somehow limited by eternal matter or by other beings in the universe? Is His Word true and clear or is it tentative and vague, subject to man's shifting opinions? These are the ultimate issues, and genuine believers ought to be united on them.

Unfortunately man is an inconsistent creature, often governed by emotion and temporarilites rather than by sound reasoning and eternal verities. Not all evolutionists are "bad guys," some are highly moral and spiritual in their personal relations. By the same token, not all creationists are "good guys"; some are opinionated cranks and some even self-seeking charlatans.

Such inconsistencies in human belief and behaviour, however, do not vitiate the consistency of the immutable God and His infallible Word. The character of God demands the doctrine of special creation and the word of God clearly reveals it. These fundamental truths constitute the only sound foundation for the development of all other doctrines. Unity in these is, therefore, prerequisite to any true unity in other doctrines. It is just such unity which is excitingly developing today among godly creationist Christians in all denominations.

The Importance of Creationism

One of the most frustrating problems which we encounter in trying to encourage and strengthen belief in creationism is the indifference of so many Christian people to the importance of this issue. "I don't believe in evolution anyhow, so why should I waste time in studying or promoting creationism?" "Why get involved in peripheral and controversial issues like that — just preach the Gospel!" "The Bible is not a textbook of science, but of how to live." "It is the Rock of Ages which is important — not the age of rocks!" "Winning souls is the principal thing — not winning debates."

Platitudes such as the above, however spiritual they sound, are really cop-outs. They tend to become excuses for avoiding serious thought and the offense of the cross. In the name of evangelism and of appealing to large numbers, a least-common-denominator emphasis on emotional experiences and a nominal commitment of some kind has become the dominant characteristic of most Christian teaching and activity today, and this is almost as true in fundamentalist and conservative circles as it is among religious liberals.

This attitude seems to date largely from the after-effects of the infamous Scopes Trial in 1925. The fundamentalists and creationists were made to look so ridiculous by the news media covering that trial at the time (and they are still exploiting it today!) that Christians in general retreated altogether from the battle for the schools and the minds of their young people. Avoiding any further attempt to relate science and history to an inspired Bible, Christian teachers and preachers thenceforth emphasized evangelism and the spiritual life almost exclusively. The "gap theory" which supposedly allowed the earth's billions of years of evolutionary history to be pigeon-holed between the first two verses of Genesis and then ignored, provided a convenient device for saying the entire question was irrelevant.

As a consequence, in less than a generation, the entire school system and the very establishment itself — educational, scientific, political, military, industrial, and religious — was taken over by the evolutionary philosophy and its fruits of naturalism, humanism, socialism and animalistic amoralism.

For the past decade, however, a noteworthy revival of creationism has been taking place, both in the churches and, to some extent, in the schools. Thousands of scientists have become creationists, and the interest among teachers and students in creationism is higher than it has ever been.

Nevertheless, although many churches and Christian people have become actively involved in the creation issue, it is still sadly true that the majority of them are indifferent, or even antagonistic, to creationism They think it is only a peripheral biological question, of no concern in the preaching of the Gospel. Even most fundamentalists, who themselves may believe in creation, think evolution is a dead issue.

Such an attitude is based on wishful thinking, to say the least. The lead article in the latest issue of *Science*, the official journal of the prestigious American Association for the Advancement of Science, says:

> "While many details remain unknown, the grand
> design of biologic structure and function in plants

and animals, including man, admits to no other explanation than that of evolution. Man therefore is another link in a chain which unites all life on this planet." (A.G. Motulsky, "Brave New World," *Science,* Vol. 185 August 23, 1974, page 653.).

Not only did man evolve, but so did "the religions of Jesus and Buddha" (*Ibid*). That being so, not only are the supernatural aspects of Christianity open to question, but so are its ethical teachings.

"An ethical system that bases its premises on absolute pronouncements will not usually be acceptable to those who view human nature by evolutionary criteria." (*Ibid*, page 654).

Ethics and morals must evolve as well as organisms! And so must social and political systems. There are no absolutes.

This is the logical and inevitable outgrowth of evolutionary teaching. This is the logical and inevitable outgrowth of Christian indifference to evolutionary teaching.

The doctrine of special creation is the foundation of all other Christian doctrine. The experience of belief in Christ as Creator is the basis of all other Christian experience. Creationism is not peripheral or optional; it is central and vital. That is why God placed the account of creation at the beginning of the Bible, and why the very first verse of the Bible speaks of the creation of the physical universe.

Jesus Christ was Creator (Colossians 1:16) before He became Redeemer (Colossians 1:20). He is the very "beginning of the creation of God" (Revelation 3:14). How then can it be possible to really know Him as Saviour unless one also, and first, knows God as Creator?

The very structure of man's time commemorates over and over again, week by week, the completed creation of all things in six days. The preaching of the Gospel necessarily includes the preaching of creation. ". . . the everlasting gospel to preach unto them that dwell on the earth . . . worship Him that made heaven, and earth, and the sea, and the fountains of waters" (Revelation 14:6,7).

If man is a product of evolution, he is not a fallen creature in need of a Saviour, but a rising creature, capable of saving himself.

The "gospel" of evolution is the enemy of the Gospel of Christ. The Gospel of Christ leads to salvation, righteousness, joy, peace, and meaning in life. Evolution's "gospel" yields materialism, collectivism, anarchism, atheism and despair in death.

Evolutionary thinking dominates our schools today — our news media, our entertainment, our politics, our entire lives. But evolution is false and absurd scientifically! How long will Christian people and churches remain ignorant and apathetic concerning it?

Creation and Christian Witnessing

At the beginning of the book of Acts, the Lord Jesus Christ gave His great command to His disciples: "Ye shall be witnesses unto me — unto the uttermost parts of the earth" (Acts 1:8). The remainder of the book of Acts tells how the first-century believers attempted to obey His command, witnessing first in Jerusalem, then in all Judea, then in Samaria and on throughout the world as far as they were able to go. Generation after generation of Christian witnesses has continued to try to fulfill His command, but it must be admitted that no generation has ever been so effective in doing this as was that first generation.

Many reasons could be given for the remarkable spread of the gospel in the first century. One that has not been adequately considered by most modern-day witnesses, however, is the specific procedure followed by the early Christian evangelists and missionaries when they first encountered a new audience. That is, they always started preaching or witnessing at the level of faith and knowledge already shared by their listeners, and then went on from there to direct their minds and hearts eventually to Christ, building on the specific foundation corresponding to the particular background of the audience.

The initial ministry was, of course, to the Jews, and these

people already believed in God and in the inspiration and authority of the entire Old Testament. Therefore, Peter and the others always began by referring to the Scriptures, showing that Christ was indeed the fulfillment of the Messianic prophetic promises (note Acts 2:16-21, 25-31, 34-36; 3:20-26; 4:10-12; 7:48-51; 8:30-36; 10:43; etc.). Continually using two powerful Christian evidences — namely, the fulfillment of Old Testament prophecy and the bodily resurrection of Christ — they were able to win great multitudes of their Jewish countrymen to faith in Christ.

Even when they began to go to the Gentiles, they would almost always begin at the local synagogue. There were colonies of Jews in almost every city and, since these also believed the Old Testament, Paul and the other missionaries always began as they had back in Jerusalem, by reasoning out of the Scriptures (note Acts 13:5; 14-15, 32-40, 14:1; 17:2-3, 10-11; 18:4, 28; 19:8, etc.).

There are two recorded instances, however, where Paul found himself confronted by a crowd composed exclusively of pagan Gentiles. These people neither knew nor believed the Old Testament Scriptures, and it would have been futile to preach to them on the basis of a common acceptance of Biblical revelation. Therefore, Paul began be referring to the evidence of creation, which they could see and appreciate entirely apart from Scripture.

In the first case he was at Lystra, in Asia Minor, speaking to pagan worshippers of the Roman gods. To turn them away from these idols, he urged their attention to the evidence of the true God in the creation. "We — preach unto you that ye should turn from these vanities unto the living God, which made heaven, and earth, and the sea, and all things that are therein: Who in times past suffered all nations to walk in their own ways. Nevertheless, He left not Himself without witness, in that He did good, and gave us rain from heaven, and fruitful seasons, filling our hearts with food and gladness." (Acts 14:15-17).

The other occasion was at Athens, in the midst of the Epicureans, the Stoics, and other evolutionary philosophers at Mars Hill. To them he preached: "God that made the world and all things therein, seeing that he is Lord of heaven and earth, dwelleth not in temples made with hands: Neither is worshipped with men's hands, as though He needed anything, seeing he giveth to all life, and breath, and all things; And hath made of one blood all nations of men for to dwell on all the face of the earth — that they should seek the Lord, if haply they might feel after him, and find Him, though He be not far from everyone of us." (Acts 17:24-27).

In neither case, of course, was the preaching of God as Creator sufficient to bring salvation. The message must not stop there, but it often must begin there. Only when God is acknowledged as Creator and Sovereign is one able to understand his need of a Saviour.

The twentieth century in North America is far removed in space and time from first century Jerusalem. Except for a fundamentalist minority, modern skepticism concerning the Scriptures is exceeded only by modern ignorance of the Scriptures. Especially among young people, years of indoctrination in evolutionary humanism have made them almost impossible to reach simply by exposition of the Scriptures. Like the pagans at Lystra and the philosophers at Athens, they first must be made to see the majesty and love of the God of creation, and then perhaps they will listen to His Word and believe His promise on forgiveness and salvation.

Give Attendance to Reading

Since the above admonition was important for Christians in the first century (see I Timothy 4:13), it is surely much more so now. This is the age of the information explosion, and the annual publication growth rate today is nearly five times the population growth rate. The world population is increasing at a rate of 2% each year, but publications at over 9%!

People of influence in any field are always people who are informed people. Furthermore, if information is to be understood *and retained*, there is no substitute for reading. One may be stirred at the hearing of a sermon or a lecture, or by a drama he witnesses on stage or television, but the details and fine points are almost invariably quickly forgotten unless they are written down and reviewed again later. To prove this to yourself, merely try to recall in full the sermon you heard two or three weeks ago: you'll probably do well even to remember the subject!

A book can be read and re-read, as often as necessary to master its contents. It is available for reference and review whenever needed. It is significant that the Apostle Paul, in the last chapter of his last epistle, written from his dungeon on Rome's "death row" shortly before his martyrdom, still felt it important to keep on reading! "The cloak that I left at Troas with Carpus, when thou comest, bring with thee, and the books, especially the parchments," he wrote to Timothy (II Timothy 4:13).

One cannot read every book and every journal, of course. In the field of science, for example, approximately 10,000,000 scientific articles are published in 100,000 scientific journals every year!

Therefore, a conscientious Christian must be selective in his reading, spending as much time in reading and study as necessary to be the most effective person he can be in the work and ministry to which God has ordained him, yet not wasting precious time on the useless or harmful literature which is so abundantly available today.

His first responsibility, of course, is to know the Holy Scriptures, which are profitable in every part for every Christian (II Timothy 3:15-4:2). Paul's admonition to "give attendance to reading" applied first of all to the Scriptures, both to their private study and their public reading (in earlier days, before the printing press, most people had no direct access to the Scriptures, so it was vital for their pastor to read them aloud in the assembly).

His responsibility for reading goes much beyond this, however. He is commanded: "Be ready always to give an answer (literally, an "apologetic") to every man that asketh you a reason of the hope that is in you, with meekness and fear" (I Peter 3:15).

In these days of global skepticism concerning God's Word and ignorance of His divine purpose for man, one can only be an effective Christian "answerer," one whose witness will be taken seriously and whose "fruit will remain" (John 15:16) if he is both an *informed* witness and a *gracious* witness. One can only give an answer if he *knows* the answer, and the answer will only be effective if given in "meekness and fear." God uses neither ignorance nor arrogance, and the truth must be spoken in love.

All of which is possible only if the Christian spends adequate time in diligently studying both the Scriptures and other books which confirm and apply the Scriptures in the modern world.

A Testimony

It is often difficult to know just what to say when one is asked to speak on "Creation versus Evolution," or a similar subject, for a 30- to 40-minute one-time message. The subject of origins is so vast, with so many ramifications and implications, and evolutionary thinking so engrained in the minds of so many people, that it seems impossible to deal with it effectively in such a brief time. Yet people often seem to expect a creationist speaker to deal conclusively and exhaustively with the subject, answering all problems and difficulties, in a single brief message. If he doesn't deal with every such problem, the listener leaves unsatisfied and probably convinced that creationists can't answer his own particular difficulty. Furthermore, if the speaker's message becomes at all technical, many listeners feel it is over their heads and therefore unspiritual, whereas if he does *not* deal with the technical aspects of the problem, his other listeners (those with some amount of evolutionary indoctrination) decide it is merely superficial religious semantics and therefore unscientific.

We can only hope many listeners to such a one-time message will at least be sufficiently impressed by it either to attend one of our Summer Institutes, or to read some of our books on these subjects. We are convinced, of course, that

Biblical creationism is *both* spiritual and scientific, and that all Christians and non-Christians need to *know* this.

Because of these frustrating limitations of time, however, I frequently resort merely to stating my own personal convictions and testimony for whatever they are worth. I *have* read through the Bible many times, and in particular have studied thoroughly every passage (and these abound in great numbers) dealing in any way with the phenomena of nature and facts of science. In addition I have studied to some degree in most of the sciences, and have read in essence hundreds of books and journal articles, on scientific topics relating to such Biblical discussions. I have associated with scientists and other intellectuals daily for over 30 years, most of them unbelievers, and am a member of a dozen or more scientific societies.

I certainly don't know all the answers to Bible-science problems, but at least my testimony is this. *The Bible is absolutely the Word of God, fully and verbally inspired, infallibly true in every detail. There are no scientific mistakes, no contradictions, no irrelevancies, but rather hundreds of marvelous scientific and prophetic insights. The Bible is strong and sure, and one may confidently rest his eternal soul on that faith.*

chapter XII

THE IMPACT OF CREATION
— BIBLICAL AND SCIENTIFIC

IMPACT SERIES ARTICLES, 1974-1975

THE STARS OF HEAVEN*

By Henry M. Morris, Ph.D.

"The host of heaven cannot be numbered"
(Jeremiah 33:22)

Man has always been intrigued and fascinated by the heavens. The scholars of antiquity, whether in Sumeria, Egypt, China, Mexico or any of the other early civilizations were well versed in the locations and orbits of all the visible stars. They had counted and catalogued and grouped them all and had pronounced the total number to be almost two thousand stars!

But the Holy Scriptures were far ahead of these ancient scientists. According to the Bible, the stars were as great in number as the sands of the seashore (Genesis 22:17) and simply could not be numbered! The vast reaches of the

---

*Impact #10, January 1974

heavenly spaces were — and are — utterly incomprehensible to man. "For as the heavens are higher than the earth, so are my ways higher than your ways, and my thoughts than your thoughts" (Isaiah 55:9).

The giant telescopes of the present day have only begun to reveal the immense numbers and fantastic variety of the stars. With literally billions of galaxies, and billions of stars in every galaxy, the number of the stars seems to increase almost without limit. The variety is equally amazing — red giants, white dwarfs, Cepheid variables, neutron stars, pulsars, and on and on! As the Bible says in an incisive foregleam of modern astronomy: "There is one glory of the sun, and another glory of the moon, and another glory of the stars: for one star differeth from another star in glory" (I Corinthians 15:41).

Origin and Purpose of the Universe

The origin and purpose of the stars was no more perplexing to the ancient stargazers than to our modern astronomers. There is no shortage of theories, of course, and new theories are developed rather frequently purporting to explain the origin and evolution of the universe.

But, one after another, each new theory eventually seems to encounter such problems and difficulties that it falls by the wayside and is eventually abandoned. In a recent review of modern cosmology, a leading astronomer has said:

> "Is it not possible, indeed probable, that our present cosmological ideas on the structure and evolution of the universe as a whole (whatever that may mean) will appear hopelessly premature and primitive to astronomers of the 21st century? Less than 50 years after the birth of what we are pleased to call 'modern cosmology,' when so few empirical facts are passably well established, when so many different over-simplified models of the universe are still competing for attention, is it, we may ask, really credible to claim, or even reasonable to hope, that we are presently close to

a definitive solution of the cosmological problem?"[1]

The author concludes his survey of cosmology by stating:

"It seems safe to conclude that a unique solution of the cosmological problem may still elude us for quite sometime!"[2]

The two leading types of cosmological theories currently are the "steady-state" and "big bang" theories. Both of these are evolutionary theories and each includes the "expanding universe" concept, according to which the galaxies are all rapidly receding from one another. The "steady-state" theory has also been called the "continuous creation" theory, attempting to explain the decay and disappearance of matter and energy by the continual evolution (not "creation") of new matter out of nothing. The "big bang" theory is usually also known as the "oscillating universe" theory, supposing that the universe continuously alternates between processes of expansion and contraction and that its present expansion began with a super-dense state following its most recent contraction about twenty billion or so years ago.

Within the framework of either type of cosmology, numerous subsidiary theories of galactic and stellar evolution have been published, dealing with the supposed development of particular types of stars or galaxies or clusters of galaxies from other types. The very variety of stars and galaxies tends to encourage such evolutionary speculation.

Stability of the Heavens

Nevertheless, it should be quite obvious that such evolutionary processes cannot actually be observed. No astronomer has ever observed a "red giant" evolving into a "white dwarf," or a "spiral nebula" into a "globular cluster," or any other such change. Within the time of human observation, no such evolutionary changes have ever been seen to occur at all.

---

1. G. de Vancouleurs: "The Case for a Hierarchical Cosmology, *Science,* Vol. 167, February 27, 1970, p. 1203.
2. *Ibid*: p. 1212.

This being the case, there is nothing whatever to prevent us from proposing the theory that they *don't* take place! This is by far the most reasonable theory, since it is supported by all the actual astronomic measurements that have ever been collected since man first began making such observations. If we limit ourselves to real, observational *science*, rather than indulging in philosophical speculation, we would have to say that the stars and galaxies have always been just as they are now since the time they were created.

Is the Universe Expanding?

Someone may object to such a suggestion by contending that the universe is expanding and therefore evolving. This deduction is not necessary, however. In the first place, whether or not the universe is actually expanding is still an unsettled question. The famous "Doppler effect" — the red shift in the light spectra from distant galaxies — is the only observational basis for such expansion, and this interpretation has been challenged by various cosmologists, especially in view of the anomalous red shifts recently noted in quasars.

Assuming, however, that the universe really is expanding, in accordance with the standard interpretation of the red shifts, there is still no proof that this phenomenon is part of some evolutionary process. The expansion could just as well have been initiated by an act of creation at *any* arbitrary position of the various galactic components of the universe.

Fiat Creation

Not only is the concept of special complete creation most logical and consistent in accord with God's character and ability, but it is surely the concept most in accord with Biblical revelation on this subject. "For in six days, the Lord made heaven and earth, the sea, and all that in them is" (Exodus 20:11). On the fourth of these days, "He made the stars" (Genesis 1:16). "Thus the heavens and the earth were *finished*, and all the host of them" (Genesis 2:1). "By the word of the Lord were the heavens made; and all the host of them by the breath of His mouth; . . . For He spoke, and it was done; He commanded, and it stood fast" (Psalm 33:6,9).

The idea of a simple fiat creation of the entire universe in its present form may seem too naive to evolutionary astronomers and cosmologists. Nevertheless, it fits all the facts of observational astronomy more easily and directly than does any other theory. The objection that special creation is not scientific because it is non-observable is irrelevant, since exactly the same objection applies to any of the evolutionary models. Who has ever *observed* a star evolve, or a "big bang," or an evolution of matter out of nothing?

Comparison of Evolutionist and Creationist Models

Although *no* model of origins can be scientifically tested—since one cannot repeat history — any such model can be used to predict and correlate the observable data which result from that history. The model which most effectively does this is the one most likely to be correct.

Any evolutionary model of the universe must conflict with one of the most fundamental laws of science, namely the Second Law of Thermodynamics. This law formalizes the observed fact that, within those regions of space and time which are accessible to observation, the universe is decreasing in complexity and in availability of energy. The evolutionary model must, however, postulate a universe that has instead evolved upwards toward higher states of order and availability. Since the Second Law always appears to hold true in *observable* space and time, an evolutionary model must include some component which negates the Second Law in *non-observable* space and time. The steady state theory supposes that energy or matter somehow came into existence out of nothing far out in *non-observable space*. The big bang theory supposes that energy or matter somehow came into existence out of nothing (or at least out of some state of things completely incommensurate with the present state of things) far back in *non-observable* time. There is, of course, no way of testing any process which operates in non-observable space or time!

The creation model, on the other hand, specifically predicts the conditions described by the two laws of thermodynamics. It postulates a primeval perfect and complete creation, preserved in quantity (First Law) but decaying in quality (Second Law). As a matter of fact, the two laws point directly back to a period of special creation. The Second Law says the universe must have had a beginning — otherwise it would already be completely disordered. The First Law (conservation of mass-energy) says it could not have begun itself. Thus, the Cause of its beginning must be greater than the universe and external to it. The omnipotent, omnisicient, eternal God of the Bible is the only Cause adequate to produce the universe as we know it.

The Nature of the Universe

The creation model must attempt to explain the various aspects of the universe, not in terms of evolutionary development (for it assumes they did not evolve at all but were created) but rather in terms of creative purpose. This is no small task, in view of the infinite variety of stellar systems, but it is no more difficult, nor less susceptible to empirical test, than imaginary evolutionary explanations for the same things.

Why, for example, is the universe so big, and why are there so many different kinds of stars and galaxies and inter-stellar phenomena? Why are the moon and the older planets barren of life? What is the purpose of pulsars and quasars? And so on. It is obviously much easier to raise such questions than to answer them, whether in terms of evolutionary mechanisms or of creative purposes.

We can see a number of reasons for the *visible* stars at least. They are useful for light, for navigation and for chronology. They are a source of beauty and inspiration for mankind. Furthermore, every new discovery in the stellar heavens adds that much more to our amazement at the vastness of power and variety in the Creation. "The heavens declare the glory of God, and the firmament showeth His handiwork" (Psalm 19:1). Surely the enlargement of our appreciation of Him is a worthwhile purpose for the stars to have.

The barrenness of the moon and planets, as well as the intense heat of the stars, emphasizes the Biblical teaching that "the heavens are the Lord's, but the earth hath He given to the children of men" (Psalm 115:16). U.F.O. enthusiasts to the contrary notwithstanding, there is no evidence either in science or Scripture that biological life exists elsewhere in the universe. Life was created specifically for the earth, and the earth for life. Of all other bodies in the universe, the moon would be expected to have most nearly the same (evolutionary) origin as the earth, but the lunar explorations have eliminated such a notion.

> "To the surprise of scientists, the chemical makeup of the moon rocks is distinctly different from that of rocks on earth. This difference implies that the moon formed under different conditions . . . . and means that any theory on the origin of the planets now will have to create the moon and earth in different ways."[1]

The same situation apparently exists with respect to all the other planets in the solar system.

Thus the earth is unique in the solar system and, for all we know, the solar system is unique in the universe. So far as we can *observe*, there are not even any planets anywhere else, let alone a planet equipped to sustain biological life. And even if there were, with even the nearest star being four light-years distant, there is no rational possibility of our ever being able to communicate with such hypothetical space-people on such hypothetical planets.

Amazing though it may seem to evolutionary naturalists, the evidence favors the conclusion that man is unique in the universe and, furthermore, that he is the apex, not of the evolutionary process, but of God's creative purposes! Even the galaxies, therefore, are inferior to man. Isaac Asimov, certainly not a creationist, has nevertheless recognized this fact.

---

1. Jerry E. Bishop: "New Theories of Creation," *Science Digest,* Vol. 72, October 1972, p. 42.

"In man is a three-pound brain which, as far as we know, is the most complex and orderly arrangement of matter in the universe."[1]

The physical universe of space and time and all the phenomena of energy and matter and life that occur in space and time must somehow be related to man and to God's purpose for man. In the present economy of things, however, man is inescapably confined to only a tiny corner of the vast universe. The fulfillment of the Creator's purposes for man in the universe (and they *will* be fulfilled, since an omnipotent and omniscient God, by definition, cannot fail in His purposes) must therefore await the establishment of a new economy of things, in an age to come.

The Heavenly Host

In the meantime, there is still another "host of heaven," described in the Bible as an "innumerable company of angels" (Hebrews 12:22). The frequent identification of angels with stars in the Bible (note Job 38:7; Revelation 12:4; and many others) is most intriguing, especially in view of the fact that there is no similarity between them whatsoever. The same mysterious correlations are found everywhere in ancient mythology, the gods and goddesses (Jupiter, Venus, Orion, etc.) being identified with various stars, planets and constellations. The age-long influence of astrology, even on people of intelligence and culture, is another strange phenomenon. And now, in an almost unbelievable return to these ancient pagan mysteries, modern scientific speculations about the evolution of life in other worlds have been transmuted into a weird celestial drama of ancient astronauts, flying saucers, little green men and "chariots of the gods."

The reality behind all these "fearful sights and great signs from heaven" (Luke 21:11) can only be that there really is

---

1. Isaac Asimov: "In the Game of Energy and Thermodynamics You Can't Even Break Even," *Smithsonian Institute Journal*, June 1970, p. 10.

life in outer space! But these living inhabitants of the heavenly bodies are neither super-men in space ships nor blobs of protoplasm in various stages of evolution. They are, rather, "angels that excel in strength" (Psalm 103:20), "ministering spirits, sent forth to minister for them who shall be heirs of salvation" (Hebrews 1:14), none other than God's holy angels. There exists also in the heavens a vast horde of rebel angels, following "that old serpent, called the Devil, and Satan, which deceiveth the whole world" (Revelation 12:9).

These are all real beings, living a real existence in this real physical cosmos. However, they are spiritual beings, not physical, and thus are not restrained by the gravitational and electro-magnetic forces which control bodies formed of chemical elements. On occasion, however, the faithful angels have been known to have power to "materialize" themselves in human form (Hebrews 13:2), and the fallen angels, or demons, to "possess" human or animal bodies (Matthew 8:28-32).

Thus there is a host of stars without number in the heavens and also an innumerable angelic host of heaven. The latter apparently inhabit the former and are thus, in both Scripture and mythology, intimately inter-related.

But if only angels can ever reach the stars, why has God placed such a strange fascination and yearning for the heavens in the heart of man? Jesus answers: "For in the resurrection they . . . are as the angels of God in heaven" (Matthew 22:30). To the prophet Daniel, the angel said: "And many of them that sleep in the dust of the earth shall awake, some to everlasting life, and some to shame and everlasting contempt. And they that be wise shall shine as the brightness of the firmament, and they that turn many to righteousness *as the stars for ever and ever*" (Daniel 12:2,3).

In resurrection bodies, unfettered by gravity, the redeemed of the Lord will thus have an eternity of time to explore the infinitude of space. Though the earth will still be his home, man will finally reach the stars.

RICHARD LEAKEY'S SKULL*
By Duane T. Gish, Ph.D.

It is too early to assess with any degree of confidence the true import of recent finds by Richard Leakey near the east shore of Lake Rudolf in Kenya. Nevertheless, the impact on evolutionary theories related to the origin of man is potentially so explosive, these reports merit, even at this early date, a tentative evaluation. One newspaper report has said, "Because of him (Leakey's Skull 1470) every single book on anthropology, every article on the evolution of man, every drawing of man's family tree will have to be junked. They are apparently wrong." The article in *Science News*[1] was headlined "Leakey's new skull changes our pedigree . . ."

Richard Leakey is the son of Dr. Louis Leakey. Dr. Leakey acquired world-wide fame through a series of allegedly sensational finds at Olduvai Gorge in Tanzania, about 500 miles south of Lake Rudolph. Dr. Leakey's principal find was a skull of a purported "ape-man", which he called Zinjanthropus, or "East Africa Man." Through a combination of hasty judgment, exaggerated claims, and wide publicity through the *National Geographic*, other journals, and the news media, most people, including just about all evolutionists, were convinced that Dr. Leakey had indeed found the remains of a very unique creature, one that was in man's direct line of descent about two million years ago.

A more thorough and careful evaluation of Dr. Leakey's finds by experts in the field finally revealed that Dr. Leakey's "Zinjanthropus" was nothing more than a variety of Australopithecus (as Dr. Leakey, himself, eventually admitted), an ape-like creature, the remains of which had been discovered 35 years earlier by R.A. Dart in South Africa. Dr. Leakey thus had become famous for "discovering" something that had been discovered many years earlier!

---

*Impact #11, February 1974

1. *Science News*, Vol. 102, p. 324 (1972).

Although some authorities, such as Montagu[1] and von Koenigswald,[2] had long maintained that the australopithecines were outside of the line of man's ancestry, the consensus of evolutionists was that the australopithecines had been habitually bipedal man-like apes in the direct line leading to man.

Richard Leakey does not hold a Ph.D. in anthropology. In fact, he has no degree of any kind. He has never been to college. Nevertheless, he spent many years working and studying with his father, and he has assembled a team that does include Ph.D. scientists. During the past few years, his research has lent powerful support to those who claimed that the australopithecines had nothing to do with the origin of man. We have already given our evaluation of the evidence related to these creatures, evidence which we believe shows conclusively that they were apes — period.[3] If Richard Leakey's evaluation of his latest find, Skull 1470, is accepted, he will have succeeded not only in shattering completely his father's theories on man's origins, in which the australopithecines were given a central role, but everyone else's, as well.

Dr. Leakey claimed that he had found two species of his "Zinjanthropus", a less evolved and more primitive form, later designated *Australopithecus robustus*, and a more highly developed or gracile form, designated *A. africanus*. Richard Leakey now claims that these were merely the male and female members of a single species, the gracile form be-

---

1. A. Montagu, *Man: His First Million Years,* World Publishers, Yonkers, N.Y., 1957, p. 51.
2. G.H.R. von Koenigswald, *The Evolution of Man,* University of Michigan Press, Ann Arbor, 1962; see also J. Hawkes review of this book, *Science*, Vol. 204, p. 952 (1964).
3. D.T. Gish, *Evolution: The Fossils Say No!*, Institute for Creation Research, San Diego, 1973.

ing the female and the robustus form being the male.[1] [2] No evolution from primitive to advanced was involved at all.

On the basis of extremely fragmentary evidence (and of strongly preconceived ideas), the consensus of evolutionists has been that the australopithecines walked habitually upright, one of the characteristics predicted for a transitional form between man's supposed ape-like ancestor and man. Evidence produced by Richard Leakey in the past two or three years has now established strong support for the fact that the australopithecines did not walk upright, but were long-armed, short-legged knucklewalkers, similar to the extant African apes.[1] [3]

Leakey's latest find may now have delivered the final shattering blow to the australopithecines as candidates for man's ancestor; in fact, if accepted, it will destroy all presently held theories on man's evolutionary ancestry. In his lecture last year in San Diego (which the author attended) Leakey reported that what he has found destroys all that we have ever been taught about human evolution, and, he said, "I have nothing to offer in its place!"

The heretofore generally accepted ideas on the evolution of man included a hypothetical common ancestor of man and apes, variously estimated to have existed up to 30 million years or so ago, plus little else (as far as any real fossils are concerned) until the australopithecine stage was reached, supposedly about two million years ago. Later on, it was believed, these ape-like ancestors of man were succeeded by a more man-like creature (or less ape-like man!), represented in Java by *Pithecanthropus erectus* (Java Man), and in China by *Sinanthropus pekinensis* (Peking Man). These have been dated by evolutionists (purely conjecturally) at about 500,000 years, and today most evolutionists place them in a single species, designated *Homo erectus*.

1. R.E.F. Leakey, *Nature,* Vol. 231, p. 241 (1971).
2. *Science News,* Vol. 99, p. 398 (1971).
3. *Science News,* Vol. 100, p. 357 (1971).

We have discussed in some detail why we believe that the only evolution that has occurred in these creatures was the evolution of the models and descrptions of the creatures by evolutionists since they were first described![1] The early descriptions of these creatures were very ape-like, but they became more man-like in succeeding reports, culminating in the models of Franz Weidenreich, which were quite man-like. Unfortunately, all of the bones disappeared during World War II, so there is no way now to confirm whether this creature was man or ape. We are convinced that, as with the australopithecines, they were simply apes.

Thus we have the picture: common ancestor of man and ape (30 my.) —Australopithecus (ape-like man 2 my.) —Java Man, Peking Man (near-man, 0.5 my.) —modern man (it is now recognized that Neanderthal Man was fully human, *Homo sapiens*). That is precious little, considering a supposed evolutionary span of 30 million years and the fertile imaginations of evolutionists!

Richard Leakey now claims that his team has discovered a skull (designated KNMR 1470) much more modern than even "Peking Man," essentially the same, in fact, as that of a modern human (except in size), and yet it has been dated at nearly three million years![2,3] If Leakey's evaluation is supported, and, if the dates assigned to the australopithecines (2 million years), "Peking Man" (½ million years) and KNMR 1470 (3 million years) are accepted, it is obvious that neither the australopithecines nor "Peking Man" was in an ancestral line leading to man, for how could modern man, or essentially modern man, be older than his ancestors? Who ever heard of parents being younger than their children?

As reconstructed by Mrs. Richard Leakey, Dr. Bernard Wood, a London anatomist, and others, the skull is

1. D.T. Gish, Evolution? The Fossils Say No!, Institute for Creation Research, San Diego, 1973.
2. *Science News,* Vol. 102, p. 324 (1972).
3. R.E.F. Leakey, *National Geographic,* Vol. 143, p. 819 (1973).

remarkable in its similarity to modern man.[1] The skull wall is thin, its general conformation is human, and it is devoid of the heavy brow ridges, supra-mastoid crests, and other ape-like features found variously in the australopithecines and "Peking Man." Furthermore, a few miles away, but in the same strata, Dr. John Harris, a paleontologist attached to the National Museums of Kenya, discovered limb bones that reportedly are indistinguishable from those of modern man. They are presumably limb bones of creatures identical to 1470.

The cranial capacity of 1470 has been estimated by Leakey to be only about 800 cc. While it is greatly in excess of that reported for the australopithecines (450-550 cc), and, considering its alleged antiquity, it is called "large-brained," yet this is below the range for modern man (about 1000-2000 cc, with a mean of about 1450 cc). The age and sex of 1470 cannot be determined with certainty (first believed to be male, it is now believed to be female).

The small cranial capacity for this skull is difficult to reconcile with the fact that everything else about it is reportedly essentially indistinguishable from modern man (Dr. Alec Cave, an English anatomist, has described the skull as "typically human"[2]). Even the pigmy must possess a cranial capacity in excess of that reported for 1470, although an Australian aboriginal female with a cranial capacity of about 900 cc has been reported.

A recent newspaper article[3] tells of an interview with Dr. Alan Mann, an anthropologist of the University of Pennsylvania who spent four weeks with Leakey in Kenya this past summer. It is reported that Mann was initially very skeptical

1. R.E.F. Leakey, *National Geographic, Vol. 143, p. 819, (1973)*.
2. *J. Hillaby, "Dem Ole Bones", New Scientist,* December 21, 1972.
3. J.N. Shurkin (Knight Newspapers writer), The Cincinnati Enquirer, October 10, 1973, p. 6.

of Leakey's reports concerning 1470, but after his experience during the summer, he became convinced that Leakey has revolutionized anthropology. He reports that Leakey has now found a second skull, and that this skull is large enough to fit over the top of 1470.

Mann, like most other evolutionists, has been left thoroughly confused by the astounding implications of Leakey's discovery. He is reported as saying, "We just don't know what happened. There's no real theories. Everybody's sort of astounded . . . It just throws us back to 'go.' "

What about the date assigned by Leakey to his 1470, as well as the dates assigned to "Zinjanthropus" (1-¾ million years) and "Peking Man"? Is it legitimate for a creationist who believes in a young earth, and therefore who believes that the dating methods used to arrive at these dates are invalid, to use these same dates to invalidate evolutionary theories? Absolutely. *If* what Leakey reports about his 1470 is true, and *if* the dates assigned to this creature, to "Zinjanthropus," and to "Peking Man" are valid, then "Zinjanthropus" (and all of the australopithecines) and "Peking Man" are wiped out as man's ancestors, and evolutionists are left with nothing. On the other hand, if the age of the earth is in the nature of thousands of years rather than billions of years, then the whole concept of evolution becomes inconceivable. Thus, in either case, we are left without any evolutionary ancestors for man.

We would like to emphasize that at this point we are almost completely dependent upon the judgment of Richard Leakey and his colleagues as to the nature of his finds. At this early date, furthermore, we are limited to reports published in quasi-scientific journals and in newspapers. The importance and implications of Leakey's finds are thus predicated on reports that may not be completely reliable and data that have not yet been required to stand the scrutiny of critics. We must, therefore, view all of this with a great deal of caution. We can say at this point, nevertheless, that Leakey's latest report lends considerable support to creationists, who maintain that man and the apes have always been contemporary.

It has fallen as a bombshell, on the other hand, in the midst of evolutionists. Perhaps this is why, in our many discussions and debates with evolutionists during this past year or so, we have encountered no one who wanted to talk about human evolution!

Other recent developments have strengthened the creationist position. For example, Neanderthal Man used to be portrayed as a primitive sub-human creature, the immediate ancestor to *Homo sapiens*. He was believed to have possessed only a semi-erect posture and to have possessed a number of other primitive features, including heavy brow ridges, low-slung neck, stooped shoulders, and bowed legs. For many years the Field Museum of Natural History in Chicago had an exhibit of a family of Neanderthal Man depicting him as a bent-over, knuckle-dragging, hairy, grunting, sub-human, peering out from under a massive brow ridge through deep-set eyes.

This picture of Neanderthal Man had been generated by the fact that the individual whose skeleton had been used for depicting this creature had suffered severely from arthritis and other pathological conditions. Even in the 19th Century this had been pointed out by Virchow, a famous anatomist. This has been confirmed more recently by Straus and Cave who reported:

> "There is thus no valid reason for the assumption that the posture of Neanderthal man . . . differed significantly from that of present-day men. . . . It may well be that the arthritic 'old man' of La Chapelle-aux-Saints, the postural prototype of Neanderthal man, did actually stand and walk with something of a pathological kyphosis; but, if so, he has his counterparts in modern men similarly afflicted with spinal osteoarthritis. He cannot, in view of his manifest pathology, be used to provide us with a reliable picture of a healthy, normal Neanderthalian. Notwithstanding, if he could be reincarnated and placed in a New York subway — provided that he were bathed, shaved, and

dressed in modern clothing — it is doubtful
whether he would attract any more attention than
some of its other denizens."[1]

Even more recently, Dr. Francis Ivanhoe has claimed that
the teeth of Neanderthal Man show specific evidence of
rickets (caused by a Vitamin D deficiency) and that x-rays of
the bones of Neanderthal Man show the characteristic rickets
ring pattern.[2] He further reports that every Neanderthal
child skull studied so far has signs associated with severe
rickets: a large head with a high, bulbous forehead, late
closure of bone junctions and patches of defective bone, and
poor teeth.

No wonder Neanderthal Man was some sort of a slouch! His
brow ridges, bulbous forehead, sloping shoulders, bowed-legs
and other "primitive" features were due to softening of his
bones and other pathological conditions caused by his severe
Vitamin D deficiency. Cripple him further with arthritis and
you have the picture of Neanderthal Man that has graced so
many textbooks for 100 years — the picture that evolutionists
claimed to show that Neanderthal Man was a link between
modern man and ape-like creatures.

But now this picture of Neanderthal Man has been abandoned, and today he is no longer classified *Homo
neanderthalensis*, but he is classified *Homo sapiens*, just
like you and I. The Museum of Natural History in Chicago
has removed its earlier models of Neanderthal Man and has
replaced those with up-dated, much more modern appearing
models. Thus, one by one — "Nebraska Man" (constructed on
the basis of a pig's tooth!), "Piltdown Man" (built around a
modern ape's jaw!), "Zinjanthropus", or "East Africa
Man," "Peking Man," "Neanderthal Man" — our supposed
apelike ancestors have slipped away. And Richard Leakey
appeals for funds to start the search all over again!

1. W.L. Straus, Jr., and A.J.E. Cave, *The Quarterly
   Review of Biology*, December, 1957 pp. 358, 359.
2. F. Ivanhoe, *Nature*, August 8, 1970 (see also *Science
   Digest*, February, 1971, p. 35; *Prevention*, October,
   1971, p. 115).

INTERPRETING EARTH HISTORY*
By Stuart E. Nevins, M.S.
(Assistant Professor of Geology, Christian Heritage College)

Historical geology is the field of study which seeks to decipher the clues and records bearing on the earth's history. Since the historical geologist cannot observe the history he attempts to interpret (he cannot relive ancient times), scientific methods involving repeatable observation and experimentation cannot be utilized. The method relied upon is much like that used by a detective as he seeks to unravel the many evidences and furnish a tentative description of a crime. The conclusions reached by the historical geologist, as those of the detective, rely on numerous assumptions and much fragmentary evidence making scientific proof impossible. The conclusions made in any type of historical investigation — no matter how "scientific" they are claimed to be — depend largely on the basic conceptual framework (values, beliefs, and methodology) used by the investigator.

Uniformitarianism

In the seventeenth century great scientific and technological discoveries were made by the English scientists Isaac Newton, Robert Boyle, and Robert Hooke. These discoveries were fostered by *empiricism*, a philosophical theory of knowledge stressing the importance of the scientific methods of hypothesis, observation, and experimentation. Francis Bacon (1561-1626) and John Locke (1632-1704) were the early advocates of the empirical method, stressing the importance of sense experience above reasoning procedures to understand the natural causes in the physical world.

In keeping with the early success of empiricism in physics and chemistry, an attempt was made to apply the method to other fields of inquiry. If empiricism could explain natural events solely in terms of physical causes or laws, must not this apply also to the origin of religion, the writing of the Bible, and the life of Jesus Christ? Must not the action of present processes and laws also explain the origin and present

---

* Impact Series #12, March 1974

configuration of the earth? It is, therefore, not surprising that a framework for historical geology based primarily on observation of present types of processes (called *uniformitarianism*) first appeared late in the eighteenth century in Britain and Scotland.

James Hutton (1726-1797), a Scottish doctor, agriculturalist, and member of the Royal Society of Edinburgh, was one of the first advocates of the uniformitarian framework for interpreting earth history. To Hutton the earth was a giant machine composed of solid earth, oceans, and atmosphere. Understanding the *present* operation of the three-part system could be used by analogy to decipher the earth's history. The present was used as the key to the past.[1]

The essence of the Huttonian theory and his uniformitarianism was belief in the constancy of the laws of nature, and belief that geologic processes were cyclic and dynamic, operating at essentially the same rates as observed today. This prevailing uniformity and slowness of geologic processes which Hutton imagined allowed for almost unlimited amounts of time for earth history. Although Hutton credited the present operations of nature as worthy of divine wisdom, his empirical approach did not allow for an original creation or divine suspensions of the laws of nature. The earth has always existed in a state more or less like it exists today.

Charles Lyell (1797-1875), a British lawyer, was responsible for popularizing the uniformitarian framework through his published work titled *Principles of Geology*. Lyell claimed that the progress of geology had been hindered by Christian views suggesting a limited time span for earth history, catastrophes such as Noah's Flood as important geologic events, and supernatural interference in the normal course of nature. To controvert the popular catastrophist view of the early nineteenth century, Lyell proposed an empirical framework assuming both uniformity of natural laws in

---

1. James Hutton, *Theory of the Earth with Proofs and Illustrations:* Facsimile reprint, Hafner Pub. Co., New York, Vol. 1, 1959, p. 19.

space and time, and uniformity of process rates or material conditions.[1]

Not only did he maintain that natural laws were invariant through time, but he believed that the earth was essentially a balanced and steady-state system with the forces tending to produce processes with a faster rate restrained constantly by forces tending to produce processes of slower rate. Like Hutton, Lyell envisioned essentially unlimited geologic time and considered it fruitless to speculate on the origin or future destruction of the earth.[2]

Although the interpretive frameworks of Hutton and Lyell relied somewhat on rationalism to extrapolate observed rates and laws into the unseen past, their frameworks were based primarily on empiricism. We notice that Hutton and Lyell were very reluctant to speculate on the origin of geologic phenomena unless their origin could be observed in the present. Thus, one of Hutton's works was titled, "Theory of the Earth; or an Investigation of the Laws Observable in the Composition, Dissolution and Restoration of Land upon the Globe". We learn that Lyell's major work had an empirical slant from its full title, *Principles of Geology; Being an Attempt to Explain the Former Changes of the Earth's Surface by Reference to Causes Now in Operation.*

Lyell failed to adequately refute catastrophism and his extreme view soon became inconsistent with geological evidence. Study of the differences between modern oceanic sediments and ancient marine sedimentary rocks led geologists to recognize that different regimes of climate and sedimentation existed in the past. Lava flows in the ancient rock record reveal tremendous volcanic episodes dwarfing any of modern times. Meteorite impact craters in the earth's crust up to 50 miles in diameter have been well documented.

1. K.M. Lyell, *Life, Letters and Journals of Sir Charles Lyell:* London, John Murray, Vol. 1, 1881, p. 234.
2. William B.N. Berry, *Browth of a Prehistoric Time Scale Based on Organic Evolution:* San Francisco, W.H. Freeman, 1968, pp. 12, 13.

Although many modern historical geologists give lip service to the empirical framework of Lyell, few geologists are willing to accept his static, steady-state view. Most modern geologists have a dynamic, evolutionary view of earth history which is quite different from that originally proposed by Lyell.

Evolutionary Uniformitarianism

Three types of research led to the demise of the classical uniformitarian framework. These are: (1) evidences for a finite age to the earth rather than an earth eternally old, (2) evidences for unique and catastrophic processes during geologic history, and (3) theories suggesting evolution of the solid earth. Because of these, Lyell's empirical framework was significantly modified late in the nineteenth century to form an evolutionary-iniformitarian framework. Thus, the earth's history under the new approach was to be interpreted by analogy to modern laws and processes *and also* after an evolutionary model postulating an *historical* (not static), step-by-step development of the earth.

The evolutionary approach was based, to a large degree, on *rationalism*, a philosophy suggesting that the employment of certain procedures of reasoning would lead to historical knowledge about the earth. Under the philosophy of rationalism the principal measure of a good geologic theory was not necessarily how well it accorded with present process rates and natural laws, but how well it formed a logical portion of an entire conceptual history.

It is not surprising that the first of the modern rationalist philosophers, Rene Descartes (1596-1650), a French mathematician, was also the first since classical times to propose a *plausible* secular theory utilizing the innate natural processes of gaseous condensation and gravitational attraction to form the earth. This theory was modified to form the famous "nebular hypothesis" by the German rationalist Immanuel Kant (1724-1804). Kant influenced Georg Hegel (1770-1831) to found a rationalist school in Germany called "higher criticism." These rationalists later systematically discounted the supernatural elements of the

Bible as products of mythology.

The French rationalist G.L. Buffon (1707-1788) was one of the first scientists to question the account of the six days of Creation in the Book of Genesis. Buffon imagined that the earth originated through detachment of a hot portion of the sun during a near collision with a great comet. He allowed a great interval of time for the earth to cool to its present temperature.

Rationalist criticism of the Biblical account of creation was greatly promoted by Charles Darwin's book *Origin of Species by Means of Natural Selection* (1859). Darwin's observation that natural selection was an inherent process in the biological world led him to propose a rationalistic, evolutionary theory supposing that all the species had developed from a few separate stocks.

Geology of the present century has been dominated by rationalistic, evolutionary theories. Geologists have recently labored with models for the evolution of the earth's crust suggesting that a single supercontinent broke apart with fragments drifting to their present locations. For several years geologists have attempted to construct a plausible physical and chemical environment under which life could have spontaneously appeared from inorganic substances. One's mind is stretched to imagine how processes operating with extreme slowness over millions of years could cause significant changes to occur.

The evolutionary-uniformitarian synthesis of the empirical and rationalistic frameworks of earth history appeared late in the nineteenth century and is presently the popular framework among modern geologists. The popular framework is evolutionary because it visualizes an unfolding, unidirectional development of the earth through time. The popular framework is also uniformitarian because of its distaste for catastrophes and need for gradually acting processes over vast periods of time. However, Lyellian uniformitarianism has little place. The empirical uniformity is in vogue only to the extent that it helps promote the rationalistic, evolutionary view.

Biblical Catastrophism

"Faith," as the author of Hebrews says, "is the substance of things hoped for, the evidence of things not seen" (Hebrews 11:1). Faith forms a valid means of perceiving earth history for "through faith we understand that the worlds were framed by the word of God" (Hebrews 11:3). As an alternate path to the perilous way of the empiricist, who trusts in his ability to observe the regularity of nature, or the rationalist, who trusts in his ability to frame a plausible conceptual history from basic immanent characteristics of matter, the Bible-believing Christian recognizes that his unaided mind and faculties of observation cannot solve the basic problems dealing with earth history. The Christian trusts in a revealed record from God, Himself, providing a basic framework within which the data of historical geology must be interpreted. Such a revealed history from a credible observer is the only way man can have absolute knowledge about the earth's history.

The basic framework which the Christian is to accept by faith is the one plainly taught in Scripture. This framework is Biblical Catastrophism. The Bible-believing Christian accepts three great events which form a framework into which the data of geology are to be interpreted. First is the special creation of the universe by the spoken word of God (Genesis 1:1-31; Psalm 33:6, 9; Hebrews 11:3). Second is the Fall, subsequent curse, and entrance of death into the world due to man's sin (Genesis 3:1-24; Romans 5:12; 8:19-22; I Corinthians 15:21). Third is the worldwide Noachian Flood (Genesis 6-9; Psalm 104:6-9; II Peter 3:5,6). Thus, the Bible is the Christian's vital key to the past.

Among Bible-believing Christians there should be little disagreement about the status of the empirical, uniformitarian framework and the rationalistic, evolutionary framework. Both are untrue. Thus, the Apostle Peter specifically warned that scoffers would propose an empirical, uniformitarian framework supposing that "all things continue as from the beginning of the creation" (II Peter 3:4). The Apostle Paul denied the empirical philosophy when he said, "We walk by faith, not by sight" (II Corinthians 5:7).

The rationalistic approach epitomized by the evolutionary model is merely an exercise of man's wisdom, being an attempt to explain earth history by a conceptual scheme derived from the basic rudimentary and elementary characteristics inherent in nature. This system denies God from the outset. The Apostle Paul, who was well educated in the rationalism of the Greeks, gave a stern reprimand of this thinking when he admonished Christians to beware of philosophy "according to the traditions of men, after the rudiments of the world" (Colossians 2:8) which does not follow Christ. In contrast to the rationalistic approach, the truth which Paul proclaimed to the Greek Christians at Corinth was not "words which man's wisdom teacheth, but which the Holy Ghost teacheth" (I Corinthians 2:13).

The Proverbs warn us, "There is a way which seemeth right unto a man" (Proverbs 16:25). Each of us is admonished to "Trust in the Lord with all thine heart, and lean not unto thine own understanding" (Proverbs 3:5).

The previous comments do not imply that the Christian denies the validity of sense experience or reasoning procedures. Sense perception and reason were given to man by God. The problem occurs when man separates from God and attempts to place reason or perception on a higher level than the Word of God.

The Significance of Man

Each of the three approaches to interpreting earth history leads to a different view of man's condition. The empirical, uniformitarian framework supposes that everything can be explained by the interaction of the immutable laws of nature. Man in this view becomes trapped in the deterministic machine of nature. He is a helpless pawn powerless to choose his own destiny. If God exists, He is certainly unable to help man because everything continues in the same fashion under the autonomous, eternally operating system.

The rationalistic, evolutionary framework attempts to explain the origin of everything without need for a supernatural power by a naturally operating, integrative process. Man in this view is a cosmic accident, the product of the impersonal evolutionary process operating by blind chance over vast eons. On the basis of reason there is no meaning, purpose, or significance to man's existence. There is only pessimism concerning man. His condition must continue to be improved by struggle and death or his species will face extinction. A philosophy of despair is also the rational outcome of the evolutionary framework.

Not all evolutionists are pessimists. There is presently a popular movement known as "optimistic evolutionary humanism" which believes that a glorious future is ahead for man. The leaders of this philosophy insist that man's normal evolutionary method (a cruel and immoral process of struggle and death leading to the survival of the fittest) must be eliminated in the future by the acceptance of a new evolutionary mystique stressing more virtuous behavior. Thus, according to the leaders of optimistic evolutionary humanism, society will function better by believing in the existence of a god, even though no god is actually present. The philosophy involves a non-rationalistic leap of faith, for in order to be optimistic and benevolent, man must believe and function upon what his reason tells him is a lie.

In the Christian view man is created in the image of God. Although man is deliberately sinful, he continues to be God's image-bearer and is of great value to God, who made atonement through Christ for man's sin. Each person by trusting Christ as Saviour is restored to fellowship with God and given purpose and reward for all eternity. There is no reason for man to despair, for he has been given a position of dignity in God's creation. Christianity is not a nebulous set of experiences or an irrational leap in the dark, but a faith which has substantial basis in valid experience and a rational groundwork in real evidence (Hebrews 11:1).

THE AUTHOR. Stuart E. Nevins has B.S. and M.S. degrees in geology and is Assistant Professor of Geology at Christian Heritage College.

CREATION AND THE ENVIRONMENT*

By Henry M. Morris, Ph.D.

One of man's most vexing problems today is the conflict between energy and ecology, between conservation of jobs and conservation of nature. The need for expanded energy sources and more goods and services for mankind seems completely at cross-purposes with the maintenance of an unpolluted environment.

Is there a way out of this dilemma? If not, what is wrong with a world that forces us into such a situation?

As with all great issues, the way in which a person views a problem and the course of action he follows in handling it depend fundamentally upon his basic philosophy of life. The ecological crisis, in particular, points up the evolution-creation conflict in a surprising light.

Evolution and Ecology

Evolutionists in recent years have tried to claim that our environmental problems result from man's exploitation of the world's resources in the Bible-founded belief that they were all made for him and that he was to develop and use them solely for himself. The Bible, however, teaches no such thing. If there is to be any placing of blame for the problem of pollution and related ills, it should be assigned to the philosophy of evolution, where it really belongs. Furthermore, effective remedies for such problems can be found only in the context of a sound creationist philosophy.

The essence of evolution, of course, is randomness. The evolutionary process supposedly began with random particles and has continued by random aggregations of matter and then random mutations of genes. The fossil record, as interpreted by evolutionists, is said by them to indicate aeons of purposeless evolutionary meanderings, the senseless struggling and dying of untold billions of animals, extinctions of species, misfits, blind alleys. The present-day environmental ecologic complex then is nothing more than the current stage in this unending random struggle for existence.

* Impact Series #13 (April 1974)

209

Those populations of organism which have survived to this point therefore must represent the "fittest" — those that have been screened and preserved by the process of natural selection. In spite of its randomness, therefore, evolutionists believe that the net result of evolution has somehow been the development of higher and higher kinds, and finally of man himself.

This development is believed by most evolutionists to have been made possible by a peculiar combination of small populations, changing environments, and accelerated mutational pressures, a combination which supposedly enables natural selection to function in its remarkable role as "creator" of new and beter kinds of populations. It would seem therefore that anything that would change the environment today (for example, by altering the chemical components of the atmosphere and hydrosphere through pollution), decrease populations (perhaps by war, famine, or pestilence), or increase mutational pressures (such as by increasing the radioactive component of the biosphere through nuclear testing), would contribute positively to further evolution and therefore should be encouraged, at least if evolutionists are correct in their understanding of evolutionary mechanisms. In other words, the very processes which modern ecologists most deplore today are those which they believe to have been the cause of the upward evolution of the biosphere in the past. The conclusion would seem to be that evolution requires pollution!

More directly to the point, however, three generations of evolutionary teaching have had the pragmatic result of inducing in man an almost universal self-centeredness. God, if He exists at all, is pushed so far back in time and so far out in space that men no longer are concerned about responsibility to Him. As far as other people are concerned, doesn't nature itself teach that we must struggle and compete for survival? Self-preservation is nature's first law. Race must compete against race, nation against nation, class against class, young against old, poor against rich, man against man.

Two thousand years of Christian teaching linger on to some

extent, in modern social concerns and in the diluted esthetics and ethics of the day, but these are easily forgotten when one's self-interests are at stake. Conservationist groups may inveigh against the ecological destruction wrought by petroleum and utilities plants, but they do not personally wish to give up their automobiles or electrical appliances, nor to pay the higher prices required if these commodities are to be produced without damage to the environment. Furthermore, during the past 150 years especially, the very exploitation of nature — its flora and fauna, its resources, and even its human populations — against which environmentalists are protesting, has itself been carried out in the name of science and evolutionary philosophy. Thus the modern ecologic crisis is not a product of Biblical theology at all, but rather a century of worldwide evolutionary thinking and practice. It is significant that the environmental problems developed entirely within a period when the scientific and industrial establishments were totally committed to an evolutionary philosophy!

The Creationist Perspective on Nature

Recognition of the world as God's direct creation, on the other hand, transforms man's outlook on nature and his attitude toward other men. The creation is God's unique handiwork and displays His character and glory (Psalm 19:1; Psalm 148; Rev. 5:13). The design and implementation of this marvelous universe and its varied inhabitants were to God a source of great delight (Genesis 1:31; Job 38:4-7; Revelation 4:11). Man was created, not to exploit God's world, but to be His steward, exercising dominion over it (Genesis 1:26, 28) and "keeping" it (Genesis 2:15).

The primeval world as it came from God's hand was beautiful beyond imagination and perfect in every way as man's home. There was ample food for both man and animals (Genesis 1:29, 30) and each kind had its own ecological niche. Even when God stopped creating(Genesis 2:1-3), He provided abundantly for the maintenance of the creation (Nehemiah 9:6 ; Hebrews 1:3).

What Went Wrong?

With man's fall and God's Curse on his dominion, this pristine perfection changed (Genesis 3:17; Romans 8:20, 22). Every process henceforth operated inefficiently, and every system tended toward disintegration. Although the earth's resources remained constant in quantity, their quality could thereafter be maintained only with great difficulty and only at the cost of drawing excess energy from some other source.

Not only was the quantity of matter and energy to be "conserved" (as expressed formally now in our scientific Law of Conservation of Energy), but presumably also the "quality" of energy was to be maintained. Not only was energy conserved, but entropy as well; the universe was not designed to "perish," "wax old," and "be changed" (Psalm 102:25; Psalm 148:6), but to be "established forever and ever." In some unknown manner, no longer operating, the sun's energy probably was replenished cyclically from that radiated into space after some had been used to maintain terrestrial processes. On the earth itself, none of its resources were ever to be depleted and all processes were to function at perfect efficiency. A great abundance of plant and animal life was soon produced, in response to God's commands (Genesis 1:11, 20, 24), and continued to multiply, storing energy from the sun in an enlarging biosphere. All necessary disintegrative processes (e.g., disgestion, etc.) were presumably in balance with the increasing numbers of highly-structured organisms. Order and entropy were thus everywhere in balance, as well as matter and energy. Everything was "very good" (Genesis 1:31).

The Bible gives little information as to such specific energy sources before the Flood, except for the sun itself. At the time of the Deluge, however, the earth's energy balance changed drastically. Its greenhouse-like environment, which had been maintained by "waters above the firmament," (Genesis 1:5) was destroyed when the great canopy of vapor condensed and deluged the entire globe. The tremendous stores of chemical energy in the biosphere of the antediluvian world were partially converted in the resulting cataclysm into great stores of coal, oil and gas, the so-called "fossil fuels." Much of the incoming solar energy thenceforth would be needed to drive the atmospheric circulations and to maintain the post-diluvian hydrologic cycle for the earth.

It is significant to realize that today's pollution problems are derived mostly from using energy stores that were produced in the Noachian Deluge! Coal is the fossil product of the terrestrial plant life, and oil largely of the marine animal life, of the rich biosphere that had been created and developed by the Creator in the beginning. These organisms were not designed to serve as fuels for man's machines, and it is not surprising that the efficiency of heat engines using them is low and the waste products are high. Furthermore, they are exhaustible and, even now, the imminent end of economic oil and gas production is a matter of great concern.

In a sense, of course, the burning of these fossil fuels is merely hastening the process of "returning to the dust," which is the present fate of all organic life, under the Curse. The waste products, both of the processes of life and of the phenomena of death, have always posed a pollution problem to the environment, but the normal cycles of nature are able to accommodate them in part, and even utilize them (e.g., in the enrichment of the soil, etc.) as long as they are sufficiently dispersed in time and space. When concentrated in abnormal numbers of either men or animals, either in living communities or massive extinctions, however, such wastes cannot be assimilated and initiate various abnormal reactions which accelerate and accentuate environmental decay.

Retarding Environmental Decay

These deleterious changes can be corrected to some extent, but only at the cost of excess energy from other sources and therefore only at great labor and expense. Nuclear energy is one possibility but this of course creates its own pollutional problems. Geothermal energy may be a partial answer, in the few regions where it is available. Hydroelectric energy has already been developed to nearly its maximum potential in many parts of the world and is seriously limited in all parts of the world.

Solar energy is undoubtedly the best ultimate hope for an adequate energy supply, since the sun is the ultimate source of energy for all of earth's processes anyhow. To date, however, no economically efficient solar converters have been developed, except for special and limited applications. Since the sun was created to "give light upon the earth" (Genesis 1:17) and since "there is nothing hid from the heat thereof" (Psalm 19:6), we may well believe that it is possible to find ways to utilize solar energy to meet all man's legitimate energy needs and to do so with a minimal amount of further damage to the environment. Cost of the needed research should not be prohibitive, at least in relation to other energy and environmental costs.

In any case, a creationist orientation can certainly contribute more effectively to the alleviation of such problems than can an evolutionary perspective. The creationist recognizes that the world is God's handiwork and that he is God's steward. The divine commission to "have dominion over" and to "subdue" the earth is not a license for despotic exploitation of its resources, but rather a call to service, encourging him to understand its nature ("science") and then to utilize its resources ("technology") for the benefit of all men, under God.

Dead End

Eventually, however, if the present world (no matter how carefully its resources were guarded) were to continue indefinitely operating under the present laws of nature, it would die. The "whole creation" is under the "bondage of decay" (Romans 8:20-22).

But this bleak prospect will never be reached. God's eternal purpose in creation cannot fail. The creation, therefore, must be somehow redeemed and saved. Although in the present order, the Curse is universal and inexorable, the One who imposed it can also remove it. (Revelation 22:3).

The Earth Made New

The redemption price has in fact been paid in full (Colossians 1:20) and this "redemption of the purchased possession'' (Ephesians 1:14) will be completely implemented when Christ returns. At that time, everything, including the earth and its land-water-air environment, will all be "made new" again (Revelation 21:5), and will then last forever.

In the meantime, every person who has appropriated this redemption individually through an act of faith in his Creator and Redeemer has the privilege of sharing in God's work of reconciliation, for "He hath given to us the ministry of reconciliation" (II Corinthians 5:18). The work of redemption and reconciliation involves the reclamation and saving both of individual man and of man's dominion, for the eternal ages to come. We seek not only to win scientists to Christ, but even to win the sciences themselves to Christ.

"O Lord, how manifold are thy works! in wisdom hast thou made them all: the earth is full of thy riches . . . . The glory of the Lord shall endure for ever: the Lord shall rejoice in His works" (Psalm 104:24, 31).

PLANET EARTH: PLAN OR ACCIDENT?*

By Stuart E. Nevins, M.S.

From where did the earth come? By what process was it constructed? Did an everseeing Intelligence plan and direct the creation of our planet? Or, did the earth evolve by unguided chance processes without an overseeing plan? A person's answers to the above questions will significantly affect his personal viewpoint regarding the origin, purpose, and destiny of both the earth and man.

Since scientists agree that the earth has not existed eternally, simple logic dictates that no middle position exists on the

* Impact Series #14 (May 1974)

important issue of plan versus accident. *Either* a superintending Mind planned and designed our planet, *or* it all originated by a fortuitous accident without a plan and design! To help resolve the matter let us consider some amazing facts about the earth.

Earth's Surface Temperature

The average temperature at the earth's surface depends upon several factors, the two most important being the distance of the earth from the sun and the tilt of the rotational axis of the earth. Of secondary importance to the earth's surface temperature is the area of the continents, the amount of earth covered by light- and heat-reflecting masses of ice (glaciers), and the amount of carbon dioxide and water vapor affecting the transparency of the atmosphere to both incoming and outgoing heat.

The most important factor affecting the surface temperature of the earth is obviously the distance from the sun. If the earth were moved a few million miles closer to the sun, the surface of the earth would become warmer causing our glaciers to melt. With a decrease in the area of ice the total reflectivity of our planet's surface would thereby *decrease* and more of the sun's heat would be absorbed. The melting of glaciers would produce a rise of sea level, and, apart from flooding most of our modern cities, would create a larger total ocean surface area. Since seawater absorbs larger amounts of solar radiation than equal area land masses, heating of the earth would again be promoted. Furthermore, after increasing the temperature of the oceans, much of the ocean's dissolved carbon dioxide would be added to the atmosphere along with large amounts of water due to increased evaporation. The increased carbon dioxide and water vapor level of the atmosphere would again bring about a significant temperature rise. All things considered, a minor *decrease* in the sun's distance would have a drastic heating effect on the earth's surface.

What would happen if the earth were a few million miles farther from the sun? The reverse of the previous situation applies. We would have more of our planet covered by ice, with associated *increased* reflectivity of the sun's heat. The ocean would cover less of the earth's surface and the important process of absorption of heat by seawater would be *decreased*. Since the ocean would be colder, evaporation would be less with less heat-trapping water vapor in the atmosphere. Much of the carbon dioxide from the atmosphere would become dissolved in the colder ocean. Calculations show that a decrease of carbon dioxide in the air to just one-half of its present level would lower the average temperature of the earth's surface by about 7.0 degrees Fahrenheit! Thus, increasing the sun's distance would have a profound cooling effect on our planet.

From this discussion we see that the earth is just the proper distance from the sun to maintain the right surface temperature suitable for life and the many important geologic processes! To the evolutionist the distance of the earth from the sun is a strange accident, but to the creationist it is a marvelous testimony of God's planning.

Earth's Tilt and Rotation

The earth's axis of rotation is tilted 23½ degrees relative to the perpendicular of the earth's plane of orbit. This tilt causes the four seasons. During the months of May, June, and July the northern hemisphere is pointed toward the sun, causing the hemisphere to warm and bringing on the season called summer. During November, December, and January the northern hemisphere is pointed away from the sun providing colder temperatures and the season called winter. Why is this tilt 23½ degrees? Why not some other value?

What if the earth had no tilt, and the axis of rotation remained perpendicular to the plane of orbit? We would have no seasons and the surface temperature at any point on the earth would be the same during both July and January. The equatorial region of our planet would be intolerably hot all year and the poles would remain fairly cold. Ice would accumulate at the poles. The weather patterns would be stationary with permanently positioned warm and cold air masses. Some areas would continually be very humid while other areas would be quite arid. Only the mid-latitudes would be comfortable for human habitation and suitable for cultivation. Only about one half of our presently farmable lands could grow crops.

What would be the effect if the earth had double the present tilt? Temperature extremes between seasons would be much more pronounced. Even the mid-latitudes would have unbearable heat in the summer and frigid cold in the winter. Most of Europe and North America would experience very prolonged darkness in the winter and very prolonged daylight in the summer. Life on most of the earth's surface would become intolerable.

The earth rotates once every 24 hours producing the interval of time called "day." If the earth rotated more slowly, we would have more extreme day and night temperatures. Other planets have "days" which are many times that of the earth, producing scorching daytime heat followed by freezing nighttime cold. The normal daily routine of plants and animals would be impossible if the earth day were much shorter than that of the present. The 24-hour day seems to be optimum, serving to evenly heat the earth (somewhat like a turkey turning on a barbeque spit).

Thus, we could hardly improve on the present arrangement of tilt and rotation, which seems to be *planned* for both comfort and economy. Our present tilt causes seasons with associated fluctuations in weather, producing a maximum amount of farmable land and pleasant seasons. The present rotation of the earth helps to uniformly heat its surface and cause winds and ocean currents.

Earth's Atmosphere

The earth's atmosphere is composed of four important gases. The most abundant gas is nitrogen (N_2) which comprises about 78% of the atmosphere. Oxygen gas (O_2) is the second most common ingredient, being present at 21%. Argon gas (Ar) is third at slightly less than 1%. Fourth is carbon dioxide gas (CO_2), present at 0.03%.

In our study of the atmosphere we see that its gases can be divided into two main categories — inert gases and reactive gases. Argon is inert and nitrogen is relatively inactive.

These enter into very few chemical reactions. It is indeed fortunate that nitrogen gas does not readily combine with oxygen, otherwise, we could have an ocean full of nitric acid!

Oxygen gas is the most common reactive gas in our atmosphere. The presence of abundant oxygen is the feature which most distinguishes our atmosphere, for oxygen in more than trace amounts has not been discovered in the atmosphere of any other planet.

Unlike nitrogen gas, oxygen gas readily enters into reactions with other gases, with organic compounds, and with rocks. The present level of oxygen seems to be optimum. If we had more oxygen, combustion would occur more energetically, rocks and metals would weather faster, and life would be adversely affected. If oxygen were less abundant, respiration would be more difficult and we would have a decreased quantity of ozone gas (O_3) in the upper atmosphere which shields the earth's surface from deadly ultraviolet rays.

Carbon dioxide is also a reactive gas which forms an essential part of our atmosphere. Carbon dioxide is required by plants, serves to effectively trap the sun's radiation, and mixes with water to form an acid which dissolves rocks adding an important substance called bicarbonate to the ocean. Without a continuing supply of carbon from the atmosphere, life would be impossible.

Important as carbon dioxide is to the present earth and life, it comprises only a mere 0.03 of our atmosphere! This small amount, however, seems to be at the optimum value. If we had less carbon dioxide, the total mass of terrestrial and marine plants would decrease, providing less food for animals, the ocean would contain less bicarbonate, becoming more acidic, and the climate would become colder due to the increased transparency of the atmosphere to heat. While an increase in atmospheric carbon dioxide would cause plants to flourish (a beneficial circumstance for the farmer), there would be some unfortunate side effects. A fivefold increase in carbon dioxide pressure (the optimum level for organic productivity) would alone cause the average world surface temperature to be a few tens of degrees Fahrenheit warmer! Also, a large increase in carbon dioxide would so accelerate the chemical weathering of the continents that an excess of bicarbonate would form in the ocean, leading to an alkali condition unfavorable for life.

The total density air pressure of our atmosphere appears to be ideal. The density is very important for it acts as an insolating blanket protecting the earth from the coldness of space. If the earth had a greater diameter, holding a more dense atmosphere, the thermal blanketing effect would be enhanced, producing a much warmer climate. If the earth were of smaller diameter, holding a less dense atmosphere, there would be a colder climate. As suggested earlier, the earth has the correct surface temperature, showing the atmosphere has the proper density and that the earth has the proper size!

The atmosphere also serves to filter out ultraviolet light and cosmic rays. Both are harmful to life and would be much more common at the earth's surface if the atmosphere were less dense. The atmosphere also burns up meteors. Long range radio communication is possible because the atmosphere is the correct density to reflect some radio frequencies. Furthermore, the atmosphere reflects unwanted stellar noise which could interfere with radio.

This analysis shows that our atmosphere has both the correct composition and density. How, except by divine planning and design, could our atmosphere have formed?

World Ocean

Water is an extremely rare compound in space. A permanent reserve of *liquid* water, a very unlikely occurrence in space, is known to exist only on the earth. Our planet possesses an abundant supply estimated at some 340 million cubic miles of liquid water.

Water in liquid form has many unique chemical and physical properties which make it ideal as the primary component of life and the solution of the world ocean. The solvent characteristic of water, for example, makes it possible for all essential nutrients needed by life to be dissolved and assimilated. The fact that water is transparent to visible light makes it possible for marine algae to perform photosynthesis below the ocean surface and for ocean animals to be able to see through water. Water is one of only a few substances which expands when it freezes, preventing our ocean and lakes from freezing from the bottom upward.

One of the most remarkable properties of water is its high heat-capturing and heat-holding capacity. The ocean is less reflective than the land to incoming solar radiation and thereby absorbs more of the sun's energy than equal areas of land. It also takes much more heat to raise the temperature of a unit mass of seawater one degree than it does for an equal mass of the continents. Since the average temperature of the ocean is about 45 degrees Fahrenheit, the ocean will cool the hotter equatorial land portions of our planet and warm the colder polar regions. Furthermore, ocean currents caused by the earth's rotation serve to circulate seawater and prevent the equatorial seas from becoming too hot and the polar seas from becoming too cold and freezing completely.

The world ocean serves as a reservoir for some very important chemicals besides water. Most of our planet's carbon dioxide is dissolved in seawater, being in equilibrium with the atmosphere. The recent addition of large amounts of carbon dioxide to the atmosphere by burning of fossil fuels has not significantly raised the amount of that gas in the atmosphere. Most of the combustion-derived carbon dioxide has been absorbed by the ocean.

From our discussion it should be evident that the presence of an ocean on our planet is an evidence of God's planning and foresight. No other planet is known to have a permanent supply of liquid water. The chemical and physical properties of liquid water are necessary for life to survive. The world ocean regulates the earth's temperature and serves as a reservoir for many important chemicals.

Earth's Crust

The continents which cover 29% of our planet's surface have a mean elevation of about 2,750 feet above sea level. The world ocean which covers 71% of the earth's surface has an average depth of some 12,500 feet! Why do we have such lofty continents along with such deep ocean basins? We would expect, using simply probability estimates, to have an earth of nearly constant elevation.

If we were to scrape off the continents and place them in the deeper parts of the ocean to make an earth of common elevation, we would have an earth covered with approximately 8,000 feet of water! No land areas would be exposed and terrestrial life could not exist. There would be no shallow coastal seas providing ecological zones in which most marine creatures could thrive. The ocean with a constant elevation earth would be nearly void of life.

There are two main reasons that the continents remain elevated above the sea floor. First, the continents are made up of rocks which, as a whole, are less dense than the rocks of the ocean bottom. Second, the continental crust is usually over twice as thick as the oceanic crust. The difference in density and thickness between continental and oceanic crust is *just the right amount* to maintain the present "freeboard" of the continents above the ocean bottom! To the evolutionist this is a peculiar accident. To the creationist, however, these facts show God's design.

Study of meteorites has revealed that the elements iron and oxygen are about equal in abundance on the average. From what is known about the density and structure of the earth, geologists suggest that iron is the commonest element in the bulk of the earth, being slightly more abundant than oxygen. However, when the crust of the earth is considered, geologists estimate that oxygen is about *eight times* more abundant than iron! Furthermore, the earth's crust has unusually large amounts of silicon and aluminum.

If we had larger amounts of iron and magnesium in the crust, oxygen from the atmosphere would be consumed to weather these elements and an oxygen-rich atmosphere would be impossible. Our present crust, unlike other planets and meteorites, is already highly oxidized and therefore permits an oxidizing atmosphere. Thus, the composition of the crust shows God's wisdom.

Conclusion

Two different conclusions can be drawn from the data which have been presented. The data indicate either that an omniscient Mind planned and designed our amazing planet, *or* that it originated by a fortuitous accident without plan or design. There is no middle ground! One must decide — *either God or chance!*

The person who is a consistent evolutionist will attribute the many wonders of our planet (the earth's surface temperature, tilt and rotation, atmosphere, ocean, and crust) to the unguided chance. This conclusion, though not impossible, takes a great deal of faith in extremely improbable events. It is akin to supposing that the Mona Lisa came into existence from globs of paint hurled at a canvas.

The creationist, on the other hand, will recognize that the only rational deduction from the data is that the marvels of the earth owe their origin to the intelligence and handiwork of God. It was the psalmist who said:

> "In His hand are the deep places of the earth; the
> strength of the hills is His also. The sea is His, and
> He made it, and His hands formed the dry land.
> Oh, come, let us worship and bow down; let us
> kneel before the Lord our maker."
>
> (Psalm 95:4-6)

THE SOLAR SYSTEM — NEW DISCOVERIES*

By Duane T. Gish, Ph.D.

The results of recent space exploration have served to compound the mysteries of the solar system, rather than providing data predicted on the basis of evolutionary theories. Present theories on how planets were formed may have to be junked as the result of data on Mercury transmitted by Mariner 10. Earlier, Pioneer 10 cruised past Jupiter, photographing the most massive planet in the solar

---

* Impact Series #15 (June 1974)

system (318 times as massive as the earth) in detail hitherto unobservable, and finding that its largest satellite, Io, has an atmosphere. Until then, Titan, the largest of Saturn's nine satellites, was believed to be the only moon in the solar system to have an atmosphere. Furthermore, the latest data on the atmosphere of Titan add new problems for those who believe the age of the solar system to be billions of years.

Up to the present time, many theories on the origin of the universe and of the solar system have been proposed. All such theories suffer from apparently insurmountable difficulties.[1] No theory on the origin of the solar system has been able to explain the fact that although the sun has 99-6/7% of the mass of the solar system, it possesses only 2% of its angular momentum. Thus, the planets, which contain only 1/7% of the mass of the solar system, are revolving around the sun at such high speeds, while the sun is revolving so slowly, that the planets possess 98% of the angular momentum of the solar system. Yet the sun and planets supposedly were formed from the same dust and gas cloud, and thus some highly efficient mechanism would be required for transferring angular momentum from the central part of the nebula to the periphery. No plausible mechanism has yet been proposed.

If the solar system condensed out of a huge flattened disk of dust and gas, the motions of the sun, the planets, and all bodies within the solar system should exhibit a very high degree of regularity in their motions. Evolutionists are quick to point out that all nine planets move around the sun in the same direction in nearly circular orbits which lie in almost the same plane, but they neglect to emphasize other serious departures from regularity. Uranus is remarkable. Even though it rotates around the sun in the same direction as the other planets in an orbit inclined less than a degree (46') from the ecliptic (the plane of the earth's orbit around the sun), the

1. For an excellent review of cosmogonical theories see *The Origin of the Solar System* by John Whitcomb, Presbyterian and Reformed Pub. Co., Philadelphia (1964).

224

axis of rotation of Uranus is nearly in the plane of its orbit. Thus, the inclination of the equator of Uranus to the plane of its orbit is 98°, and its *axial* rotation is *retrograde*. The five moons or satellites of Uranus move exactly in the equatorial plane of the planet and they revolve in the same direction as the planet rotates. Their motion, with respect to the remainder of the solar system, is, therefore, also retrograde. Thus the direction of the axial rotation of Uranus and the motion of its satellites is opposite to that predicted on the basis of an evolutionary origin.

Saturn has nine satellites. The motion of the outermost, Phoebe, is retrograde, moving in a direction opposite to the other eight moons and opposite to that predicted, of course, from an evolutionary origin. Jupiter has twelve satellites. The five inner moons revolve around their planet in orbits only slightly inclined to the planet's equator at distances from about 110,000 miles for the innermost to about 640,000 miles for the outermost. Then there is a group of three moons whose orbits are inclined to the planet's equator by almost 30° at distances of about 7 million miles from Jupiter. These three moons also revolve around the planet in the predicted direction. The four outer moons, however, move around the planet in *retrograde* motion, or opposite to that of the other eight satellites, at distances from about 12 to 13 million miles from the planet.

Neptune has two satellites. Nereid, a small moon, moves around Neptune in the predicted direction, but Triton, one of the larger satellites in the solar system with a mass almost twice that of the earth's moon, moves in a retrograde orbit.

Thus, of the 31 planetary satellites in the solar system (in addition to those mentioned above, the earth, of course, has one and Mars has two), eleven exhibit retrograde orbits. It has already been mentioned that Uranus has a retrograde axial rotation. Venus rotates very slowly, one rotation requiring about 240 earth days. Goldstein and Carpenter[1] have found

---

1. R.M. Goldstein and R.L. Carpenter, *Science,* Vol. 139, p. 910 (1963).

that this planet may also possess a retrograde axial rotation. These exceptions to motions predicted on the basis of an evolutionary origin of the solar systems cannot be brushed aside as minor exceptions, but speak of a created universe rather than a universe produced merely by matter in motion.

Analysis of the reams of data produced by Mariner 10 as it flew past Venus on February 5 and Mercury on March 29 is still proceeding, of course, but one of the most startling findings that has come out of the space program has already been revealed (startling to evolutionists, that is).[1] The data from Mariner 10 revealed that Mercury has a lightweight crust. Since the density of Mercury is 4.5 - 5.0 g/cc (the density of the earth is 5.5), it must have a heavy core. Mercury, just like the earth, then, is differentiated into a light crust and a heavy core. According to all previous theories on the evolution of the solar system, planets were formed from a uniform cloud of some kind. Differentiation, during which lighterweight material aggregates and floats to the surface and heavy material sinks to the core, would require the planet to reach a molten state. Such a molten state would erase all primordial surface features. Scientists who have examined photographs of Mercury believe, however, that they are looking at the essentially undisturbed primordial surface features of Mercury, that no change has taken place in these surface features since Mercury was formed. In other words, even though Mercury is differentiated into a light crust and a heavy core, it is in the original created state. How then, did it become differentiated? The creationist has a direct and simple answer, of course, but the evolutionist must somehow reconcile data that appear to be irreconcilable.

Another unexpected feature of Mercury is its possession of a magnetic field. About 20 minutes before the spacecraft reached its closest approach to Mercury (about 466 miles), magnetometers revealed clear signs of a bow shock, a shock front formed by the solar wind ricochetting off the planet's enveloping magnetic field. This magnetic field is very weak

---

1. *Science News,* Vol. 105, p. 220 (1974)

(about one-hundredth as strong as the magnetic field of the earth) but it poses another problem for evolutionary cosmogonists: its source. One of the most popular theories on the source of the earth's magnetic field is the self-generating dynamo theory. Such a theory requires that the planet have a relatively high speed of rotation. Mercury, however, rotates very slowly, revolving once in 88 earth days. Therefore, the self-generating dynamo theory won't work for Mercury. Some new theory must be hatched to account for Mercury's magnetic field.

These results indirectly support the contention of Dr. Thomas Barnes that the self-generating dynamo theory of the magnetic field of the earth is not only unnecessary, but impossible.[1] There are so many problems with the self-generating dynamo. If Mercury can have a magnetic field without such a dynamo, why not the earth? Barnes has shown that in the absence of such a dynamo the earth's magnetic field must be generated by the flow of an electric current. Since the earth's magnetic field is decaying, extrapolation back into the past more than about 10,000 years predicts a current flow so vast that the earth's structure could not survive the heat produced. Thus, the earth cannot be much older than 10,000 years.[1]

Since Kuiper's discovery[2] of methane in the spectrum of Titan, a large satellite of Saturn, it has been realized that Titan must have an atmosphere. The presence of hydrogen-rich molecules (methane is CH_4) on such a compact body is surprising because it would indicate an evolution contrary to that of the oxidized atmospheres of the compact terrestrial planets.[3] Now Trafton has discovered the presence of

1. T.G. Barnes, *Origin and Destiny of the Earth's Magnetic Field,* Institute for Creation Research, San Diego, Calif. (1973).
2. G.P. Kuiper, *The Astrophysical Journal,* Vol. 100, p. 378 (1944).
3. L. Trafton, *The Astrophysical Journal,* Vol. 175, p. 285 (1972).

hydrogen in Titan's atmosphere, [1] and, because the gravity of tiny Titan isn't strong enough to hold hydrogen, it must be flying away from this moon at a tremendous rate.

Earlier, Allen and Murdock[2] discovered a brightness temperature for Titan of 125° K (0° Kelvin is absolute zero and 270° Kelvin is 0° centigrade). This is significantly higher than the equilibrium temperature which corresponds to its rate of rotation and other features (about 87° K). The fact that Titan exhibits a surface temperature in excess of that predicted strongly suggests a greenhouse effect.[3] In other words, Titan must have an atmosphere capable of absorbing and retaining solar radiation.

The hydrogen in Titan's atmosphere could not be a remnant of its original atmosphere if one assumes an age for the solar system of billions of years. Because of Titan's small size and consequent low escape velocity, any original atmosphere would have rapidly been lost from the new-born satellite.[1] Even the earth is believed by some scientists to have lost its original atmosphere.[4,5] Where is all this hydrogen coming from that supposedly has been pouring forth from this satellite for billions of years? Some means must be proposed for converting Titan into a huge hydrogen generator.

Trafton[1] and Sagan[3] have proposed that outgassing from Titan's interior is the most reasonable solution to the problem. But how can there be volcanism on a body which has a surface temperature almost 200° below the freezing point of water? Sagan[3] accepts the suggestion of Lewis[6] that the low

---

1. L. Trafton, *The Astrophysical Journal,* Vol. 175, p. 285 (1972).

2. D.A. Allen and T.L. Murdock, *Icarus,* Vol. 14, p. 1 (1971).

3. C. Sagan, *Icarus,* Vol. 18, p. 649 (1973).

4. G.P. Kuiper, *The Astrophysical Journal, Vol. 100, p. 328 (1944).*

5. P.H. Abelson, *Proceedings National Academy of Science,* Vol. 55, p. 1365 (1966).

6. J.S. Lewis, *Icarus,* Vol. 15, p. 174 (1971).

density of Titan and its probable content of radioactive materials imply an interior composition of a molten slush of methane, ammonia, and water, not many tens of kilometers below the surface. Heat released by radioactive decay is supposed to keep the slush warm enough to cause gasses containing methane, water, and ammonia to pour through fissures on the satellite's surface. Ultraviolet light of the sun would then photochemically break down these gasses to produce hydrogen as one of the products.

According to the calculations used, the highest outgassing rate estimated, even if constant over 5 billion years, would correspond to only about 10^5 g/cm^2, or a few kilometers of equivalent ice outgasses. [1] Of course, it can be surmised that the assumptions made in these calculations were such as to prevent things getting out of hand. One is still faced with the problem of the origin of a body with an interior containing methane, ammonia, and water.

Kuiper had constructed a hypothetical composition for Titan, based on its density, of a water-ice, silicate-metal combination. Now it is being proposed that Titan may be some kind of an icy mud ball. It is proposed that Titan has a rocky core surrounded by a deep layer of liquid water, ammonia, and methane. This is topped by a frozen surface composed of these three compounds.

It has been theorized that the earth lost all of the gasses associated with the material from which it accreted during the accretion process. [2] The mass of the earth and its gravitational attraction was too small to retain such gasses as methane, ammonia, and water. It supposedly started life with no atmosphere, but an atmosphere was soon generated by volcanic outgassing of gasses that were originally combined with silicates and other material which made up the rocks.

---

1. C. Sagan, *Icarus,* Vol. 18, p. 649 (1973)
2. P.H. Abelson, *Proceedings National Academy of Science,* Vol. 55, p. 1365 (1966)

Now if an accreting planet the size of the earth was not massive enough to retain such constituents as ammonia, methane, and water, how could a body as small as Titan, with only about 0.0235 the mass of the earth, retain such huge quantities? Why didn't Titan end up merely as an orbiting rock pile?

It is always possible, of course, to invent new mechanisms through secondary and tertiary assumptions to salvage the basic theory, even though the assumptions are unproven and inherently unprovable. Many such mechanisms cannot stand a searching inquiry, however, since they cannot be reconciled with established physical theories. It is predicted that as more and more is learned about our solar system, the more incompatible this knowledge will become with evolutionary theories concerning its origin. The words of the Psalmist ring even stronger today than 3500 years ago when written: "The heavens declare the glory of God and the firmament showeth His handiwork" (Psalm 19:1).

PHYSICS: A CHALLENGE TO "GEOLOGIC TIME"*
By Thomas G. Barnes, D.Sc.

(Professor of Physics, University of Texas at
El Paso, and Visiting Professor at
Christian Heritage College)

I. Lord Kelvin Urged Geologists to Accept Limitations Set by Physics on the Earth's Age.

In contrast to the narrow specialization of present-day scientists some great physicists in the nineteenth century made significant contributions to numerous branches of science. England recognized this breadth and depth in Sir

---

* Impact Series 16 (July 1974)

William Thomson and elevated his title to Lord Kelvin. It was Kelvin's brilliant thermodynamic analysis that gave us the absolute temperature scale that bears his name. When the Atlantic cable was laid it took the ingenious electromagnetic developments of Kelvin to make it a workable device. His best papers are to be found in a six volume set, *Mathematical and Physical Papers, Lord Kelvin,* (Cambridge University Press, 1911). Many of those papers employed physics to expose the errors inherent in the long-age concepts held by uniformitarian geologists. One paper was entitled: "The 'Doctrine of Uniformity' in Geology Briefly Refuted"; another was entitled: "On the Age of the Sun's Heat." Many of his papers dealt with the age of the earth.

In reference to the President of the Geological Society, Kelvin stated: "I believe . . . Professor Huxley . . . did not know that there was valid foundation for any estimates worth considering as to absolute magnitudes" (greatest possible age of the earth). When Kelvin pressed Sir Andrew Ramsay for strict physical limitations on geological time, Ramsay begged the question with the remark, "I am as incapable of estimating and understanding the reasons which you physicists have for limiting geological time as you are incapable of understanding the geological reasons for our unlimited estimates." Kelvin replied, "You can understand perfectly, if you give your mind to it" and "Physicists are not wholly incapable of appreciating geological difficulties."

In later years Kelvin thought that geologists had accepted the limitations in the earth's age imposed by the principles of physics, which Kelvin had logically set forth. He wrote: "It was only by sheer force of reason that geologists have been compelled to think otherwise, and to see that there was a definite beginning, and to look forward to a definite end, of this world as an abode fitted for life." But Kelvin's optimism was premature. Evolutionary geologists had not and still have not accepted the limits imposed by physics upon "geological time"; their evolutionary tug has always been for more time. The compiler of Kelvin's papers points out that the geologists never accepted Kelvin's limits on the earth age: " . . . the complaint had become widely prevalent that in the hands of Lord Kelvin and the physicists the evolution of the terrestrial strata, and of the life of which they contain the evidence, had been hurried up too much."

Kelvin faced up to the *miracle of the creation of life*. He had no respect for the materialistic views of the origin of life and stated plainly: "Mathematics and dynamics fail us when we contemplate the earth, fitted for life but lifeless, and try to imagine the commencement of life upon it. This certainly did not take place by any action of chemistry, or electricity, or crystalline grouping of molecules under the influence of force, or by any possible kind of fortuitous concourse of atmosphere. We must pause, face to face with the mystery and miracle of creation of living creatures."

II. Analyses that Yield Limits on the Age of the Earth.

In order to understand how physical measurements and logical analyses may lead physicists to the conclusion that the earth is relatively young, one needs to understand how a "constraint" may be applied in physics. The constraint may be a limit placed on the *initial state* or original condition of the earth. For example, Kelvin assumed that in no case could the initial temperature of the earth have been greater than a *white hot* temperature. That constraint set the upper limit on any initial temperature to be assumed for the earth. Hence even though the constraint chosen is somewhat arbitrary, it is still based upon a very reasonable assumption.

This analysis finds an extreme limit. Whereas the actual value may be much smaller, at least a "lid" had been imposed on possible values to consider. Kelvin never said that the age limits set by his physical reasoning gave the actual age of the earth. He simply said its age was not greater than those limits.

Once a particular constraint, or initial state, has been assumed, the physicist methodically derives his conclusion from the laws of physics. We shall be particularly concerned with the laws of thermodynamics, mechanics, gravitation, and electro-magnetism. These laws govern the respective physical processes that change the value of the earth's physical parameters from those that were there in its initial state. These processes always involve *decay*. The physicist recognizes at least three kinds of decay that have been taking place on the earth: (1) The rate of rotation of the earth has been slowing down as a result of tidal friction and other factors, including some less known effects such as that of the solar wind drag on the earth's magnetic field. (2) Thermal energy within the earth has been decaying through the process of conduction to the surface of the earth and radiation out into space from the surface of the earth. (3) Magnetic energy associated with the earth's dipole magnet has been decaying, causing a growing diminution of the magnetic field that shields the earth from cosmic and solar radiation hazards.

The measured decay rates associated with each of these decay processes, together with reasonable constraints on their initial state, enable physicists to find limits to the possible age of the earth. Kelvin used the first two decay processes to establish limits of: (1) less than a billion years; (2) less than 24 million years; respectively, on the earth's age. Of course the shorter limit is the controlling one and Kelvin held to less than 24 million years for the earth's age. More recently, the author has taken some clues from theoretical work by Sir Horace Lamb, some extensive observational data, assumed a reasonable constraint on the upper limit of the earth's magnetic field, and the laws of electro-magnetism to arrive at an age of the earth's magnet of less than 10,000 years. Since there is no known geophysical means for starting up such a huge magnet in the earth within that period, one also concludes that the age of the earth itself is less than 10,000 years.

III. Kelvin's First Physical Argument Against the Vast Earth-Age.

Kelvin investigated the deceleration of the earth's rate of rotation due to the energy lost through tidal currents. He showed that, if the earth had been here for 7.2 billion years, its initial rate of rotation would have been twice its present rate (the days being only 12 hours long). That would have yielded *four times as much centrifugal force as at present*. If, as historical geologists claim, the earth was molten in its initial state, the centrifugal force would have *bulged out the mass in the equatorial region*, making the earth's radius 86 kilometers greater at the equator than at the poles (the radius of the earth's sea level is presently only 21.5 kilometers greater at the equator due to the centrifugal force with its present rate of spin). Kelvin reasoned that if the earth had consolidated at that time, the land masses would have retained most of that greatly oblated shape, four times its present oblateness. As the years passed the centrifugal force would have been reduced and the oceans would have settled into two very deep basins, one at the north polar region and the other at the south polar region. The continents would in that case now be extremely high in the equatorial regions, 40 miles higher than they actually are!

Kelvin noted that, even if the earth had been molten and consolidated *at some time appreciably less than a billion years ago*, it would still have evidences of that centrifugal effect and *its continents would run east and west around the equator rather than the present configuration of continents running more or less north and south*. Today there is evidence that the earth's rate of rotation is slowing even more than the value used by Kelvin. Hence his physical argument is even stronger today. No one has ever really challenged his physics. Geologists just chose to ignore it. Nevertheless the actual configurations of the continents and seas refute "historical geology's" claim of a 4.6 billion year age for the earth. The continents stand as testimony to a recent creation of the earth, at the maximum of, not more than, say, about 500 million years old by this evidence alone.

IV. Kelvin's Second Physical Argument Against the Vast Earth-Age.

The mean surface temperature of the earth is, so far as we know, in equilibrium. The surface of the earth receives thermal energy from the sun and stars; a small amount (one part in 3000) flows up to the surface from inside the earth. The surface of the earth radiates back into space an amount equal to the sum of that thermal influx to its surface. In fact, one can compute the mean surface temperature of the earth from this known influx of heat and Stefan's law that governs the radiation from the surface.

Kelvin assumed that even if the earth's surface were originally white hot, its surface temperature would have dropped quickly to approximately the same mean temperature it has now. The reason for this rapid surface cooling is that the cooling radiation rate at the surface is, by Stefan's law, proportional to the *fourth power* of the temperature (in degrees Kelvin), and the crust of the earth is a very poor thermal conductor. The cooling would then progress very, very gradually inward from the surface, penetrating inch by inch deeper into the earth. When the cooling had progressed only one foot inward, there would be a large *temperature gradient*, the temperature changing from very hot to the relatively cool surface temperature in just one foot. As the cooling progressed to two feet inward, the temperature gradient would have decreased to roughly half the previous value, etc.

Kelvin was able to compute the *temperature gradient near the surface of the earth as a function of time lapsed from its initial state*. He then assembled enough data on the earth's temperature gradient to evaluate the time lapsed since the assumed initial state. His best value for the earth's age limit, found by this method, was 24 million years.

Some scientists claimed that radioactivity in the earth would alter this limit upward, but none has given any clear analysis of how much it would alter Kelvin's value. Kelvin was well aware of radioactivity, as is demonstrated by the fact that he wrote several papers on it. That did not appear to him to alter the problem at all. He was working from an actual measured thermal flux gradient and a knowledge of thermal conductivity of the crustal rocks and was still confident that he had shown that the earth's age does not exceed 24 million years.

V. Analysis of the Decay of the Earth's Magnetic Energy Sets a Shorter Limit on the Earth's Age.

The earth's magnet is vastly stronger than any man-made magnet. Its *magnetic moment* (the vector that denotes the strength and direction of the magnet) has a present value of 8 x 10^{22} ampere meter^2, a huge value. Even so, this magnet was much stronger in the ages past. The decay rate of this magnet is the most remarkable worldwide geophysical decay phenomenon ever measured. The author has employed the fundamental laws of electro-magnetism (Maxwell's Equation), together with a reasonable assumption about the initial state of the earth's magnet and the measured decay rate of the earth's magnetic moment, to derive a limit on the age of the earth's magnet.[1] Although there is not enough space here to give the details, both the layman and scientist will find sufficient information, physics, and analysis in the monograph to verify this physical means of arriving at a limit on the age of the earth's magnet and, by inference, a limit on the age of the earth itself. The pertinent points and physical arguments are reviewed in the following portion of this paper.

There is a logical physical reason why this magnet is decaying. Its source is *real* electric current, freely circulating in the molten core of the earth. Like any electric current in a conductor, it expends energy. Its present rate of energy loss is 813 million watts. This loss is not being resupplied. That is evident from the decreasing value of the earth's magnetic moment and its associated magnetic energy. As is true of other sources of energy on this earth, *the earth is running out of its magnetic energy.*

This is a serious problem to evolutionary geologists. None of them seems willing to admit that the earth's magnetic energy is dying out, but the data and physics unequivocally

---

1. Barnes, T.G. Origin and destiny of the earth's magnetic field. I.C.R. Technical Monograph 4, Institute for Creation Res. San Diego 1973.

show that it *is* dying out. A publication of the Department of Commerce[1] itemizes the values of the earth's magnetic moment for the last 130 years and states that, if the decrease in the earth's magnetic moment persists, their analysis shows "that the dipole moment will vanish in A.D. 3991."

The irony of this whole problem is that its solution is a simple one when one accepts the actual physics and sees that it does imply a young earth. The gradual collapsing of the earth's magnetic field as the magnet decays is sensed in the core of the earth as a rate of change of magnetic flux through it. *The process of self-induction, operating off of that rate of change of magnetic flux, generates the back electromotive force that drives the electric current in the core of the earth.* This *self-induction* process is sufficient to explain the observed data on the decay of the earth's magnetic moment. If there *were* a workable dynamo down there in the core of the earth, it in fact would have to be turned off, because this self-induction process is already producing all of the six billion amperes of current flowing in the core of the earth. Any added amount from a dynamo would be contrary to the actual value of current that is known to exist in the core, and that is produced by self-induction. One thing that is certain is that self-induction cannot be shut off so long as there is a decay in the strength of the magnet, as indicated by the data.

VI. Half-life of the Earth's Magnetic Energy is 700 Years.

To evaluate the magnetic moment of the earth requires the reduction of a tremendous amount of worldwide data. The data from scores of magnetic observatories around the world are collected for at least a year's continuous measurements. These data are reduced through an elaborate mathematical process to arrive at *one value and direction for the earth's magnetic moment for that year.* The famous

---

1. Analysis of earth's magnetic field from 1835 to 1965, Essa Tech. Rept. IER, 46-IES 1 U.S. Gov. Printing Office, Wash. D.C. 1967, p.1.

mathematician and physicist, Gauss, developed the mathematics and the instrumentation, gathered the worldwide data, and made the first evaluation in 1885. Since then there have been additional evaluations every few years. We now have 130 years of actual data.

A computer analysis of these data has shown that the decay is an exponential one, as expected from the physics, and that the half-life of the *magnetic moment* is 1400 years. Because the energy is proportional to the square of the magnetic moment, the half-life of the magnetic *energy* is only half of this time, namely 700 years. This is perhaps the most meaningful value, 700-year half-life for the energy, because the energy supply is the most fundamental quantity.

VII. Deduction of 10,000-Year Age Limit on the Earth.

Knowing the half-life of the earth's magnetic moment, one may easily work backwards to set up an historical schedule of the earth's magnetic moment and of the associated magnetic field. If that is done, it will be seen that the value of the earth's magnetic field approaches that of a magnetic star if the earth's magnetic field goes back 10,000 years. But a magnetic star has a magnetic field generated by a huge *nuclear* power source. Surely it is reasonable to assume the constraint that the earth never had such a powerful source and, therefore, never had a magnetic field equal to that of a magnetic star. With that constraint, physics implies a limit on the age of the earth's magnet of less than 10,000 years.

Because there is no known geophysical means, within the last 10,000 years, of starting up the huge magnet in the earth, one is led to conclude that the origin of the magnet was concurrent with the creation of the earth. Hence, the earth also has an age limit of less than 10,000 years.

THE YOUNG EARTH*
Henry M. Morris, Ph.D.

It should be recognized that it is impossible to determine with certainty any date prior to the beginning of historical

*Impact Series #17, (September 1974)

records — except, of course, by divine revelation. Science, in the proper sense, is based on observation, and we have no records of observation except historical records. Natural processes can be used to *estimate* prehistoric dates, but not to *determine* such dates. The accuracy of the estimates will depend on the validity of the assumptions applied to the use of the processes in making such calculations.

Assume, in the general case, a simple process in which there are two main components, one "parent" and one "daughter" component — call them A and B, respectively. The initial magnitudes of these components at zero time (that is, the time when the particular system came into existence) are A_0 and B_0. After an additional time T these magnitudes have changed to A_T and B_T. The average time-rate at which A changes into B during the time T is R_T. The instantaneous rate may either be constant or may change in some fashion with time, in which case it may be expressed in functional form as:

$$r_t = f(A_0, B_0, t), \qquad (1)$$

since it may possibly depend on the process components as well as on time.

If the process is not a closed system, then there may be changes in A and B which result from extraneous influences, other than those expressed in the normal rate function. Let such changes be represented by the quantities Δa and Δb where Δa may be either positive or negative and represents the modification in A brought about during the time T by such external influences. A simlar definition applies to Δb.

Putting all these quantities together, the following equations express the effect of these changes in A and B.

$$A_0 \pm \Delta a - (R_T)T = A_T \qquad (2)$$

$$B_0 \pm \Delta b + (R_T)T = B_T \qquad (3)$$

Subtracting equation (3) from equation (2):

$$(A_0 - B_0) \pm (\Delta a \mp \Delta b) - 2R_T(T) = (A_T - B_T) \qquad (4)$$

from which the time T is calculated as follows:

$$T = \frac{(B_T - B_0) + (A_0 - A_T) \pm (\Delta a \mp \Delta b)}{2R_T} \qquad (5)$$

This equation is relatively simple, involving only two components in the chronometric system. Many processes would involve more than this. Some, of course, might involve a change in only one component.

To solve the equation and obtain the duration T, it is obvious that all the terms on the righthand side of equation (5) would have to be known. The problem, however, is that only A_T, B_T and r_T (the *present* magnitudes and rate) can actually be measured.

There is no way by which the average rate R_T can be determined unless the functional relationship expressed in equation (1) is known. Mathematically this average rate could be expressed as follows:

$$R_T = \frac{\int_o^T r_t\,(dt)}{T} \tag{6}$$

This cannot be calculated, however, unless the equation for rt is known. It is customary simply to assume that $R_T = (r_t)$ as it is measured at present. In other words, it is arbitrarily assumed that the process rate has been constant throughout the period T. This is an unrealistic assumption since, in the real world, there is no such thing as a process rate which cannot be changed.

Furthermore, there is no way by which Δa and Δb can be determined, since there is no way of knowing what extraneous influences may have affected the system in the prehistoric past. The common assumption is that the system has always been a closed system and thus both Δa and Δb are zero, but this assumption is likewise unrealistic since, in the real world, all systems are open systems.

Similarly, there is no way of knowing the initial magnitudes of the parent and daughter components, A_0 and B_0, since no scientific observers were present to measure them at the time. Again, however, it is commonly assumed that there was no daughter component present initially, so that B_0 is zero, and that the initial parent component has been modified only by the amount corresponding to the present daughter component, so that $A_0 = B_T + A_T$.

If all these assumptions are made, then equation (5) becomes:

$$T = \frac{(B_T - 0) + (B_T + A_T - A_T) + (0 + 0)}{2R_T} = \frac{B_T}{R_T} \quad (7)$$

Since both B_T and r_T can be measured, it is thus easily possible to calculate T. However, the resulting date is obviously only as accurate as the assumptions.

To recapitulate, any geochronometric calculation is based on at least the following assumptions:

1. Constant process rate (or known functional variation of process rate).
2. Closed process system (or known external effects on the open system).
3. Initial process components known.

It is significant that not one of these three vital assumptions is provable, or testable, or reasonable, or even possible! Therefore, no geochronometric calculation can possibly be certain.

Since the magnitude of the error in the assumptions obviously will vary quite widely from process to process, one would expect to get a wide range of "apparent ages" from different processes.

In Table I have been listed 76 different processes for calculating the age of various integral parts of the earth and, thus, presumably of the earth itself. All of them yield an age of much less than a billion years, whereas the present standard evolutionary estimate is approximately five billion years.

The presently-favored geochronometric methods (that is, those that give long ages, such as uranium-lead, rubidium-strontium, and potassium-argon) have not been included in the tabulation, nor are they discussed in this paper. However, it has been shown elsewhere (1, 5, 6, 7) that these can also easily be reconciled with young-age concepts.

The most obvious characteristic of the values listed in the table is their extreme variability — all the way from 100 years to 500,000,000 years. This variability, of course, simply reflects the errors in the fundamental uniformitarian assumptions.

Nevertheless, all things considered, it seems that those ages on the low end of the spectrum are likely to be more accurate than those on the high end. This conclusion follows from the obvious fact that: (1) they are less likely to have been affected by initial concentrations or positions other than "zero"; (2) the assumption that the system was a "closed system" is more likely to be valid for a short time than for a long time; (3) the assumption that the process rate was constant is also more likely to be valid for a short time than for a long time.

Thus, it is concluded that the weight of all the scientific evidence favors the view that the earth is quite young, far too young for life and man to have arisen by an evolutionary process. The origin of all things by special creation — already necessitated by many other scientific considerations — is therefore also indicated by chronometric data.

Finally, the reader should note that these conclusions were reached with no reference at all to the testimony of the Bible relative to chronology. It is, therefore, all the more significant that these results correspond closely to the brief chronology of terrestrial and human history given long ago by divine revelation in the Holy Scriptures.

TABLE I
Uniformitarian Estimates — Age of the Earth

(Unless otherwise noted, based on standard assumptions of closed systems, contant rates, and no initial daughter components.)

Process	Indicated Age of Earth	Reference
1. Efflux of Helium-4 into the atmosphere	1,750—175,000 years	1
2. Influx of meteoritic dust from space	too small to calculate	1
3. Influx of radiocarbon to the earth system	5,000—10,000 years	1
4. Development of total human population	less than 4,000 years	1
5. Influx of uranium to the ocean via rivers	10.000—100,000 years	1
6. Influx of sodium to the ocean via rivers	260,000,000 years	1
7. Influx of nickel to the ocean via rivers	9,000 years	1
8. Influx of magnesium to the ocean via rivers	45,000,000 years	1
9. Influx of silicon to the ocean via rivers	8,000 years	1
10. Influx of potassium to the ocean via rivers	11,000,000 years	1
11. Influx of copper to the ocean via rivers	50,000 years	1
12. Influx of gold to the ocean via rivers	560,000 years	1
13. Influx of silver to the ocean via rivers	2,100,000 years	1
14. Influx of mercury to the ocean via rivers	42,000 years	1
15. Influx of lead to the ocean via rivers	2,000 years	1
16. Influx of tin to the ocean via rivers	100,000 years	1
17. Influx of aluminum to the ocean via rivers	100 years	1
18. Influx of carbonate to the ocean via rivers	100,000 years	2
19. Influx of sulphate to the ocean via rivers	10,000,000 years	2
20. Influx of chlorine to the ocean via rivers	164,000,000 years	2
21. Influx of calcium to the ocean via rivers	1,000,000 years	2
22. Leaching of sodium from continents	32,000,000 years	2
23. Leaching of chlorine from continents	1,000,000 years	2
24. Leaching of calcium from continents	12,000,000 years	2
25. Influx of sediment to the ocean via rivers	30,000,000 years	3
26. Erosion of sediment from continents	14,000,000 years	3
27. Decay of earth's magnetic field	10,000 years	4
28. Efflux of oil from traps by fluid pressure	10,000—100,000 years	5
29. Formation of radiogenic lead by neutron capture	too small to measure	5
30. Formation of radiogenic strontium by neutron capture	too small to measure	5
31. Decay of natural remanent paleomagnetism	100,000 years	5
32. Decay of C-14 in pre-Cambrian wood	4,000 years	5
33. Decay of uranium with initial lead	too small to measure	6
34. Decay of potassium with entrapped argon	too small to measure	6
35. Influx of juvenile water to oceans	340,000,000 years	7
36. Influx of magma from mantle to form crust	500,000,000 years	7
37. Growth of active coral reefs	10,000 years	7
38. Growth of oldest living part of biosphere	5,000 years	7
39. Origin of human civilizations	5,000 years	7
40. Formation of river deltas	5,000 years	8
41. Submarine oil seepage into oceans	50,000,000 years	9
42. Decay of natural plutonium	80,000,000 years	10
43. Decay of lines of galaxies	10,000,000 years	11
44. Expanding interstellar gas	60,000,000 years	12

45. Formation of Carbon 14 on meteorites	100,000 years	13
46. Decay of short-period comets	10,000 years	14
47. Decay of long-period comets	1,000,000 years	15
48. Influx of small particles to the sun	83,000 years	15
49. Maximum life of meteor showers	5,000,000 years	15
50. Accumulation of dust on the moon	200,000 years	15
51. Deceleration of earth by tidal friction	500,000,000 years	16
52. Cooling of earth by heat efflux	24,000,000 years	16
53. Accumulation of calcareous ooze on sea floor	5,000,000 years	17
54. Influx of lithium into ocean via rivers	20,000,000 years	18
55. Influx of titanium into ocean via rivers	160 years	18
56. Influx of chromium into ocean via rivers	350 years	18
57. Influx of manganese into ocean via rivers	1,400 years	18
58. Influx of iron into ocean via rivers	140 years	18
59. Influx of cobalt into ocean via rivers	18,000 years	18
60. Influx of zinc into ocean via rivers	180,000 years	18
61. Influx of rubidium into ocean via rivers	270,000 years	18
62. Influx of strontium into ocean via rivers	19,000,000 years	18
63. Influx of bismuth into ocean via rivers	45,000 years	18
64. Influx of thorium into ocean via rivers	350 years	18
65. Influx of antimony into ocean via rivers	350,000 years	18
66. Influx of tungsten into ocean via rivers	1,000 years	18
67. Influx of barium into ocean via rivers	84,000 years	18
68. Influx of molybdenum into ocean via rivers	500,000 years	18
69. Influx of bicarbonate into ocean via rivers	700,000 years	19
70. Escape of high-velocity stars from globular clusters	40,000 years	20
71. Rotation of spiral galaxies	200,000,000 years	20
72. Accumulation of peat in peat bogs	8,000 years	21
73. Accumulation of sediments for sedimentary rocks	20,000 years	21
74. Lithification of sediments to form sedimentary rocks	20,000 years	21
75. Instability of rings of Saturn	1,000,000 years	15
76. Escape of methane from Titan	20,000,000 years	15

REFERENCES

1. Henry M. Morris (Ed.), *Scientific Creationism for Public Schools* (San Diego, Institute for Creation Research, 1974).

2. Dudley J. Whitney, *The Face of the Deep* (New York, Vantage Press, 1955).

3. Stuart E. Nevins, "Evolution: The Ocean Says No.", *Impact Series, ICR Acts and Facts,* Vol. 2, No. 8., October 1973.

4. Thomas G. Barnes, *Origin and Destiny of the Earth's Magnetic Field* (San Diego, Institute for Creation Research, 1973).

5. Melvin A. Cook, *Prehistory and Earth Models* (London, Max Parrish, 1966).

6. Harold S. Slusher, *Critique of Radiometric Dating* (San Diego, Institute for Creation Research, 1973).

7. John C. Whitcomb, Jr., and Henry M. Morris, *The Genesis Flood* (Philadelphia, Presbyterian and Reformed, 1961).

8. Benjamin F. Allen, "The Geologic Age of the Mississippi River", *Creation Research Society Quarterly,* Vol. 9 (September 1972), pp. 96-114.

9. R.D. Wilson *et al.*, "Natural Marine Oil Seepage", *Science* (Vol. 184), May 24, 1974, pp. 857-865.

10. "Natural Plutonium", *Chemical and Engineering News,* September 20, 1971.

11. Halton Arp, "Observational Paradoxes in Extragalactic Astronomy", *Science,* Vol. 174 (December 17, 1971, pp. 1189-1200.

12. V.A. Hughes and D. Routledge, "An Expanding Ring of Interstellar Gas with Center Close to the Sun",

Astronomincal Journal, Vol. 77, No. 3 (1972), pp. 210-214.

13. R.S. Boekl, "Search for Carbon 14 in Tektites", *Journal of Geophysical Research,* Vol. 77, No. 2 (1972), pp. 367-368.

14. Harold S. Slusher, "Some Astronomical Evidences for a Youthful Solar System", *Creation Research Society Quarterly,* Vol. 8 (June 1971), pp. 55-57.

15. Harold S. Slusher, "Age of the Earth from some Astronomical Indicators", Unpublished manuscript.

16. Thomas G. Barnes, "Physics, A Challenge to Geologic Time", *Impact Series 16, ICR Acts and Facts,* Institute for Creation Research, July 1974.

17. Maurice Ewing, J. I. Ewing & M. Talwan, "Sediment Distribution in the Oceans-Mid-Atlantic Ridge", *Bulletin of the Geological Society of America,* Vol. 75 (January 1964, pp. 17-36).

18. *Chemical Oceanography,* Ed. by J.P. Riley and G. Skirrow (New York, Academic Press, Vol. 1, 1965), p. 164. See also Harold Camping, "Let the Oceans Speak", *Creation Research Society Quarterly,* Vol. 11, (June 1974), pp. 39-45.

19. Stuart E. Nevins, "How Old is the Ocean?", Unpublished manuscript.

20. George Mulfinger, "Critique of Stellar Evolution," *Creation Research Society Quarterly,* Vol. 7 (June 1970), pp. 7-24.

21. Henry M. Morris, Unpublished calculations.

MIMICRY*

By Lane P. Lester, Ph.D.
(Extension Scientist, I.C.R.)

As more and more scientists adopt the creation model, there ought to be an increasing emphasis on examining data from a creationist viewpoint and a decreasing emphasis on searching out failures of the evolution model to make true or testable predictions. More than enough of the latter has been done than is needed to convince anyone not hindered by non-scientific considerations, such as ignorance, prejudice or philosophy. Although creationists will continue to call attention to unfounded assumptions and conclusions made by evolutionists, increased effort should now be spent on building a more comprehensive creation model. In addition to re-interpreting the data produced by evolutionists, we hope to see creationists increase their emphasis on carrying out studies specifically designed to test and refine the creation model. Although no one seems to think it was unscientific for Watson and Crick to use the data of others in developing the DNA model, a favorite aspersion cast by evolutionists is the paucity of original creationist research, particularly in biology. This article will follow the trend described above in that, while the data were gathered by others, the interpretation will be aimed toward an increased sophistication of the creation model, rather than a refutation of the evolutionary model.

---

* Impact Series #18 (October 1974)

In 1862, H.W. Bates[1] reported finding in South American butterflies a number of color patterns common to various species which otherwise were distinctly different. From these observations, he developed what is known as the Batesian hypothesis, namely that at least one species (the model), having a particular color pattern, is distasteful to birds, while the other species (the mimics) having a similar pattern benefit in that birds will mistake them for the model and not eat them. Bates believed that the mimics had evolved to look like the model.

The Batesian hypothesis has not been universally accepted, and a number of studies have been made to test its predictions. J. Brower[2,3,4] found that when various distasteful models were placed in a cage of jays, the jays learned to avoid them after tasting a few. The jays then would avoid also any mimics which were introduced to the cage. In order to still objections to his interpretation of the classic case of the peppered moth, H.B.D. Kettlewell[5] filmed the birds capturing moths resting on the tree trunks. Studies such as these

1. H.W. Bates: "Contributions to an insect fauna of the Amazon Valley. Lepidoptera: Heliconidae", *Transactions of the Linnaean Society of London*, Vol. 22, 1862, pages 495-566.
2. J. Brower: "Experimental studies of mimicry in some North American butterflies. I. *Dannaus plexippus* and *Limenitis archippus archippus*," *Evolution*, Vol. 12, 1958, pages 32-47.
3. J. Brower: "Experimental studies of mimicry in some North American butterflies. II. *Battus philenor* and *Papilio troilus, P. polyxenes* and *P. glaucus*," *Evolution*, Vol. 12, 1958, pages 123-136.
4. J. Brower: "Experimental studies of mimicry in some North American butterflies. III. *Danaus gilippus bernice* and *Limenitis archippus floridensis*," *Evolution*, Vol. 12, 1958, pages 273-285.
5. H.B.D. Kettlewell: "Further selection experiments on industrial melanism in the Lepidoptera," *Heredity*, Vol. 10, 1956, pages 287-301.

build confidence that birds are influenced by coloration in their predation on butterflies.

Natural selection is an integral part of the current creation model, in which it serves two purposes. The first purpose is the protection of each species from degeneration by mutation. Mutations are almost always harmful, and one of their consequences is the reduction of their possessor's reproduction potential. By the inability of a mutant to perpetuate itself, the fitness of the species is maintained. The second role played by natural selection is effected when a population encounters a new environment, either through local changes or the movement of the population into a new area. If, within the gene pool of the population, there exist genes that produce characteristics better adapted to the new environment, these genes will, through natural selection, increase in frequency, increasing the fitness of the population as a whole. The illustration drawn from photographs by Sheppard[1] shows a series of models and mimics occurring in African butterflies. Numbers 1-5 are the distasteful models *Bematistes poggei, Danaus chrysippus, Amauris albimaculata, Amauris niavius dominicanus,* and *Amauris niavius niavius,* respectively. Numbers 6-10 are the mimics and are varieties (not races) of the species *Papilio dardanus.* They are *planemoides, trophonius, cenea, hippocoonides* and *hippocoon,* respectively. Each of the models lives in a different geographical area in Africa, thereby producing a different selection pressure on the variety of *P. dardanus* living in that particular area. Thus the genetic variability found in the species *P. dardanus* provides the potential for coping with different environments, in this case the different distasteful models.

What is the source of the variability which enables *P. dardanus* to mimic the distasteful species with which it is sympatric (occupying the same area)? The creationist recognizes

---

1. P.M. Sheppard: "The Evolution of Mimicry; a Problem in Ecology and Genetics," *Cold Spring Harbor Symposia on Quantitative Biology,* Vol. 24, 1959, page 134.

four sources of variability within each baramin (created kind[1]). The first is the genetic diversity placed there by the Creator, both in differences between members of the same kind and heterozygosity (different gene forms controlling the same characteristic) within each individual. A second source of variation would be mutations, failures in reproduction to correctly transmit the genetic information. These failures form a continuum from mistakes in the replication of single genes to the loss or gain of whole chromosomes to changes involving whole sets of chromosomes. Recombination, the rearrangement of genetic material through sexual reproduction, provides a third method for individuals within a population to vary, a simple example being the way a child exhibits a combination of the traits of each parent. Finally, the environment itself produces variation among individuals in a population, which is not inherited such that two individuals with identical genes for body size may differ due to differences in their diet. What evidence is there that might indicate the relative importance of the four sources of variability in the mimicry of *P. dardanus*?

Genetic crosses by Clarke and Sheppard[2] indicated that the various mimicry patterns in *P. DARDANUS* WERE CONTROLLED BY ONE GENE WITH AT LEAST ALLELES (different forms of the same gene). In this case, environment does not seem to be directly producing a significant part of the variation in wing patterns. Recombination between individuals carrying the genes for different mimicry patterns does not produce a third mimicry pattern, but rather the offspring look like only one of the parents, either completely or imperfectly. This leaves us with only two important sources of variation, creation or mutation.

---

1. F.L. Marsh: *Evolution, Creation, and Science,* 2nd edition, Review and Herald Pub. Assn., Washington, D.C., 1947, pages 161-201.
2. C.A. Clarke and P.M. Sheppard: "The Evolution of Later considerations by Clarke and Sheppard[1] alleviated 14, 1960, pages 73-87.

From all we know about mutations occurring today, they are virtually always harmful or, at best, neutral. Of all the variations which appear to be true mutations, one can count on one hand the examples that can be considered as possibly beneficial. Because of this, the creation model predicts that almost never would adaptive variation in the pre-historic past be due to mutations, but rather would be a result of created variability. This raises a problem in the present case, because we are faced with the need for the creation of ten alleles of the same gene. This is no problem as far as the original creation is concerned, but the historical record of the world-wide flood indicates that, of most land animals, only one pair survived. Each individual carries only one pair of each gene, so, at most, only four alleles could have been preserved. There is the possibility of later intragenic recombination, but this is unlikely to produce the ten particular alleles with which we are concerned.

Later considerations by Clarke and Sheppard[1] alleviated this problem in that they showed that the mimicry is controlled not by a single gene, but rather by a supergene, a set of genes located so closely together on the chromosome that they behave as one. With several genes involved, there is no problem as to the required variability being preserved in one pair of individuals. Therefore, it is not necessary to hypothesize favorable mutations, which would run counter to what we know about mutations. So we see that the entire array of variability in the mimicry of *P. dardanus* most probably results from that introduced by the Creator into the baramin of which *P. dardanus* is the whole or part.

We have not by any means exhausted the possibilities for fruitful study in this rich example of genetic variability. For example, a point not raised earlier is the fact that only female *P. dardanus* are mimics. The males are all of a similar, non-mimetic pattern. Furthermore, in the isolated

---

1. C.A. Clarke and P.M. Sheppard: "Super-Genes and Mimicry," *Heredity,* Vol. 14, 1960, pages 175-185.

population on the island of Madagascar, the females look just like males. How do these observations contribute to the creation model? When we see the possibilities within a single species, we get a glimpse of the vast opportunities for developing a comprehensive creationist biology.

MODEL   MIMIC

CLUES REGARDING THE
AGE OF THE UNIVERSE*

By Harold S. Slusher, M.S.
(Chairman, Geoscience Department,
Christian Heritage College)

INTRODUCTION

The age of the universe has been the object of intense study and wide speculation. There are certain fundamental unknowns in the problem that seem impossible of determination. The inability of scientists to describe the origin of things, the explaining of all things in an evolutionary framework, and the feeling that the uniformitarian geologist is right about the age of the earth has led astronomers to push the age of the universe further and further back in time, hiding all the unsolvable problems behind a veil of time. The beginning of the universe, if one follows the "big-bang" model, would be at 15 to 20 billion years ago. If one believes the "continuous-creation" model, though it is in rather ill-repute today, he would say the universe is infinitely old, having no real beginning and, supposedly, no end. The opposing position to these naturalistic views is that the universe was created a short time ago with all the celestial bodies that make up the universe coming into existence simultaneously. This position maintains that there is a Creator, which is basic and original, "which exists on its own." This Creator has caused all the other things (the universe) and the universe will cease to exist if the Creator ceases to maintain it.

The age of the universe is hard to come by, and it is very easy to approach the problem with ready-made answers. However, it is possible to pick up some clues which will tell us whether it is old or young. If the universe is very old (on the order of billions of years), it should show certain signs of age. Let's assume, for the discussion, the "big-bang" model of the origin of the universe, since this version holds the center stage of cosmogony today. From this model we should expect the universe to show its age by certain appearances.

* Impact Series 19 (November 1974)

Let's see if this old age for the stellar system is really the case or if a youthfulness is more the appearance of the stars, galaxies, and dust and gas in space.

The Big-Bang Model

The "big-bang" model starts with all the matter in the universe concentrated in a superdense core with a density of 10^{94}gm/cm^3 and a temperature in excess of 10^{39} degrees absolute. The alleged initial superdense, hot cosmic fluid was a mix of the strongly interacting elementary particles composed of mesons, protons, neutrons, etc., and a smaller proportion of photons and the lighter-weight muons, electronics, neutrinos, etc. Supposedly there was anti-matter present also. At the near instantaneous origin of time by this scheme, there was the annihilation of heavier elementary particles into gamma radiation resulting in a huge fireball. Then the light-weight particles annihilated each other continuing the tremendous fireball. The fireball stage ends as radiation decouples from matter. Quasars and clusters of galaxies condense. And, finally, galaxies and stars form and, it is said, they are still forming today. There you have it — the "big-bang" — tremendously exciting but not a shred of evidence to prove it and much to disprove the notion in the first place!

Using the conventional model of star formation based on the above described "big-bang," as matter expanded outward from the explosion, stars were formed by gravitational collapse of huge, turbulent clouds of hydrogen. The cloud temperature was raised as gravitational potential energy was given up when the cloud collapsed. At some stage thermonuclear reactions were possible because of the high temperatures supposedly generated in the cloud and hydrogen was converted to energy and helium according to processes similar to the proton-proton cycle and the Einstein mass-energy equivalence relation. With the passage of time the various heavier chemical elements should be formed in the stars. As time elapses the chemical composition of the stars and, of course, the interstellar medium (material

254

between the stars) should change considerably, says this model. After 15 to 20 billion years there should be rather tremendous chemical evolution of the universe. This, then, is one of the signs of aging for the universe.

Chemical Composition of The Stellar System

The spectra of a wide variety of stars show atmospheric compositions for them very similar to that of the sun. The similarity in abundances for stars of as widely differing "ages" as a Bo star, which according to the evolutionary scheme formed only a few million years ago, and a red giant or the planetary nebulae, which again by the evolutionary scheme should be among the oldest objects in the galaxy and, hence, 7 or more billion years old, indicate that the interstellar medium has hardly changed at all. There is this serious lack of evidence for chemical evolution. In other words, the Sun; a very "young" Bo star, Tau Scorpii; planetary nebulae; a red giant ϵ Virginis; and many other "normal" stars all have the same chemical composition, within the limits of observational error. This is significant because the alleged ages of these objects cover the whole supposed lifetime of the Milky Way (our Galaxy).

These analyses show that throughout this supposed lifetime of the Galaxy the interstellar matter has had an almost unchanged composition. There are small numbers of exceptional stars, however, that do show a quite different chemical make-up than the other stellar bodies. But the stars that are suspected of being the oldest show abundances of the elements from carbon to barium that are 2 magnitudes smaller than the "younger" stars like the sun. This evidence would seem to indicate that the universe is nothing near its alleged age since it shows practically no change or that the energy generation processes in the stars and their exchange with the interstellar medium are not remotely understood, or both!

Galaxies

The formation of galaxies seems to be an insurmountable difficulty for all the various naturalistic cosmogonies. There

255

are some observations that would lead one to believe that galaxies are of recent origin: (1) Galaxies never appear to occur singly. They are only found in pairs or in larger aggregates. (2) In general, the masses of galaxies that are members of a physically well-isolated group or cluster seem to be smaller than the mass that would be required to bind the galaxies gravitationally. Thus, the groups or clusters of galaxies must be of recent origin or they would have long ago disintegrated the groupings by their tremendous velocities. (3) Some pairs or multiple galaxies are joined by bridges of luminous matter. In a few cases the speeds of the galaxies along the radial direction alone are of the order of several thousand kilometers per second so that these galaxies cannot be gravitationally bound and would separate quite rapidly. They therefore must have originated recently — and it would seem as completely formed galaxies!

Further, a galaxy is an assemblage of stars that cannot rotate as a rigid body; the inner parts revolve in shorter times than the outer, and an enormous difficulty which all theories that propose a large age for the universe encounter is that any spiral arm structure will be wound up into a near circle in one to a few (at most) revolutions of the galaxy — 100 million to 500 million years. The magnetic field which runs through the gases in a spiral arm is not strong enough to give the arm appreciable rigidity, and further the stars in the arms are not coupled to this magnetic field. In other words, the galaxy will wrap itself up in a relatively short time. This analysis does not, of course, determine the age of the universe, but certainly seems to put an upper limit on its age. This limit is far smaller than the time called for by the evolutionist astronomer.

Stellar Energy

Another problem regarding the ages of the stars comes from the mass-luminosity law that has to do with the rate at which stars burn up their energy. Very massive stars burn up their energy so much faster than less massive stars that they cannot last nearly as long. The mass-luminosity law says that the power radiated by a star is proportional approximately to the cube of its mass. It is argued that the very bright and hot stars (O and B) must be of recent origin since if they were born at the alleged beginning of things with their present masses, they should have burnt out long ago. It used to be thought that all the stars were the same age. There is the co-existence of giants (20 x Sun's mass) and dwarfs (1 Sun's mass) in the same clusters. They must have had the same origin from the same source, so how could they differ in age? If we imagine time to run backward from the present instant, it is found by R.A. Lyttleton that a star's mass will build up to infinity in a small fraction of the time that it would take for the hydrogen content of the star to diminish by one-half with time running the ordinary way. If you assume the old age of the galaxy and the manner of evolution advocated by most astronomers (though no one has seen a star go through a lifetime), it is somewhat marginal whether the Galaxy is old enough for a one-solar mass star to have evolved to the white dwarf stage, but it certainly is not old enough for a star of one-half solar mass to have done so. Yet white dwarfs with masses this small are known. How then can the age estimates be correct at all? It would seem that the universe was created with stars of all forms and appearances. Some of the "oldest" galactic clusters appear to have little compositional differences from the youngest ones even though they approach the globular clusters in age. I think this a further clue arguing for a recent origin.

Olbers' Paradox

Suppose that space were uniformly filled with stars. Light emitted by stars in a shell at some distance from an observer at its center would be proportional to the surface area of the shell and its thickness. Of this light a fraction inversely proportional to the square of the radius of the shell would be incident on the observer's telescope, since light intensity drops as the inverse square of the distance. From each spherical shell of some thickness an observer would therefore receive an amount of light proportional to that thickness alone. On adding these effects of the stars along out to infinite distance from the observer, we find that the light received by the observer should have infinite brightness. This infinity arises only because we have not taken into account the self-shadowing of stars. A foreground star will prevent an observer from seeing a star in a more distant shell, provided both stars lie along the same line of sight. When shadowing is taken into account, it is found that the sky should only be as bright as the surface of a typical star, not infinitely bright. Of course, that still is much brighter than the daytime sky; and the night sky is fainter still.

This argument, called Olbers' paradox, cannot be circumvented by introducing curved space. It could be argued that inter-stellar dust might absorb the light. But in an infinitely old universe, dust would come into radioactive equilibrium with stars and would emit as much light as was absorbed. The dust would then either emit as brightly as the stars, or else it would evaporate into a gas that either transmitted light or else again emitted as brightly as the stars.

Unless we wish to suggest that no laws of physics hold for the phenomena there are three possible conclusions:

(1) The density or luminosity of stars at large distances diminishes.

(2) The constants of physics vary with time.

(3) There are large systematic motions of stars that give rise to spectral shifts.

Argument (1) would hold if the universe were very young — stars would only have been radiating a short time.

Argument (2) forms the basis of some cosmologies that postulate that such quantities as the gravitational constant might vary from one epoch to the next. There is great doubt as to whether this is true.

Argument (3) states the expanding universe need not be bright since the radiation from distant galaxies is less intense by the time it reaches the observer as photons reach the observer from points closer to the cosmic horizon, where the red shift of galaxies approximates infinity, their energy and arrival rate approaches zero. However, the expansion of the universe has been challenged considerably on a number of counts. If the red shifts do not represent a real expansion of the universe, then the argument has no meaning. The universe having a dark night sky would then be persuasive evidence of a young age.

Break-up of Star Clusters

There are groupings of stars much smaller than the galaxies called clusters. These clusters are of different types according to their shape, constituents, and distribution in the Galaxy. These star clusters are breaking up due to high velocities of the component stars that overcome the self-gravitation of the cluster. The stars are diverging from a common point so fast that in some cases if their motions were projected backwards to this common point the cluster could have originated only several thousand years ago. Most astronomers believe that the stars and the cluster came into existence at roughly the same time. We have many star clusters that are disintegrating so rapidly that their ages can in no way be on the order of a billion or billions of years. There is no evidence for the formation of stars now. This seems to argue strongly for a young age of the stars and clusters.

CONCLUSIONS

These clues do not exactly determine the actual age of the universe but do put upper limits on the age. These upper limits deny the huge time span necessary for the evolutionist's case. The signs say the universe is young.

EVOLUTION AND THE
POPULATION PROBLEM
By Henry M. Morris, Ph.D.

Few issues today are more emotionally charged than that of population control. Sociological alarmists insist that the growth of human populations must be stopped by whatever means are available. Not only the usual contraception

---

* Impact Series #21, (November 1974)

methods, but such anti-Scriptural practices as abortion and homosexuality, have been promoted as desirable to help attain the goal of zero population growth.

The intellectual and educational establishments today assume it as self-evident that population growth should be halted. Famed anthropologist Margaret Mead, in the lead editorial in a recent issue of *Science*, says:

> "The United Nations Population Conference, which concluded on 31 August in Bucharest, passed by acclamation a World Plan of Action that dramatized the growing global concern for the planet's plight . . . At Bucharest it was affirmed that continuing, unrestricted worldwide population growth can negate any socio-economic gains and fatally imperil the environment.
>
> Those governments for which excessive population growth is detrimental to their national purpose are given a target date of 1985 to provide information and methods for implementing these goals."[1]

So urgent do the experts consider this problem to be that the United Nations Organization actually proclaimed 1974 to be "World Population Year." It can be shown, in fact, that if the population continued to increase at the rate of 2% per year, in less than 700 years there would be one person for every square foot of the earth's surface. Obviously, the present growth rate cannot continue indefinitely.

Nevertheless, many creationists find such arguments unconvincing. Since the evidence for a purposeful Creator of the world and mankind is exceedingly strong, the creationist can be confident that the world God made for man is large enough and productive enough to accomplish His purpose. That purpose will surely have been consummated before the population exceeds its divinely-intended maximum.

---

1. Margaret Mead: "World Population: World Responsibility," *Science*, Vol. 185, September 27, 1974, p. 1113.

According to the Biblical record of creation, immediately after the first man and woman were created, God instructed them as follows:

"Be fruitful and multiply, and replenish (literally, 'fill') the earth, and subdue it." (Genesis 1:28). Essentially the same commandment was given to the handful of survivors of the great Flood (Genesis 9:1). Since man has not yet come anywhere near to *filling* the earth (the total population currently averages less than one person for every 400,000 square feet of land area), even to its maximum feasible "carrying capacity," it seems unlikely that the earth has yet reached its optimal population, as far as the purposes of the Creator are concerned.

Throughout the Scriptures, a large family is considered to be a blessing from the Lord (note Psalm 127:3-5; 128:1-6; etc.), not a problem to society, assuming, of course, that these children are going to be brought up" in the nurture and admonition of the Lord." (Ephesians 6:3).

The historic fact of creation is prophetic of the future fact of consummation. That is, since God created the world for His own good purposes, we are justified in believing He will bring these purposes to completion at the proper time. Many current trends seem to have been predicted in the Bible and, therefore, suggest that the return of Christ and the end of the age may be near at hand. It is, therefore, at least a possibility that the Creator's work of consummation may solve the population problem long before it becomes critical.

Even apart from Biblical revelation, however, there is no good reason for alarm over population. The earth is quite able to support a much larger population than it now possesses. Even with the present status of technology (available water for irrigation, potentially arable land, modern methods of soil treatment and improved crop yields, etc.), authorities estimate that the earth's reasonable "carrying capacity" is about 50 billion people.[1] Future advances in technology (solar

1. Donald Freedman and Bernard Berelson, "The Human Population," *Scientific American,* Vol. 231, September 1974, p. 31.

energy, saline conversion, etc.), may well increase this still more.

Thus, even at the present annual increase of 2%, it will still be 135 years before this maximum population will be reached. However, in order for this population to be achieved, modern technological knowledge will have to be employed worldwide, in the underdeveloped countries as well as in the developed nations. In turn, experience in the latter shows that population growth rates tend to drop off as a society's technology increases. Revelle comments on this as follows:

> "Here we are faced with a paradox: attainment of the earth's maximum carrying capacity for human beings would require a high level of agricultural technology, which in turn calls for a high level of social and economic development. Such developments, however, would be likely to lead to a cessation of population growth long before the maximum carrying capacity is reached."[1]

It is interesting that, for the most part, those intellectuals who are most vocal in support of population limitation (Margaret Mead, for example), are also strong believers in human evolution. This is probably because of their refusal to recognize divine purpose in the world. If there was no creation and therefore no purpose or goal in creation, then neither is there any reason to believe the Creator will accomplish His purpose at the end of history. Just as man's past evolution was dependent solely on random natural processes, so must his future be controlled by naturalism, the only difference being that man now knows how to control those processes — or so he hopes.

One of the strange aberrations of the modern drive for

---

1. Roger Revelle, "Food and Population," *Scientific American*, Vol. 231, September 1974, p. 168. Revelle is Director of the Center for Population Studies at Harvard.
2. *Ibid,* p. 169.

ecological and population controls is the notion that the "environment crisis" is an outgrowth of the Biblical teaching that man should multiply numerically and subdue the earth. Professor Lynn White of U.C.L.A. first popularized the notion that this Genesis mandate has served as man's justification for the exploitation of the earth's resources.[1] Professor Richard Means and others have even proposed that we should all revert to belief in a pantheistic polytheism in order to have a proper regard for all aspects of the world and its living things as they have evolved.[2]

This idea is a prime example of evolutionistic confusion of thinking. Christians who believe and understand the Biblical teachings on this subject have never used Genesis 1:28 in support of the careless use and waste of any of the earth's resources. To the contrary, since everything is presented in Scripture as the product of God's creative design and purpose, Biblical creationist Christians regard themselves, and man in general, as stewards of the creation, accountable directly to the Creator for its proper development and use.

On the other hand, it is very significant that all of the earth's serious environmental problems, even its population crisis, have developed during that one century (say, from about 1860 to the present) when the evolutionary philosophy had replaced creationism in the thinking of practically all of the world's leaders in education, science and industry. The earth has been exploited not because of any divine mandate, but because of social Darwinism, economic and military imperialism, secular materialism, anarchistic individualism, and other such applications of the "struggle and survival" rationale of modern evolutionism.

As far as reverting to pantheism is concerned, this is simply another variant of evolutionism and will inevitably lead to

----

1. Lynn White, "The Historical Roots of our Ecological Crisis," *Science,* Vol. 155, March 10, 1967, pp. 1203-1207.
2. Richard L. Means, "Why Worry about Nature," *Saturday Review,* December 2, 1967.

similar results. The most pantheistic of nations (e.g., India with its Hinduism, China with its Buddhism and Confucianism, etc.) are precisely those nations in which the population/resource ratios have been most severe. It has not been the Judaeo-Christian nations in which population has become a problem, but those with religions of pantheism. How then can pantheism solve the very problems it nurtures?

But there is an even greater inconsistency in evolutionary thinking relative to population. The same population statistics which supposedly presage a serious population problem in the future also indicate a very recent origin of man in the past, and therefore a special divine purpose for man in the future.

To illustrate the problem, assume that the human population increases geometrically. That is, the increase each year is equal to a constant proportion of the population the previous year. This relation can be expresssed algebraically as follows:

$$P_n = P(1+r)^n \qquad (1)$$

in which P is the population at any certain time, r is the proportionate annual increase in population, and P_n is the population n years later. For example, if the present population is 3.5 billion and the planet's permissible population is 50 billion, the number of years before this number will be reached at the present 2% annual increase can be calculated as follows:

$$50 \times 10^9 = 3.5 \times 10^9 \, (1.02)^n$$

from which
$$\log \frac{50}{3.5} = n \log 1.02$$

and
$$n = \frac{1.156}{0.0086} = 135 \text{ years}$$

264

We have already discussed this result, however. Looking toward the past, instead of the future, equation (1) will also indicate how long it would take to produce the present population at 2% growth per year, starting with two people. Thus:

$$3.5 \times 10^9 = 2 \, (1.02)^n$$

from which

$$n = \frac{9 + \log \frac{3.5}{2}}{\log 1.02} = 1075 \quad \text{years}$$

That is, an initial population of only two people, increasing at 2% per year, would become 3.5 billion people in only 1075 years. Since written records go back over 4,000 years, it is obvious that the average growth rate throughout past history has been considerably less than the present rate.

As a matter of interest, we can also use equation (1) to determine what the average growth rate would have to be to generate the present population in 4,000 years. Thus:

$$3.5 \times 10^9 = 2(1+r)^{4000}$$

from which

$$r = (1.75 \times 10^9)^{\frac{1}{4000}} - 1 = \tfrac{1}{2}\%$$

Thus, an average population growth rate of only $(\tfrac{1}{2})\%$ would generate the present world population in only 4000 years. This is only *one-fourth* of the present rate of growth.

Now, although it is obvious that the present rate of growth (2%) could not have prevailed for very long in the past, it does seem unlikely that the long-time growth rate could have averaged significantly less than $(\tfrac{1}{2}\%)$. Very little is known about the world population in earlier times, but everything that *is* known indicates the population has steadily increased throughout recorded history.

Dr. Ansley J. Coale, Director of the Office of Population Research at Princeton University, has discussed the paucity of such data in an important recent study.

"Any numerical description of the development of the human population cannot avoid conjecture, simply because there has never been a census of all the people of the world . . . The earliest date for which the global population can be calculated with an uncertainty of only, say 20 per cent is the middle of the 18th century. The next earliest time for which useful data are available is the beginning of the Christian era, when Rome collected information bearing on the number of people in various parts of the empire."[1]

The usually-accepted estimates of world population for these two dates are, respectively, about 200 million in A.D. 1 and about one billion in A.D. 1800. The first, however, may be vastly in error, since no one really knows the population in most parts of the world at that early date.

For earlier periods than A.D. 1, absolutely *nothing* is *known concerning world populations. It should be emphatically stressed that all* estimates of earlier populations except that recorded in the Bible (namely, that immediately after the great Flood, the world population consisted of eight people) are based solely on evolutionary concepts of human technological development.

"For still earlier periods (than A.D.1) the population must be estimated indirectly from calculations of the number of people who could subsist under the social and technological institutions presumed to prevail at the time. Anthropologists and historians have estimated, for example, that before the introduction of agriculture the world could have supported a hunting and gathering culture of between five and ten million people."[1]

Such guesses are useless, however, because they are based

---

1. A.J. Coale, "The History of the Human Population," *Scientific American,* Vol. 231, September 1974, p. 41.

on a discredited model, that of human evolution. The creation-cataclysm model of earth history fits all the known facts of man's history much better than the evolution model does[1], and it recognizes that man's agriculture and other basic technologies are essentially as old as man himself.

In 1650 the world population has been estimated with perhaps reasonable accuracy to have been 600 million. In 150 years this had grown to approximately one billion. The average rate of increase for this period, therefore, is:

$$r = \left(\frac{10}{6}\right)^{\frac{1}{150}} - 1 = 1/3\%$$

Since this period from 1650 to 1800 antedated the great advances in medicine and technology which have stimulated the more rapid population growth of the 19th and 20th centuries, and also since this is the earliest period of time for which population data are at all reliable, it seems likely that this figure of $(1/3)\%$, rather than the $(\frac{1}{2})\%$ previously calculated, could be used as the norm for population growth throughout most of past history.

In that case, the length of time required for the population to grow from 2 people to one billion people, at $1/3\%$ increase per year is:

$$n = \frac{\log\left(\frac{10^9}{2}\right)}{\log(1.00333)} = 6100 \text{ years}$$

To this should be added the 175 years since 1800. Thus, the most probable date of human origin, based on the known data from population statistics, is about 6,300 years ago.

This figure, of course, is vastly smaller than the usually assumed million-year history of man. Nevertheless it correlates well not only with Biblical chronology but also with other ancient written records as well as with even the usual evolutionary dates for the origin of agriculture, animal

---

2. See *Scientific Creationonism* (San Diego, Creation-Life Publishers, 1974), pp. 171-201.

husbandry, urbanization, metallurgy and other attributes of human civilization.

By artitrary juggling of population models, of course, the evolutionist can manage to come out with any predetermined date he may choose. People should realize, however, that this does require an arbitrary juggling of figures, based solely on the assumptions of human evolution. The actual data of population statistics, interpreted and applied in the most conservative and most probable manner, point to an origin of the human population only several thousands of years ago. The present population could very easily have been attained in only about 6000 years or so, even if the average population growth rate throughout most of history were only one-sixth as much as it is at present. The burden of proof is altogether on evolutionists if they wish to promote some other population model.

The Biblical model for population growth starts with eight people (Noah, his three sons, and their wives) right after the great Flood. The date of the Flood is not certain; the Ussher chronology dates it about 2350 B.C., but possible gaps in the genealogies of Genesis 11 may justify a date as far back as say, about 6000 B.C., with the probabilities favoring the lower limit rather than the upper limit.

Even using the short Ussher chronology, it is quite reasonable, as we have seen, for the population to have grown from 8 people to 3.5 billion people in 4350 years. This growth represents an average annual increase of only 0.44%, or an average doubling time of 152 years. Such figures are quite consistent with all known data of population statistics, especially in light of the fact that the human death rates were very low for many centuries after the Flood, and family sizes quite large. Thus, in all likelihood, the population growth was very substantial in the early centuries, at least as great as it has become in the present century. In turn, this means that the rate may have been much less than 0.44% during the long period in between.

In any case, the conclusion is well justified that the Biblical chronology, even in its most conservative form, fits well into all the known facts of population growth, much more so than does the evolutionary chronology of human history.

For further discussion, with a different analytical approach, on the evolutionary implications of population growth, see *Biblical Cosmology and Modern Science,* by Henry M. Morris, Chapter VI, "World Population and Bible Chronology" (available from I.C.R.)

THE AMINO ACID RACEMIZATION DATING METHOD*
By Duane T. Gish, Ph.D.

At a widely publicized news conference in August of 1972, Dr. Jeffrey Bada of Scripps Institute of Oceanography announced the "discovery" of a new dating method based on the rate of racemization of amino acids in fossil material. He was quoted as saying that he had discovered the basis of the method in 1968, and that it was so obvious and simple he was amazed it hadn't been discovered earlier.

As a matter of fact, the basis of this method had been discovered earlier and had been reported in a series of papers published by Hare, Mitterer and Abelson in 1967, 1968, and 1969 (1-3). Hare and Mitterer actually reported an estimated age for fossil shell material based on amino acid racemization (3).

Amino acids are the "building blocks," or sub-units, of proteins. About 20 different kinds of amino acids are found in proteins. Each amino acid has two chemical groups, an amino group and a carboxyl group, which can form chemical bonds with other amino acids. The amino group of one amino acid can combine with the carboxyl group of a second amino acid to form a "peptide" bond, and its carboxyl group can

* Impact Series # 23, (April 1975)
NOTE: References for this Impact Article are keyed with numbers in parentheses and appear in the list on pages 276-277.

combine with the amino group of a third amino acid, and the chain can thus be extended indefinitely. The amino acids combine with each other like the links of a chain to form a long protein chain. Proteins contain from 50 to several hundred amino acids.

All of the amino acids which occur in proteins, except for glycine, which is the simplest amino acid, have at least one asymmetric carbon atom, and can exist as one of two possible stereoisomers. That is, the chemical groups attached to this particular carbon atom are all different and can be arranged in space in two different ways. When there is only a single asymmetric carbon atom, these two different forms are known as optical isomers. Chemically, there is very little difference between them, but biologically, there is as much difference as night and day. The two forms are known as L-amino acids and D-amino acids, the L and D designating the direction in which solutions of these amino acids rotate plane-polarized light. They are mirror-images of each other, and one cannot be superimposed on the other, just as is true of left and right hands.

All amino acids in proteins (except glycine) are L-amino acids. These amino acids spontaneously tend to slowly change to the D-form. The D-form tends to revert to the L-form, and eventually an equilibrium is obtained, as illustrated here for alanine:

Mixture of equal mounts of the L- and D-forms,

$$
\begin{array}{ccc}
\overset{\text{H}}{\underset{\text{NH}_2}{\text{CH}_3\text{-C-COOH}}} & \rightleftharpoons & \overset{\text{NH}_2}{\underset{\text{H}}{\text{CH}_3\text{-C-COOH}}} \\
\text{L-Alanine} & & \text{D-Alanine}
\end{array}
$$

The process by which an L-amino acid changes into a mixture of the L-and D-forms (or the D-form changes into a mixture of the L- and D-forms) is called racemization. Racemization is complete when equal amounts of the L- and D-forms are obtained. Complicating things somewhat is the fact that some amino acids have two asymmetric carbon atoms and can exist in four different forms, known as distereoisomers. Two of these amino acids, isoleucine and threonine, are commonly found in most proteins. L-Isoleucine racemizes (technically in this case, since there are two asymmetric carbon atoms, the correct term is epimerization rather than racemization) almost exclusively to one form, called D-alloisoleucine. Ordinarily it is difficult to separate an L-amino acid from its D-form, but L-isoleucine is easily separated from D-alloisoleucine. The racemization of L-isoleucine to D-alloisoleucine is, therefore, of special interest in the amino acid racemization dating system.

Since the amino acids in proteins of living things are of the L-form, but upon death of the plant or animal spontaneously tend to change to mixtures of the L- and D-forms, the extent of this racemization process could possibly serve as a dating method. Thus, the older a fossil shell or bone, the greater should be the extent of racemization of the amino acids which are contained in the proteins found in the bone or shell.

Hare and Mitterer (3) measured the rate of racemization of L-isoleucine to D-alloisoleucine in modern shell fragments heated in water at high temperatures and extrapolated these data to lower temperatures in order to estimate the rate of racemization of L-isoleucine in fossil shells to obtain what they believed to be an approximate age for these fossil shells.

Later, Bada and his co-workers (4,5) reported on their application of the amino acid racemization method for the dating of marine sediments. In other studies, Bada and co-workers have applied this method to the dating of fossil bones (6-10), and have even applied amino acid racemization rates to the determination of past temperatures by measuring the extent of racemization in several radiocarbon-dated bones (11). Kvenvolden. Peterson and Brown (12) have measured the rates of amino acid racemization in marine sediments. Wehmiller and Hare (13) have also reported on their application of the rate of racemization of amino acids to the dating of marine sediments.

In the study by Bada and Schroeder (5), the rate of

racemization in marine sediments under laboratory conditions was determined by heating sediments with sea water in sealed ampoules at various temperatures from 100° C to about 150° C over various lengths of time. The material was then hydrolyzed in 6 molar hydrocholoric acid (the material is hydrolyzed to break up the protein into free amino acids), and the extent of conversion of L-isoleucine to D-alloisoleucine was determined. The rates obtained at these temperatures were extrapolated to 2° C and to 4° C, the present average temperatures where the deep-sea cores containing the sediment samples were obtained.

These data are believed to yield the rates at which L-isoleucine was converted to D-alloisoleucine in the sediment through geological time. The extent of conversion of L-isoleucine to D-alloisoleucine in core sediment samples from various depths was then determined and conclusions based on the above rates were used to estimate the ages of the sediments from various core depths.

The studies carried out with bone were similar (6). Fragments of bone recovered from the Arizona desert and believed to be 2-3 years old were sealed in glass ampoules and heated at various temperatures. The fragments were then hydrolyzed in 6M hydrochloric acid and the extent of racemization of L-isoleucine to D-alloisoleucine was determined. Based on the rates at these elevated temperatures (rates at lower temperatures would be too low to measure), the rates at lower temperatures were estimated. From a combination of conclusions based on these rates, the actual extent of racemization of isoleucine in fossil bones, and the estimated average temperatures at which these fossil bones are believed to have existed, ages were calculated. In other work, the rate of racemization of aspartic acid, instead of isoleucine, was used (8-10).

The rate of racemization is highly temperature dependent. The study with bone indicated that an uncertainity of 2° would yield an age with an error of 50%. Additional uncertainties are introduced by the possible contamination of the fossil with free amino acids from the environment, and the possibility of racemization during the acid hydrolysis of the protein in the fossil. The former would reduce the apparent age of the fossil by introducing amino acids from recent material which would have undergone little racemization. Racemization which occurs during acid hydrolysis would, of course, increase the apparent age.

Under most circumstances amino acids undergo little racemization during acid hydrolysis, and thus acid hydrolysis is used routinely for the hydrolysis of protein. Under some circumstances, especially effects caused by the nature of the neighboring amino acids, considerable racemization of individual amino acids can occur during acid hydrolysis (14). This necessary step in the preparation of the sample, that is, the hydrolysis of the protein, can itself, therefore, cause the apparent age to be older than the real age.

In amino acide racemization dating methods the above effects, except for the error introduced by uncertainty of temperature, would not ordinarily cause a serious error in the results. There are several factors, however, which the writer believes render amino acid racemization rates useless as a dating method.

Bada and others working in this field have generally assumed that the only two important factors that have influenced the extent of racemization of amino acids in bone, shell, or sediment have been those of time and temperature. It has either been assumed that the nature of the environment has had little influence on the rate of racemization, or that the effect of the environment on the rate has been empirically determined in laboratory experiments.

For example, in the experiments with bone, the rate of racemization was determined in 2-3 year old bone fragments. These data were then applied to fossil bones believed to be several thousand to several million years old. The assumption was, therefore, obviously made that a recent, non-fossilized bone, dried and sealed in a glass ampoule, provides essentially the same environment furnished by a bone undergoing fossilization while standing in soil percolated by groundwater of varying mineral content and of differing pH (the pH is a measure of acidity or alkalinity). This could hardly be the case.

When a bone is deposited in soil, decomposition of the organic material in the bone begins, and the components in the bone undergo a series of chemical reactions with the material contained in the soil. As the organic material decomposes, it is replaced by the minerals contained in the ground water which seeps through the soil. Furthermore, the inorganic material in the bone undergoes change or replacement by minerals contained in the soil. These changes, being a function of the material found in the soil, are irregular, and are governed by the local environment, including mineral content, pH, and temperature. Fossilization, therefore, can occur at greatly differing rates, under circumstances and by processes that vary considerably. The rates of racemization determined by heating dry, fresh bone fragments sealed in glass ampoules could, and most likely would, differ widely from the rates occurring in a bone undergoing fossilization.

Amino acids are especially sensitive to racemization during either the formation of the peptide bond which links the amino acids together, or the breaking of this bond during the hydrolysis of proteins or of peptides (peptides are fragments of proteins of much shorter length than the intact protein). With many years of experience in the synthesis of peptides and in the determination of the structure of proteins, which involves hydrolysis of the protein, the writer can speak from personal experience.

In peptide synthesis, which involves the chemical combination of amino acids in chains of varying length, racemization during synthesis is an ever present concern. Reviews on peptide synthesis always devote special note to this problem (15). Careful choice of reagents, solvents, temperature, and procedure must be made to minimize racemization.

Amino acids, as noted above, are also sensitive to racemization during the breaking of the peptide bond, or hydrolysis. Furthermore, the rate of racemization during hydrolysis is strongly affected by pH. Ordinarily, hydrolysis in strong acid results in little racemization, especially in the absence of impurities. Hydrolysis of a protein in strong alkai, on the other hand, which requires only a fraction of the time required for acid hydrolysis, results in complete racemization of all of the amino acids. Hydrolysis in weak alkali also results in much higher racemization rates compared to hydrolysis at neutral or acid pH. It has been noted that even the rate of conversion of free L-isoleucine to D-alloisoleucine is greatly accelerated in alkaline solution.

It is thus proposed, as has also been suggested by Wehmiller and Hare (13), that most of the racemization that occurs in amino acids of fossil material occurs during the hydrolysis of the protein. It is further suggested that the rate of this hydrolysis, and especially the rate of racemization, is governed mainly by the chemical environment of the fossil material, especially the pH. Temperature could thus play a minor role in determining the extent of racemization determined by laboratory experiments under some assumed set of conditions which would likely have little or no relevance to the rate of racemization occurring in bone or shell during fossilization.

Local increases in pH, even though temporary, could greatly accelerate the rate of hydrolysis and the rate of racemization, and therefore could result in an apparent age in racemization dating methods vastly older than the real age. Many other chemical effects that occur during fossilization, as yet undetermined, could also have a profound influence on racemization rates. These same general considerations would apply to fossilization that occurs in marine sediments and in other sites.

Bender (16) has recently strongly questioned the reliability of the amino acid racemization dating method. He points out that bones obtained from different levels in the Muleta Cave of Mallorca, when dated by the amino acid racemization method, the radiocarbon method, and by the Thorium-239 method, as reported by Turekian and Bada (7), gave strongly discordant ages. He maintains that amino acide racemization rates are extremely sensitive to the environment. In support, he cited the fact that Kvenvolden and Peterson (17) had found that the extent of amino acid racemization in a supposedly 25,000-year-old bone from a saber-toothed tiger recovered from the LaBrea tar pits hardly exceeded that of modern fresh bone.

Bada (18), in his reply to Bender's criticisms, strongly disagreed that racemization rates in bone are extremely sensitive to the environment. Yet in this same paper, he admits that the results on the material from the tar pits are anomalous, stating (p. 380) that "This type of environment is, however rare and extreme." These results, nonetheless, conclusively demonstrate that the environment can exert a pronounced influence on amino acid racemization rates. The amino acids in these bones were protected from the environmental influences of soil and groundwater, and consequently suffered practically no racemization. It might be expected, on the other hand, that had these bones been subjected to these environmental factors, the rates of racemization of the amino acids contained in these bones would have far exceeded those obtained in laboratory experiments on bone in the absence of such influences.

There is no doubt that proteins in bone and shell and other fossil material undergo hydrolysis and that the amino acids contained in them suffer racemization with increasing age of fossil material. To use rates of racemization as a dating method, however, the entire history of the fossil material would have to be known, including temperature and the entire diagenetic process, especially the chemical environment that contributed to this process, and most especially the pH. Since all of these factors, most of which accelerate racemization rates, cannot be known, it is suggested that the apparent ages obtained by this method are unreliable and, with few exceptions, are much older than the real ages.

References

1. P.E. Hare and R.M. Mitterer, Non-protein Amino Acids in Fossil Shells, **Yearbook Carnegie Institution of Washington**, Vol. 65, p. 362-364 (1967).

2. P. E. Hare and P. H. Abelson, Racemization of Amino Acids in Fossil Shells, ibid, Vol. 66, p. 526-528 (1968).

3. P. E. Hare and R. M. Mitterer, Laboratory Simulation of Amino-Acid Diagenesis in Fossils, **ibid**, Vol. 67, p. 205-208 (1969).

4. J. L. Bada, B. P. Luyendyk, and J. B. Maynard. Marine Sediments: Dating by the Racemization of Amino Acids, **Science**, Vol. 170, p. 730732 (1970).

5. J. L. Bada and R. A. Schroeder, Racemization of Isoleucine in Calcareous Marine Sediments: Kinetics and Mechanism, **Earth and Planetary Science Letters**, Vol. 15, p. 1-11 (1972).

6. J. L. Bada, The Dating of Fossil Bones Using the Racemization of Isoleucine, **ibid**, Vol. 15, p. 223-231 (1972).

7. K. K. Turekian and J. L. Bada, The Dating of Fossil Bones, in **Calibration of Hominoid Evolution**, ed. by W. W. Bishop and J. A. Miller, The Wenner-Gren Foundation for Anthropological Research, New York, 1972, p. 171-185.

8. J. L. Bada and R. Protsch, Racemization reaction of Aspartic Acid and Its Use in Dating Fossil Bones, **Proceedings National Academy of Science**, Vol. 70, p. 1331-1334 (1973).

9. J. L. Bada, K. A. Kvenvolden, and E. Peterson, Racemization of Amino Acids in Bones. **Nature**, Vol. 245, p. 308-310 (1973).

10. J. L. Bada, R. A. Schroeder, and G. F. Carter, New Evidence for the Antiquity of Man in North America Deduced from Aspartic Acid Racemization, **Science**, Vol. 184, p. 791-793 (1974).

11. R. A. Schroeder and J. L. Bada, Glacial-Postglacial Temperature Difference Deduced from Aspartic Acid Racemization in Fossil Bones, **ibid**, Vol. 182, p. 479-482 (1973).

12. K. A. Kvenvolden, E. Peterson, and F. S. Brown, Racemization of Amino Acids in Sediments from Saanich Inlet, British Columbia, **ibid.**, Vol. 169, p. 1079 (1970).

13. J. Wehmiller and P. E. Hare, Racemization of Amino Acids in Marine Sediments, **ibid.**, Vol. 173, p. 907-917 (1971).

14. J. M. Manning and S. Moore, Determination of D- and L-Amino Acids by Ion Exchange Chromatography as L-D and L-

L Dipeptides. **Journal of Biological Chemistry**, Vol. 243, p. 5591-5597 (1968).

15. See for example Duane T. Gish, Peptide Synthesis, in **Protein Sequence Determination**, ed. S. B. Needleman, Springer-Verlag, New York, 1970; **Peptides**, ed. L. Zervas, Pergamon Press, New York, 1966, p. 121-155; E. Schroder and K. Lubke, **The Peptides, Vol. I, Methods of Peptide Synthesis**, Acadmic Press, New York, 1965, p. 323-325; M. Bodanszky and M. A. Ondetti, **Peptide Synthesis**, Interscience Publishers, New York, 1966, p. 18-19.

16. M. L. Bender, Reliability of Amino Acid Racemization Dating and Paleotemperature Analysis on Bones, **Nature**, Vol. 252, p. 378-379 (1974).

17. K. A. Kvenvolden and E. Peterson, Amino Acids in Late Pleistocene Bone from Rancho LaBrea California, **Geological Society of America Abstracts with Programs**, 1973, p. 704 (see also Ref. 9).

18. J. L. Bada, Dr. Bada Replies, **Nature**, Vol. 252, p. 379-381 (1974).

SOME RECENT DEVELOPMENTS
HAVING TO DO WITH TIME*

Harold S. Slusher, M.S.

This paper discusses some recent data, observations, and developments that have significance regarding the age of things. If Earth and the Universe are quite young, the implications are tremendous, since all evolutionary theories are meaningless without immense time.

The "Missing" Mass

Galaxies and clusters of galaxies are objects of much concerted study today. Galaxies in clusters are bound together by gravitational forces and, thus, provide a sort of laboratory for observations of interactions of incredible amounts of

---

*Impact Series #27, (September 1975)

matter. Galaxies never appear to occur singly. They are only found in pairs or in larger aggregates. Some pairs or multiple galaxies are joined by bridges of luminous matter. In a few cases the velocities of the galaxies along the radial direction alone are of the order of many thousand kilometers per second so that it is not likely that these galaxies are gravitationally bound. They would, therefore, seem to have originated quite recently. In general, the mass of galaxies that are members of a physically well isolated group or cluster seem to be smaller than the mass that would be required to bind the galaxies gravitationally.

A galaxy is a collection of some hundred billion stars held together by gravity. Our galaxy, the Milky Way, is a member of a cluster consisting of about twenty galaxies in all, called the Local Group. The Local Group is very small compared to most of the hundreds of clusters thus far observed and catalogued. An average cluster has one or two hundred members, while the largest contains several thousand galaxies.

The nearest cluster outside of the Local Group is thought to be about 500 billion kilometers away in Euclidean space. The most distant known clusters lie around 200 times farther away, at the very edge of the observable universe. The distances are obtained by rather indirect methods based on assumptions difficult to prove. This should always be kept in mind when distances of astronomical objects are given. Two of the richest clusters, one in the direction of the constellation Virgo and one in Coma Berenices, are at relatively small distances and have been studied carefully.

For the galaxies studied in the Coma cluster, the average velocity of recession is about 7000 kilometers per second. This is determined from studies of the red-shifts of the light from these galaxies, which is considered to indicate a radial motion toward or away from the observer, assuming the redshift of the starlight is an actual Doppler effect. Each individual galaxy ordinarily has some smaller, random motion inside the cluster. This speed is around several hundred kilometers per second with reference to the neighbor galaxies. Thus, the members should eventually escape from the Coma cluster and wander off into intergalactic space if there is not enough force to keep them in the cluster. If the Universe is at least 4.5 billion years old, the random motions of the galaxies should have long ago disrupted the cluster and the galaxies could not possibly be as close together as they are now. As a matter of fact, there should be no cluster at all. The force that would counteract this escape tendency is the gravitational force of the mass of the cluster on the galaxy. The gravitational force of the matter in the earth pulls back a baseball thrown from its surface. In the Coma cluster, the random motions of the galaxies would have to be balanced by the gravitational attraction of the matter in the cluster if the cluster is to stay together. This random motion of the galaxies in the cluster is called the velocity dispersion.

The velocity dispersion of the cluster can be calculated from the measured red-shifts of the galaxies. The mass of a galaxy is related to its brightness. When the total mass of all the galaxies in the cluster is determined, the gravitational force can be calculated and compared with the observed velocity dispersion. The result has surprised and astonished astronomers no end. In the Coma cluster the mass is too little to counter-balance the velocity dispersion, by a factor of seven. In other words, for every 7 kilograms of mass necessary to hold the cluster together, only one kilogram can be accounted for. This is not a trivial matter. There is only fourteen percent of the matter in the cluster that should be there in order for the cluster to stay together. Astronomers have looked high and low for this "missing mass' but it is nowhere to be found. Things get worse in this search when other clusters than the Coma cluster are studied: from two to ten times the needed mass is missing.

Some have thought that the "missing mass" is located in intergalactic space. To be detected, the matter would have to emit some form of electromagnetic radiation such as x-rays, visible light, or radio waves. The background x-radiation that is incident on the earth's atmosphere can be explained by other means than the presence of a diffuse intergalactic material permeating space and emitting x-rays. If cold matter exists between the galaxies, radio waves might be emitted and the radio astronomer could detect this. However, this has not been observed, and if small quantities of cold matter did escape detection they would be far too small in an amount to keep the clusters together. A hot gas would emit x-rays. Certainly x-radiation has been observed associated with some galaxies. But the presence of the radiation has been explained rather well in terms not involving an intergalactic medium. A slightly warm material would be hard to detect since the radiation would be in the ultraviolet range of wavelengths, which are mainly strained out by our atmosphere. However, using detection equipment in high-altitude rockets, balloons, and satellites there has been no indication of a slightly warm gas between the galaxies. The "missing mass" is not in the form of a diffuse gas in intergalactic space.

Further conditions have been placed on this "missing mass." A study of the dynamics of the dispersion of the galaxies would indicate that the matter cannot be postulated as existing in one very massive object that does not have luminosity. The matter has to be distributed as a common constituent of intergalactic space. If someone says that alleged "black holes" (which if they exist at all would have such a tremendously large gravitational pull that light cannot escape from their surfaces and, thus, they would be invisible) account for this matter they would have to suppose these "black holes" to be as commonly located as galaxies. As Margon[1] points out, there would have to be hundreds or thousands of them. There is no evidence for this situation. Again Margon[2] says the same objection applies to "dead" galaxies (non-luminous) or the large number of cool stars.

The obvious conclusion seems to be that the "missing mass" is not really missing since probably it wasn't there to

---

1. Margon, Bruce. *The Missing Mass!,* Mercury, January/February 1975, p. 6.
2. Ibid, p.6.

start with. The Universe could be quite young, and other lines of evidence strongly indicate this. The break-up time for these clusters (the time for dispersion of the galaxies so that there are no clusters) is far, far less than the alleged evolutionary age of the Universe. This means that the clusters, since they have not been destroyed, are young, as well as the galaxies that form them. These galaxies contain stars that are alleged by the evolutionists to be the oldest objects in the Universe (nine to twenty billion years old in the evolutionary scheme of things). This rapid break-up of the clusters coupled with their presence still in the Universe would indicate that these allegedly old stars are not old at all. The Coma cluster could not be younger than the Milky Way. So if the cluster is young, the galaxy is young and the objects within the galaxy are young. The breakup times of clusters are on the order of just a few millions of years at most. So the present existence of clusters argues that the Universe has not reached anywhere near that age, even much less the age demanded by the evolutionists.

It has been noted that the motions of the clusters look like those of bound systems which are not breaking up. If that is so, then the clusters would certainly be young, not having reached a stage where they are showing a looseness of organization indicative of much age.

To avoid the conclusions regarding time which are at the heart of evolutionary hypotheses, astronomers go to great lengths in inventing explanations regarding the "missing mass." Margon[1] suggests that "we have reached an impasse, almost to the point Thomas Kuhn has called a scientific revolution." Apparently, unless the experimental data are blatantly in error, it is inevitable that some cherished astronomical or physical principle must fall. It would seem that the axe should fall upon the supposed aeons-long time age that is assigned a priori to the Universe, the Solar System, and Earth, for this concept of huge quantities of time

---

1.   Ibid, p.6

leads to contradictory and illogical position in certain aspects of astrophysics.

The Variable "Constants"

Radioactivity was discovered in the late 1800's. It was stated early that no external effects could change the disintegration constants of radioactive elements. Radioactive elements are those chemical elements that decay into daughter elements by emission or absorption of energy and particles in the nuclei of their atoms. On the basis of experimental evidence in those early years of study of these elements it was concluded that radioactive decay rates do not change, that these rates cannot be affected by external means, and that only the nuclei of the atoms of these radioactive elements were involved in the decay processes.

The geologists immediately seized upon these decay processes as constituting clocks to determine when geological events occurred and the age of the earth. If uranium decays into lead at a constant rate and if a rock from some mountain contains uranium and lead, the age of the rock and the mountain, perhaps, may be found by simply calculating the time to obtain the lead by decay from the uranium. It is more involved, of course, but that is the essence of the method by which the radiometric "clocks" work.

Among a number of requirements for a radioactive element and its daughter product to constitute a "clock" for geological events is the necessity that the "clock" run without variation. Well, evolutionist geologists have long ignored the evidence of variability in the radii of pleochroic haloes, which shows that the decay rates are not constant and would, thus, deny that some radioactive elements such as uranium could be clocks. But now there is excellent laboratory evidence that external influences can change the decay rates.[1] Fourteen different radionuclides have had their decay properties changed by effects such as pressure,

---

1. Emery, G.T. *Perturbations of Nuclear Decay Rates,* Ann. Review Nucl. Science, Vol. 22 (1972).

temperature, electric and magnetic fields, stress in monomolecular layers, etc.[1]

Dudley[2] has proposed, "Rather than assuming that radioactivity is a series of (spontaneous) unrelated events occurring without prior cause, a theoretical approach was developed which translates the 'neutrino sea' concept of astrophysics and cosmology to nuclear physics. This postulates a radioactive atom to be a 'linear resonant system, subject to parametric excitation.' " Thus, the decay constant used in the equations for obtaining ages of geological events becomes a variable dependent on the energy state of all the atom and not just the nucleus. Half-lives would not be constants. The decay constant would instead be a stability index of the element.

If this is the case, as the evidence seems to point, then the forces and the tremendous amounts of energy involved in some processes and happenings in the universe could strongly alter the "decay" rates. The alleged radiometric "clocks" are then not really useable as age determiners at all. Actually though, they have been used as window-dressing, mainly by the geologists, since the preconceived views of theoretical historical geology of evolutionary persuasion set the ages of earth history before even radioactivity was discovered.

How Long to Form an Interstellar Grain?

The space between the stars is composed of atoms, molecules and grains of matter. The stars allegedly formed by gravitational collapse from clouds of this material. It is rather baffling how an interstellar grain of matter forms since the density of matter in interstellar space is so low.

Consider the growth rate of a grain which starts with some radius that, of course, will change with time. If this grain forms in space by the sticking of interstellar atoms and molecules to this nucleus as they impinge on it at some speed, the growth rate can be calculated. Using the most favorable

---

1. Dudley, H.C. *Radioactivity Re-Examined,* Chemical and Engineering News, April 7, 1975, p. 2.
2. Ibid, p.2.

conditions and the maximum possible sticking ability for grains Harwit[1] has determined a growth rate of $(10)^{22}$ centimeters per second (or one-ten-thousand-billion-billionth centimeter per second). To reach a size of just a hundred-thousandth of a centimeter in radius under these most favorable conditions it would take about three billion years. Using more likely values for sticking ability of particles, it would take times greater than the alleged age of the galaxy — more than twenty billion years. Of course, this supposes the grain will form, though this seems impossible, since the hydrogen that would be deposited on the grain would ordinarily evaporate right back off very rapidly. Sputtering by fast moving protons can easily jar loose the atoms of the surface of the grain even after they become attached. The formation of molecules poses just as great a difficulty as the formation of dust grains. It is easy to destroy them but very difficult, if not impossible, to form them in interstellar space.

If it takes as long to form such a simple object as an interstellar grain as the calculations indicate under the most hopeful of conditions (that do not actually exist at all), how can the huge ages for the stars and galaxies have any credibility and be taken seriously? Effects such as evaporation, sputtering, and vapor pressure would seem to destroy any grains that might form.

Conclusions

The myth that unlimited time is available in which the evolutionists may frame their schemes to explain things has been around for quite a while now. However, the scientific evidence continues to accumulate labelling the huge ages of the universe, the solar system, and the earth as a fable — not a conclusion reached by an adherence to scientific proof.

1. Harwit, M. *Astrophysical Concepts,* New York (John Wiley and Sons, Inc., 1973) p. 394.

LANGUAGE, CREATION AND THE INNER MAN*
Henry M. Morris, Ph.D.

The Uniqueness of Human Speech

Probably the most important physical ability distinguishing man from apes and other animals is his remarkable capacity of language. The ability to communicate with others of his own kind in abstract, symbolic speech is unique to man, and the evolutionist has never been able to bridge the tremendous gulf between this ability and the grunts and barks and chatterings of animals.

Some researchers have, of course, made extravagant claims as to the potentiality of teaching chimpanzees to speak, for example, or have developed highly imaginative speculations as to how animal noises may have evolved into human languages. Such notions are, however, not based on real scientific observation or evidence.

Man's brain is quite different from that of chimpanzees, especially in that portion which controls speech, Isaac Asimov notes this:

> "Once speech is possible, human beings can communicate thoughts and receive them; they can consult, teach, pool information . . . Once speech was developed then, the evolution of intelligence proceeded rapidly. The chimpanzee lacks Broca's convolution, but it may have the germs of communication, which could develop rapidly if it ever evolved that part of the brain."[1]

Unfortunately, one does not acquire a brain capable of abstract thought and intelligent speech (even if "Broca's convolution" is really all the brain needs to do this) merely by allowing "evolution" to create one because it might be helpful. Two top authorities on supposed human evolution, David

---

1. Isaac Asimov, "Chimps Tell Us About Evolution," *Science Digest,* November 1974, p. 89.

* Impact Series #28, (October 1975)

Pilbeam and Stephen Gould, anthropologist at Yale and geologist at Harvard, respectively, have pointed out that man's brain shape is not a mere scaled-up replica of the ape's, but is qualitatively distinct in critical ways.

> "*Homo sapiens* provides the outstanding exception to this trend among primates, for we have evolved a relatively large brain and small face, in opposition to functional expectations at our size . .
>
> . *Australopithecus africanus* has a rounded braincase because it is a relatively small animal; *Homo sapiens* displays this feature because we have evolved a large brain and circumvented the expectations of negative allometry. The resemblance is fortuitous; it offers no evidence of genetic similarity."[1]

Though creationists do not share the credulous faith of the evolutionists that man's unique brain has simply "evolved," they do concur with the inference that this uniqueness has placed an unbridgeable gap between man and any of the higher animals.

Evolutionist George Gaylord Simpson has admitted that there is little possibility of tracing an evolutionary connection between animals and men as far as language is concerned.

> "Human language is absolutely distinct from any system of communication in other animals . . . It is still possible, but it is unlikely, that we will ever know just when and how our ancestors began to speak.[2]

Since Simpson is a biologist and paleontologist, rather than a linguistics scientist, certain of the younger speculative linguists may feel that he was speaking out of his field and that it may yet be possible to trace such an evolutionary

---

1. David Pilbeam and Stephen Jay Gould, "Size and Scaling in Human Evolution," *Science,* Vol. 186, December 6, 1974, pp. 899, 900.
2. George Gaylord Simpson, "The Biological Nature of man," *Science,* Vol. 152, April 22, 1966, pp. 476, 477.

origin of human language. However, most modern linguistic specialists today acknowledge Dr. Noam Chomsky, Professor of Linguistics at Massachusetts Institute of Technology, to be the "world's foremost linguist" (a term recently applied to him by Dr. John Oller, Chairman of the University of New Mexico Department of Linguistics, while discussing this subject with the writer), and Dr. Chomsky says:

> "Human language appears to be a unique phenomenon, without significant analogue in the animal world."[1]

As to whether the gap between animal noises and human language was ever bridged by evolution, Dr. Chomsky states:

> "There is no reason to suppose that the 'gaps' are bridgeable. There is no more of a basis for assuming an evolutionary development of 'higher' from 'lower' stages, in this case, than there is for assuming an evolutionary development from breathing to walking."[2]

In other words there is no comparison at all!

The Underlying Unity of Human Language

Chomsky and many other modern linguists have found, not only that there is no connection between animal sounds and human speech, but also that there is a deep commonality between the basic thought patterns of all men, regardless of how diverse their individual languages may be. That is, there is a fundamental connection between all human languages, but no connection at all between human language and animal "language."

In an important recent study, Dr. Gunther S. Stent (Professor of Molecular Biology at the University of California in Berkeley), has drawn the further inference from Chomsky's studies that man has a certain fundamental being which is incapable of being reached by scientific analysis.

---

1. Noam Chomsky, *Language and Mind,* Harcourt, Brace, Jovanovich, Inc., New York, 1972, p. 67.
2. Ibid, p. 68.

> "Chomsky holds that the grammar of a language
> is a system of transformational rules that deter-
> mines a certain pairing of sound and meaning. It
> consists of a syntactic component, a semantic
> component, and a phonological component. The
> surface structure contains the information rele-
> vant to the phonological component, whereas the
> deep structure contains the information relevant
> to the semantic component, and the syntactic com-
> ponent pairs surface and deep structures."[1]

Chomsky and his associates have developed what they call
structural linguistics, with its concepts of the "deep"
structure and the "surface" structure. The latter involves the
ordinary phenomena of different languages and their translation one into the other. The mere fact that people are able to
learn other languages is itself evidence of the uniqueness and
fundamental unity of the human race. No such possibility exists as between man and animals.

The "deep structure" is the basic self-conscious thought
structure of the man himself, and his intuitive formulation of
discrete thoughts and chains of reasoning. The vocal sounds
which he uses to transmit his thoughts to others may vary
widely from tribe to tribe, but the fundamental thought-
system is there and is universal among mankind.

> "The semantic component has remained invariant
> and is, therefore, the 'universal' aspect of the un-
> iversal grammar, which all natural languages em-
> body. And this presumed constancy through time
> of the universal grammar cannot be attributable
> to any cause other than an innate, hereditary
> aspect of the mind. Hence, the general aim of
> structural linguistics is to discover this universal
> grammar."[2]

Presumably, if this "universal grammar" could ever be

---

1. Gunther S. Stent, "Limits to the Scientific Understanding
   of Man," *Science,* Vol. 187, March 21, 1975, p. 1054.
2. Ibid, p. 68.

ascertained, it would supply the key to man's original language — perhaps even its phonology and syntactical structure, as well as its semantic content.

The Unique Origin of Man

Evolutionists, as well as creationists, have in recent years come to believe in the monophyletic origin of all the tribes and races of mankind. Most of the earlier evolutionists, however, believed in man's polyphyletic origin, thinking that each of the major "races" had evolved independently from a different hominid line. This idea, of course, easily leads to racism, the belief that one race is innately superior to another race. That is, if each race has a long, independent evolutionary history, slowly developing its distinctive character by the lengthy process of random mutation and natural selection, then it is all but certain that there has been a differential rate of evolution as between the different races, with some evolving to higher levels than others. That such racist beliefs were held by all nineteenth-century evolutionist scientists (Darwin and Huxley included) has been thoroughly documented.[1]

Modern evolutionists, however, repudiate racism, which has become sociologically unpopular in the twentieth century. They now agree (with the Bible) that "God hath made of one blood all nations of men for to dwell on all the face of the earth" (Acts 17:26). Although they are now in practically complete agreement that all present groups of men came originally from one single population of ancestral men, they are currently in complete disarray as to exactly what that lineage may have been. The Australopithecines and the Homo erectus group of supposed hominids are no longer considered man's progenitors, since fossils of true man have been found which are dated earlier than any of these.

"Theorists of human evolution, who may not yet have fully assessed the impact of Leakey's 1972

---

1. John S. Haller, Jr., *Outcasts from Evolution,* University of Illinois Press, Urbana, 1971, 28 pp.

discovery, now face an even knottier problem. If members of the human genus flourished as long as four million years ago, then the time when the genus first branched from its ancestral primate stem would necessarily be even earlier. As Taieb and Johanson assert, 'All previous theories of the origin of the lineage which leads to modern man must now be totally revised.' "[1]

Maurice Tieg, of the French National Center for Scientific Research, and D. Carl Johanson, of Case Western Reserve University, have thus (with their discoveries of three fossil human jaws in Ethiopia) demonstrated that man is "older" than his supposed "ancestors." Creationists do not accept the date of four million years as the age of these jaws, of course, but merely note that the "relative" stratigraphic date has to be "older" than the stratigraphic date of Pithecanthropus, Zinjanthropus, Australopithecus, etc., as accepted by evolutionists.

Not only do these discoveries indicate that man's unique bodily structure has (so far as actual fossil evidence goes) always been distinct from that of apes, but also that he has always had his unique capacity of communication.

"There is even the possibility, Johanson says, that he had 'some kind of social cooperation and some sort of communication system.' "[2]

Back to the very beginning of human existence, therefore, in so far as it can be elucidated by archaeological excavation and anthropological analysis, man has always been man, culturally and linguistically as well as physically and mentally.

The Origin of the Different Languages

Consider this ancestral human population, whenever and however it first appeared — whether several million years

---

1. *Scientific American,* Volume 231, December, 1974, p. 64. (news items).
2. "Ethiopia Yields Oldest Human Fossils," *Science News, Vol. 106, November 2, 1974, p. 276.*

ago, newly arrived by an unknown evolutionary process from unknown evolutionary ancestors, or else several thousand years ago, representing the descendants of the handful of survivors of the great Flood. In either case, they must have constituted an originally coherent body of true men, all with the same language and culture.

The question is, how did the different languages ever develop? If the "semantic component" of language, as Chomsky puts it, is still the same for all men, how did the "phonologic component" ever become so diverse and variegated? Gradual changes are understandable (as in the gradual accretion of Latin words, Greek words, Germanic words, etc. to produce the modern English language), but how could such vastly different linguistic systems as the Indo-European languages, the agglutinative languages of the Africans, and the tonal languages of the Mongols ever develop from a single ancestral language?

Furthermore, the more ancient languages seem to be the more complex languages, as do the languages of the more apparently "primitive" tribes living today.

> "Even the peoples with least complex cultures have highly sophisticated languages, with complex grammar and large vocabularies, capable of naming and discussing anything that occurs in the sphere occupied by their speakers. The oldest language that can reasonably be reconstructed is already modern, sophisticated, complete from an evolutionary point of view."[1]

Not only so, but the history of any given language, rather than representing an increasingly complex structure as the structure of its users supposedly evolved into higher levels of complexity, seems instead to record an inevitable decline in complexity.

---

1. George Gaylord Simpson, "The Biological Nature of man," *Science,* Vol. 152, April 22, 1966, p. 477.

> "The evolution of language, at least within the historical period, is a story of progressive simplification."[1]

It seems necessary to assume either of two alternatives in order to explain these strange linguistic phenomena:

(1) An original population of men, at least 100,000 years ago and possibly up to four million years ago, with a highly complex language and culture. This original population (its origin completely unknown and apparently inexplicable on evolutionary grounds) somehow broke up into a number of separate populations, each then developing independently of the others for such a very long time that its extreme peculiarities of linguistic phonology and syntax could emerge as a deteriorative remnant of the ancestral language.

(2) An original population of men several thousand years ago (as dated not only by the Bible but also from the known beginnings of civilization in Sumeria, Egypt and other ancient nations). This population once used the postulated complex common ancestral language, but somehow broke up into the assumed smaller populations. However, this break-up was not a slow evolutionary process over hundreds of thousands of years, but rather was accomplished in some kind of traumatic separation, accomplished essentially instantaneously by a sudden transmutation of the one phonology into a number of distinctively and uniquely different phonologies.

The Dilemma of the Evolutionary Linguist

Note that neither of these alternatives is amenable to an evolutionary interpretation, since neither accounts for the original ancestral complex language and since both involve a subsequent deterioration (rather than evolution) of language

---

1. Albert C. Baugh, *A History of the English Language,* Appleton-Century-Crafts, Inc., New York, 1957, p. 10.

complexity. The former, however, is favored by evolutionists because the great time spans involved seem more suitable to a uniformitarian philosophy, and because the latter clearly involves catastrophic, even supernaturalistic, intervention in human history.

The long-time span interpretation, however, necessarily involves the evolution model once again in its racist connotations. For how are populations going to be separated long enough to develop such drastically different languages without also developing drastically different physical features and mental abilities? As long as they were together, or even closely enough associated to be in communication with each other (and such association would surely be to their mutual advantage), they would retain an essentially common language, would intermarry, and thus retain common physical and mental characteristics as well.

Yet the languages and cultures and physical features are, indeed, quite different, and have been since the dawn of recorded history! A genetics professor at Stanford says:

> "When we look at the main divisions of mankind, we find many differences that are visible to the unaided eye . . . It is highly likely that all these differences are determined genetically, but they are not determined in any simple way. For example, where skin color is concerned there are at least four gene differences that contribute to variations in pigmentation."[1]

If such an apparently simple and obvious difference as skin color is determined in such a complex fashion, and if all such gene factors have developed originally by mutation (as evolutionists believe), then a very long period of racial segregation must have been necessary.

---

1. L. L. Cavalli-Sforza, "The Genetics of Human Populations," *Scientific America,* Vol. 231, September, 1974, p. 85.

"The simplest interpretation of these conclusions today would envision a relatively small group starting to spread not long after modern man appeared. With the spreading, groups became separated and isolated. Racial differentiation followed. Fifty thousand years or so is a short time in evolutionary terms, and this may help to explain why, genetically speaking, human races show relatively small differences."[1]

Furthermore, if obvious differences such as skin color and facial morphology can arise by mutation and selection in 50,000 years, then surely subtle differences in mental abilities could also arise in such a time, and these would have considerably more selection value for survival than would skin pigmentation. The inferences for racism are again very obvious.

As a matter of fact, as creationists have repeatedly pointed out, there is no empirical evidence of mutations that confer any kind of "beneficial" effect in the natural environment upon either the individuals or populations that experience them. The various physical changes (skin color, etc.) can be much more easily explained as *created* genetic factors that were latent in the human genetic system ever since the creation but which could become openly expressed only in a small population being forced to reproduce by inbreeding after segregation from its ancestral population.

If the initial population were somehow forced to break up into small reproductively isolated populations, only a relatively small number of generations would be required to allow distinctive physical characteristics (all representing created genetic factors already present, though latent, in the

---

1. Ibid, p. 89. From what has been noted, however, it is obvious that even the author's 50,000 year estimate is much too small in the evolutionary framework. Even this, however, would surely involve significant racist connotations.

larger population) to become manifest and fixed in different combinations in the different tribal clans. The enforced segregation would most expeditiously be arranged by the postulated sudden transmutation of the ancestral phonology (spoken language) into a number of uniquely different phonologies. No other traumatic changes would be necessary, as the physical changes would easily and quickly develop genetically from the linguistic segregation.

Furthermore, no basic change in human nature would be involved. All would still "think" in the same way and would still be, distinctively, men. The "deep structure" of human consciousness and communicative ability would be unaffected even by a traumatic change in the "surface structure." Dr. Stent makes a fascinating comment in this connection.

> "Hence it is merely the phonological component that has become greatly differentiated during the course of human history, *or at least since the construction of the Tower of Babel.*" (emphasis ours)[1]

The Creationist Answer

Whether or not Dr. Stent believes in the confusion of tongues at Babel as a real event of history, it is at least symbolic to him of the fact that there must have at one time been some such division, and that no normal evolutionary development could accomplish it. To the creationist, of course, Babel is not only symbolic but actual. The supernatural confusion of phonologies, with its resultant tribal dispersions throughout the world and its logical genetic consequences in the rapid emergence of distinctive tribal (not "racial" — the Bible knows nothing of the racial categories of evolutionary biology) characteristics, fits all the known facts of philology, ethnology and archaeology beautifully.

---

1. Gunther S. Stent, "Limits to the Scientific Understanding of Man," *Science,* Vol. 187, March 21, 1975, p. 1054.

Furthermore, man's universal semantic consciousness is at once an attestation of his uniqueness in the living world and of the inability of naturalistic science to comprehend this deep inner nature of man. Dr. Stent himself has recognized this:

> "No matter how deeply we probe into the visual pathway, in the end we need to posit an 'inner man' who transforms the visual image into a precept. And as far as linguistics is concerned, the analysis of language appears to be heading for the same conceptual impasse as does the analysis of vision."[1]

Chomsky and the other structural linguists have found it necessary to postulate a "deep structure" of self-consciousness, but they do not know where this comes from nor how it functions. Materialistic science can explain much with its chemical and physical equations, but it founders when it reaches the domain of "soul" and "spirit." Stent continues in this vein:

> "That is to say, for man the concept of 'meaning' can be fathomed only in relation to the self, which is both ultimate source and ultimate destination of semantic signals. But the concept of the self . . . cannot be given an explicit definition. Instead, the meaning of 'self' is intuitively obvious. It is another Kantian transcendental concept, one which we bring a priori to man just as we bring the concepts of space, time and causality to nature."[2]

The concept of "self" may be intuitively obvious, but its *cause* is not so obvious, at least to an evolutionist. Its reality is found to be necessary, even by naturalistic science, but as an "effect," it requires an adequate "cause," and no naturalistic cause is available to explain it. A supernatural Creator is required!

---

1. Gunther S. Stent, "Limits to the Scientific Understanding of Man," *Science,* Vol. 187, March 21, 1975, p. 1054.
2. Ibid, p. 1057

All of which leads to the conclusion that the *ultimate* purpose of language is not merely for communication between man and man, but even more for communication between man and his Maker. God speaks to man through His Word and man responds in praise and prayer to God.

MULTIVARIATE ANALYSIS:
MAN ... APES ...
AUSTRALOPITHECINES ...*
Duane T. Gish, Ph.D.

For many years it has been the consensus among evolutionists that the australopithecines (various species within the genus *Australopithecus*) were intermediate between Man and the apes, indicating that this creature was on the direct evolutionary line between Man and the hypothetical common ancestor of apes and Man (see *Evolution: The Fossils Say No!*, D.T. Gish, pp. 72-112). The first specimen was discovered by Dr. Raymond Dart in 1924. Dr. Louis Leakey and his wife Mary in 1959 uncovered the skull of a creature they named *Zinjanthropus bosei*, which they claimed at the time was hitherto unknown and was an important link in man's evolution. Later research by others and by Leakey, himself, established that his *Zinjanthropus* ("East Africa Man") was simply another variety of *Australopithecus* ("Southern Ape"). Leakey even began to suggest the possibility that the australopithecines were outside of the direct line leading to man — a sterile sidebranch.

Two aspects of the australopithecine morphology that were hailed by evolutionists most widely as indicating a transitional status for this creature were his dental characteristics and the alleged evidence for habitual bipedal

* Impact Series #29, (November 1975)

gait. The dental evidence cited is the fact that, although these creatures, believed to have weighed 60-70 pounds, had cheek teeth as large as those found in 400-pound gorillas, thus possessing massive jaws, their front teeth (incisors and canine teeth) were relatively small in comparison with their cheek teeth when compared to the relative size of incisors and canines to cheek teeth in modern apes.

Based on very little fragmentary evidence, it has been claimed by most evolutionists, as mentioned above, that the australopithecines had walked upright. Recently, Richard Leakey, the son of Louis Leakey, has challenged this claim, asserting that more complete remains of the forelimbs and hindlimbs of this creature he had found indicated that this creature did not walk upright.[1,2]

A recent article entitled "Australopithecus vs. the Computer" in the *University of Chicago Magazine* (Winter 1974, p. 8) by Dr. Charles F. Oxnard, professor in the Departments of Anatomy and Anthropology, reports the results of his computerized multivariate analysis of *Australopithecus* in comparison with similar analyses of Man and modern apes (this article is adapted from his book, *Uniqueness and Diversity in Human Evolution: Morphometric Studies of Australopithecines,* published in 1975 by the University of Chicago Press). According to Dr. Oxnard, his analyses show that *Australopithecus* was not intermediate between Man and the apes but was uniquely different. *Australopithecus* was, in fact, as different from both Man and the apes as either is from the other. This should be sufficient to banish *Australopithecus* as a candidate for Man's alleged ape-like ancestor, and thus to practically clear the field of supposed transitional forms between Man and the apes.

It is rather difficult to give a simplified description of the statistical multivariate analysis method. Particular points on, say the pelvis of a chimpanzee, may be measured with

---

1. R.E.F. Leakey, *Nature*, Vol. 231, p. 244 (1971).
2. *Science News,* Vol. 100, p. 357 (1971).

respect to a three-dimensional coordinate system. These same points on the pelves of other apes, Man, and *Australopithecus* can likewise be measured using the same axes used for the chimpanzee pelvis. After correlating these swarms of points, the relations among the swarms are then determined with respect to some other set of coordinate axes. Geometrically this is the equivalent of constructing and viewing from one position a three-dimensional model of the swarms and then rotating and viewing the model from a new position that best separates the swarms. In order to analyze the data from an object on which many measurements have been made in several species, a computer must be used, but this method allows a comparison of an anatomical feature of various creatures from a multitude of vantage points. It results in an objective evaluation of a large amount of data rather than a subjective assessment of a limited amount of data.

According to Oxnard's multivariate analyses of Man, various apes, and fossil material of *Australopithecus,* the australopithecines were uniquely different from any living form to a degree comparable to the difference between Man and any of the apes, or between any of the apes themselves. He believes further that these creatures, in exhibiting unique morphology, may also have been *functionally* unique, using a form of locomotion unlike any known form.

The result of analyzing all available features of the pelvis, for example, of fossil *Australopithecus,* Man, and the apes showed that the fossil australopithecine pelvis is not intermediate between the pelves of ape and Man but is in fact uniquely different from the pelves of both living forms. A similar analysis of a finger bone of "*Homo habilis,*" so-named by Louis Leakey but judged by Oxnard, and others[1,2] to be simply a variety of the australopithecines, indicated

1. D.R. Pilbeam, *The Evolution of Man,* Funk and Wagnalls, New York, 1970.
2. J.T. Robinson, *Nature,* Vol. 205, p. 121 (1965).

that this creature would have been inefficient at knuckle-walking but efficient in a hanging-climbing mode of locomotion. A multivariate analysis of the toe bones of Man, the apes, and a fossil australopithecine, Olduvai Hominid 10, showed that the fossil is uniquely different from both Man and African apes.

In fact, multivariate analyses of several anatomical features, including the shoulder, pelvis, ankle, foot, elbow, and hand, according to Oxnard, suggest that the "common view," that these fossils are similar to modern man or that on those occasions when they depart from a similarity to man they resemble African great apes, may be incorrect. He suggests instead that most of these fossil fragments are in fact uniquely different from both Man and "man's nearest living genetic relatives, the chimpanzee and gorilla."

While making clear that he does not wish to imply a genetic affinity of *Australopithecus* with the orang-utan, Oxnard states that to the extent the australopithecines resemble living forms, they tend to be with the orang-utans, not Man. Oxnard's conclusion is that "We may well have to accept that it is rather unlikely that any of the australopithecines, including *'Homo habilis,'* can have had any direct phylogenetic link with the genus *Homo.*"

Oxnard reviews evidence produced by Richard Leakey and others of fossil material indistinguishable, or nearly indistinguishable, from modern man allegedly three to four million years old (see *Evolution: The Fossils Say No!*, pp. 105-107; also D.T. Gish, ICR Impact Article ¼ 11, "Richard Leakey's Skull 1470," 1974). He also mentions the view commonly held by evolutionists that the speed of psycho-social evolution is enormously greater than the rate of biological evolution. If, as now increasingly accepted by evolutionists, Man was present on the earth four million years or more ago, this poses two problems for evolutionists. It not only makes Man older than his alleged ancestors (which are being eliminated by the latest research anyhow), but also presents the problem of why his psycho-social evolution stood still for nearly four million years after his biological evolution was complete. We strongly suggest the alternative view that biological evolution has not occurred, and that the evidence for Man's first use of agriculture, domestication of animals, and urban living sometime within the last 10,000 years, at the most, indicates a recent creation of man rather than biological evolution over a span of many millions of years.

The Checkered History of Australopithecus

From the time of Dart's announcement of his find of *Australopithecus*, this creature has generated considerable controversy. Most workers at first dismissed Dart's *Australopithecus* as simply an ape with some interesting but irrelevant parallel features with Man. As time progressed, and especially because of Louis Leakey's early sweeping claims, *Australopithecus* gained the consensus of evolutionary anthropologists as lying in the direct line that led to man. There have always been dissenters to this view, however. For example, the well-known evolutionist Ashley Montagu asserted that, " . . . the skull form of all australopithecines is extremely ape-like . . . the australopithecines show too many specialized and ape-like characters to be either the direct ancestor of man or of the line that led to man."[1]

Louis Leakey's early assessment of his "Zinjanthropus" (*Australopithecus bosei*) was that this creature was in the direct line leading to man. Later a growing consensus held that there were two species of the australopithecines, *Australopithecus robustus* (equated with *Australopithecus bosei*), and *Australopithecus africanus*. *A africanus* had no saggital crest, or bony ridge, running along the top of the skull, which is typical of some apes, and was the more gracile of the two, so it has been held that *A. africanus* was the creature that evolved into man's progenitors, while *A. robustus* was a sterile side branch. Richard Leakey, the elder Leakey's son, however, has found the remains of *A. robustus* and *A. africanus* in the same

---

1. A. Montagu, *Man: His First Million Years,* World Publishers, Yonkers, New York, pp. 51, 52 (1957).

deposit, and he has thus been led to believe that they are of a single species; africanus, the gracile form, being the female, and robustus being the male.[1,2]

During some of Louis Leakey's later excavations, he discovered remains of a creature resembling the australopithecines but which Leakey believed was more advanced. He gave this creature the name *Homo habilis* ("handy man"), because he believed that it was sufficiently advanced to be placed in the genus *Homo* and that it was the user of the so-called "pebble tools" he had earlier assigned to his "Zinjanthropus." As mentioned earlier, Oxnard and others insist that *H. habilis* is simply a variety of the australopithecines.

The so-called Java Man and Peking Man creatures are supposed to represent an even more advanced form, and have been placed in a single species, *Homo erectus*. Even some creationists have accepted *H. erectus* as being fully human. I have earlier detailed why I believe the evidence indicates that Weidenreich's model of Peking Man, on which these opinions have been based, borders on fraud, and that Java Man and Peking Man were most likely large monkeys or apes of some kind. Eugene Dubois, the discoverer of Java Man, maintained during the last 15 years of his life that his Java Man was merely a giant gibbon.

There are a few fossils found elsewhere which have been assigned to *H. erectus* which might actually be true men, since it is said by some that these fossils would have been assigned to Neanderthal Man except for the fact that their supposed ages were too old to include them with Neanderthal Man. It is most likely that the dates assigned to these samples are much too old, and that these creatures were actually remains of Neanderthal Man, now known to be as human as you and I.

Evidence that seems in itself sufficient to completely invalidate an *Australopithecus - Homo habilis - Homo*

---

1. R.E.F. Leakey, *Nature,* Vol. 231, p. 241 (1971).
2. *Science News,* Vol. 99, p. 398 (1971).

erectus - Homo sapiens evolutionary line was uncovered by Louis Leakey himself. Leakey has reported that he found the remains of a juvenile *Homo habilis* in Bed I at Olduvai Gorge at a *lower* level than he had found an australopithecine in the same bed. Furthermore, Leakey has found evidence of both *Australopithecus* and *Homo habilis* above Bed I in Bed II, contemporary with *Homo erectus*.[1,2] This would establish the contemporaneous existence in the same area of Africa of *Australopithecus, Homo habilis,* and *Homo erectus,* hardly conducive to the idea that *Australopithecus* had evolved into *H. habilis,* which had then evolved into *H. erectus.*

Even more astounding (to evolutionists) was Leakey's report that he had found the remains of what appeared to be a circular stone habitation hut right at the bottom of Bed I![3,3] It has long been held that deliberate manufacture of shelters could have been performed only by modern Man. This evidence clearly indicates then that *Australopithecus* (and the so-called *H. habilis), H. erectus,* and modern Man were contemporary inhabitants of the same area.

This evidence is inconsistent with an evolutionary origin of Man and the apes. Kelso reacts to this evidence in the first edition of his book by casting doubt on Leakey's data and interpretations simply because these do not fit into evolutionary assumptions.[2] In the second edition of his book, published in 1974, he solves the difficulty by simply eliminating any mention of the circular stone habitation hut, and replacing his discussion in the text of Leakey's report of the contemporaneous existence of *Audtralopithecus, H. habilis,* and *H. erectus* by a brief reference in a table,[4] thus

---

1. M.D. Leakey, *Olduvai Gorge,* Vol. 3, Cambridge U. Press, 1971, p. 272.
2. A.J. Kelso, *Physical Anthropology,* 1st Edition, J.B. Lippincott Co., New York, 1970, p. 221.
3. M.D. Leakey, *op. cit.,* p. 23-24.
4. A.J. Kelso, *Physical Anthropology,* 2nd Edition, J.B. Lippincott Co., New York, 1974, p. 178.

effectively suppressing this evidence. As more and more evidence accumulates, the creationist position strengthens and evolutionary interpretations become more and more untenable.

CREATION AND THE VIRGIN BIRTH*
Henry M. Morris, Ph.D.

The Mystery of the Incarnation

The incarnation of Jesus Christ is such an important doctrine of the New Testament that without it there can be no true Christianity. "Every spirit that confesseth that Jesus Christ is come in the flesh is of God: And every spirit that confesseth not that Jesus Christ is come in the flesh is not of God" (I John 4:2,3).

But how can the one who "was God" (John 1:2) from the beginning be the same one who "was made flesh, and dwelt among us?" (John 1:1, 14). How can He truly be "Emmanuel, which being interpreted is, God with us?" (Matthew 1:23). How can the infinite, eternal God become finite and temporal? Such a concept seems impossibly paradoxical, yet millions quite properly believe it to be a real and vital truth.

Perhaps the most amazing aspect of the incarnation is that a God who is absolute holiness could reside in a body of human flesh. Is it not true that "they that are in the flesh cannot please God?" (Romans 8:8). Our human bodies have been formed through many generations of genetic inheritance from Adam himself, and "in Adam all die" (I Corinthians 15:22).

The paradox is partially resolved, of course, when it is realized that Jesus Christ came in a body which was not of

* Impact Series #30, (December 1975)

sinful flesh. His body was truly "in the flesh," but only "in the *likeness* of sinful flesh" (Romans 8:3).

But even this doesn't resolve the dilemma completely, for how could His body be of flesh (carbon, hydrogen, amino acids, proteins, etc.), received by the normal process of reproduction of the flesh of his parents, without also receiving their genetic inheritance, which is exactly what makes it *sinful* flesh? "Behold, I was shapen in iniquity; and in sin did my mother conceive me" (Psalm 51:5). "Man that is born of a woman is of few days, and full of trouble . . . Who can bring a clean thing out of an unclean? not one" (Job 14:4).

The Problem of Inherited Physical Defects

Not only is there the problem of inherent sin, but also of inherent physical defects. Over many generations, the human population has experienced great numbers of genetic mutations, and these defective physical factors have been incorporated into the common genetic pool, affecting in some degree every infant ever born. Yet the Lamb of God, to be an acceptable sacrifice for the sins of the world, must be "without blemish and without spot" (I Peter 1:19). The very purpose of the incarnation was that God could become the Saviour of men as well as their Creator, but this required that in His humanity He must be "holy, harmless, undefiled, separate from sinners" (Hebrews 7:26), and this would have been absolutely impossible by the normal reproductive process.

The solution could only be through a mighty miracle! He could not be conceived in the same manner as other men, for this would inevitably give him both a sin-nature and a physically defective body, and each would disqualify Him as a fit Redeemer. And yet He must truly become human. "Wherefore in all things it behoved Him to be made like unto His brethren, that He might be a merciful and faithful high priest in things pertaining to God, to make reconciliation for the sins of the people" (Hebrews 2:17).

It is not surprising, therefore, that the Christian doctrine of the Virgin Birth of Christ has always been such a watershed between true Christians and either non-Christians or pseudo-Christians.[1] Without such a miraculous birth, there could have been no true incarnation and therefore no salvation. The man Jesus would have been a sinner by birth and thus in need of a Saviour Himself.

On second thought, however, one realizes that it was not the virgin birth which was significant, except as a testimony of the necessity of the real miracle, the supernatural conception. The birth of Christ was natural and normal in every way, including the full period of human gestation in the womb of Mary. In *all* points, He was made like His brethren, experiencing every aspect of human life from conception through birth and growth to death. He was true man in every detail, except for sin and its physical effects.

The miracle was not His birth, but His conception. And here we still face a mystery. Conception normally is the result of the union of two germ cells, the egg from the mother and the seed from the father, each carrying half the inheritance and thus each, of course, sharing equally in the transmission of the sin-nature as well as all other aspects of the human nature.

> "Each individual gets exactly half of his chromosomes and half of his genes from his mother and half from his father. Because of the nature of gene interaction, the offspring may resemble one parent more than the other, but the two parents make equal contributions to its inheritance."[2]

Each parent thus also makes an equal contribution of defective physical and mental characteristics due to inherited mutations. Both mental and physical traits are inherited in this way.

---

1. For answers to the various objections to the doctrine of the virgin birth, see the writer's discussion in *Many Infallible Proofs* (San Diego, Creation-Life Publishers, 1974).), pp. 54-63.

2. Claude A. Vilee (Harvard University), *Biology* (Philadelphia, W.B. Sanders, Co., 1962), p. 462.

Some writers have tried to make the virgin birth appear more amenable to human reason by comparing it to the process of *parthenogenesis*, which has been known to occur in some insects and even in some mammals, by which process the female egg begins to divide and grow into a mature animal without ever being fertilized. Others have compared it to the process of *artificial insemination*, by which the sperm is artifically introduced into the egg without actual copulation.

In addition to the rather crude concept of the work of the Holy Spirit which such suggestions involve, neither solves the problem of how the contribution of inherent defects contained in the *mother's* germ cell are kept from the developing embryo. If genetic inheritance in any degree is received from either parent, there seems to be no *natural* way by which the transmission of the sin-nature, as well as physical defects, could have been prevented.

The Necessity of Special Creation

Therefore, even though He was nurtured in Mary's womb for nine months and born without her ever knowing a man, it was also necessary for all this to have been preceded by supernatural intervention, to prevent His receiving any actual genetic inheritance through her. The body growing in Mary's womb must have been specially created in full perfection, and placed there by the Holy Spirit, in order for it to be free of inherent sin damage. Christ would still be "made of the seed of David according to the flesh" (Romans 1:3), because His body was nurtured and born of Mary, who was herself of the seed of David. He would still be the Son of Man, sharing all universal human experience from conception to death, except sin. He is truly "the seed of the woman" (Genesis 3:15), His body formed neither of the seed of the man nor the egg of the woman, but grown from a unique Seed planted in the woman's body by God Himself.

That is, God *directly* formed a body for the second Adam just as He had for the first Adam (Genesis 2:7). This was nothing less than a miracle of creation, capable of accomplishment only by the Creator Himself. "That holy thing

308

which shall be born of thee shall be called the Son of God"
(Luke 1:35).

Surely God would devote no more attention to the design
and construction of the body of "the first man, of the earth,
earthy" than He would to that of "the second man, the Lord
from heaven" (I Corinthians 15:47)!

The Marvel of Inheritance and Pre-Natal Growth

For that matter, the formation of every human body is a
marvelous testimony to the power and wisdom of the Creator
of the first human body, and so is His provision for its
reproductive multiplication into the billions of bodies of distinctive individuals who have lived through the ages. "I will
praise thee; for I am fearfully and wonderfully made"
(Psalm 139:14).

The 139th Psalm contains a remarkably beautiful and scientifically accurate description of the divine forethought in the
processes of heredity and embryonic growth. Verses 15 and 16
of this psalm (with explanatory comments interspersed) are
as follows:

"My substance (literally, *my frame*) was not hid
from thee, when I was made in secret, and curious-
ly wrought (literally *embroidered* — probably a
foregleam of the intricate double-helical structure
of the DNA molecule as it carries out its function
of template reproduction of the pattern provided
by the parents) in the lowest (or *least seen*) parts
of the earth (God originally made the dust of the
earth — the basic elements — then man's body
from those elements, and then the marvelous
ability to multiply that body)." (Verse 15)

"Thine eyes did see 'my substance yet being un-
perfect" (all one word, meaning *embryo*, in the
original; note the embryo is not *imperfect*, but *un-
perfect*, still in the process of being completed);
and in thy book all my members were written,
which in continuance (literally *which days* —
that is, all the days of development and growth
were planned from the beginning) were fashioned

(same word as *formed*, used in Genesis 2:7 for
the formation of Adam's body) when as yet there
was none of them (the whole amazing process was
written into the genetic code even before actual
conception)." (Verse 16)

The Body of Christ

With such careful divine care and attention given to the
development of every one of the billions of human bodies conceived since the days of Adam and Eve, how much greater
must have been the extent of the divine preparation of the
body of God's own Son! As a matter of fact, the design for His
body was prepared before the very foundation of the world
itself (I Peter 1:20; Hebrews 10:5). It is probable that, in
some degree at least, God had this very body in mind when
He undertook to make Adam "in our image after our
likeness" (Genesis 1:26). That is, God formed for Adam a
body patterned after that perfect body which had already
been planned for the divine incarnation, when the time would
come.

Then, "when the fulness of the time was come, God sent
forth His Son, made of a woman — that we might receive the
adoption of sons" (Galatians 4:4,5).

"Wherefore when He cometh into the world, He saith,
sacrifice and offering thou wouldest not, but a body hast thou
prepared me"(Hebrews 10:5). The verb "prepared" in this
verse is striking. It is the same word in the Greek (i.e.,
katartizo) as used in the next succeeding chapter in
Hebrews, in one of the greatest of all those verses in the Bible
describing the Creation. "Through faith we understand that
the worlds were framed by the word of God, so that things
which are seen were not made of things which do appear"
(Hebrews 11:3).

The "preparation" of Christ's body by God was the same
process as the "framing" of the worlds by God! As the latter
were created *ex nihilo* ("not out of things which do
appear"), so must have been the former. The word is also
translated "make perfect" (Hebrews 13:21, etc.).

To the possible question as to whether such a specially-created human body could be a truly *human* body, the conclusive answer is that the *first* Adam had a specially-created human body, and he was true man — in fact, the very prototype man. It is entirely gratuitous to say that God could not create a second human body which would be truly human in every respect (except for the inherent defects associated with the sin-nature). Furthermore, nothing less than a true miracle of creation could really accomplish the formation of a true human body which would not be contaminated with sin and its marks.

Thus, the body of Christ, was prepared by the great Creator, with no dependence on prior materials, and was made in total perfection, ready to receive Him as its occupant. In that perfect body, which would one day be "made sin" and would "bear our sins" on the tree (II Corinthians 5:21, I Peter 2:24). He would dwell forever after its resurrection and glorification (Revelation 1:14-18).

When God created the world, it was only a little thing (Isaiah 40:15-17), but the formation of any human body required the special planning of divine omniscience, eliciting the inspired testimony. "How precious also are thy thoughts unto me, O God! how great is the sum of them!" (Psalm 139:17).

The greatest of all creations, however, was that of the body in which His Son would take up His eternal abode. Miraculously created and conceived, then virgin-born, God's eternal Son became the perfect Son of Man.

There is yet another "body of Christ," of which all believers become members, now in process of formation, with Christ the head (Ephesians 4:15, 16). This body also is being supernaturally formed by the Holy Spirit (I Corinthians 12:13), with no genetic inheritance from sinful flesh. Its members are "born, not of blood, nor of the will of the flesh, nor of the will of man, but of God" (John 1:13), so that when complete it also will be a body "not having spot, or wrinkle, or any such thing; but that it should be holy and without blemish" (Ephesians 5:27).

Here is another mighty act of special creation, repeated again and again whenever a new member is added to Christ's body, when a new son of God is born. "But as many as received Him, to them gave He power to become the sons of God, even to them that believe on His name" (John 1:12). "Therefore if any man be in Christ, he is a new *creation*" (II Corinthians 5:17). These have "put on the new man, which after God is *created* in righteousness and true holiness" (Ephesians 4:24). "Ye have put off the old man with his deeds; and have put on the new man, which is renewed in knowledge after the image of Him that *created* him" (Colossians 3:10). "For we are His workmanship, *created* in Christ Jesus unto good works" (Ephesians 2:10).

The virgin birth of Jesus Christ thus testifies of the marvelous creation of His human body, which then speaks symbolically of the marvelous member-by-member creation of His spiritual body.

THE GOSPEL OF CREATION
AND THE ANTI-GOSPEL OF EVOLUTION*
Henry M. Morris, Ph.D.

Before His return to heaven, after His resurrection, the Lord Jesus Christ gave the great commission to all His disciples: "Go ye into all the world, and preach the gospel to every creature" (March 16:15).

In order to obey this most important commandment, it is essential that believers understand exactly what the gospel is. The word itself (Greek *euaggelion*) as applied to the true Gospel, occurs 74 times in the New Testament, and a related word *(euaggelizo)* is translated "preach the gospel" 22 times and "bring glad (or good) tidings" 5 times. The word means "the good news," and in all 101 of the above occurrences is applied to the good news concerning the Lord Jesus Christ.

It seems very significant that, of these 101 references to the gospel of Christ, the *central* reference is I Corinthians 15:1.

NOTE: All references appear at the end of this section on pages 320-321.

The passage (I Corinthians 15:1-4) is, above all others, the *definition* passage for the gospel. It is here defined as the good news "that Christ died for our sins according to the scriptures; and that He was buried, and that He rose again the third day according to the scriptures." Thus, the central focus of the true gospel is the substitutionary death, physical burial and bodily resurrection of Jesus Christ.

Note also four vital facts concerning this gospel: (1) it is something to be "received" and "believed" by faith, once for all; (2) it is the means by which we are "saved," continually and forever; (3) it is the fact upon which we firmly "stand;" (4) it is emphatically to be defined, understood and preached "according to the scriptures."

Although this is the central and key verse for the gospel, all other 100 occurrences are likewise important, if it is truly to be preached "according to the scriptures." It is especially important to study its first and last occurrences.

The first occurrence is in Matthew 4:23, which speaks of Jesus Himself "preaching the gospel of the kingdom." Thus, at the "beginning of the gospel of Jesus Christ, the Son of God" (Mark 1:1), it was vital that those who believed and preached the gospel stress its final consummation, when Jesus Christ would finally be acknowledged by every creature to be "king of Kings and Lord of Lords" (Revelation 19:6).

The last occurrence of the word is in Revelation 14:6, which says the gospel is "the everlasting gospel" that must be preached to all nations and furthermore, that its greatest emphasis must be to "worship Him that made heaven, and earth, and the sea, and the fountains of waters" (Revelation 14:7). Thus, the first occurrence of "gospel" looks ahead to the consummation of all things and the last occurrence stresses the initial creation of all things. As the consummation approaches, it is increasingly important that men look back to the creation. But the creation was saved and the consummation assured when the great Creator and Consummator paid the infinite price for the world's redemption, when He died on the cross and rose again.

The gospel thus entails the full scope of the work of Jesus Christ, from creation to consummation, involving the whole sweep of His redemptive purpose in history. Only this is the gospel "according to the scriptures." One does not truly preach the gospel without emphasizing both the final consummation of God's purpose in creation itself, as well as the central core of the gospel, the atoning death and triumphant victory over death achieved by the incarnate Creator and Redeemer.

The same threefold work of Christ is expounded in Colossians 1:16-20. "By Him were all things created." Then, "by Him all things are being conserved (or saved.)" Finally, "by Him all things are reconciled." Similarly, in Hebrews, 1:2, He "made the worlds," then "upholds all things," and ultimately becomes "heir of all things." "For of Him, and through Him, and to Him, are all things: to whom be glory forver. Amen." (Romans 11:36).

The gospel of the Lord Jesus Christ therefore encompasses the threefold work of Christ — Creation, Conservation, Consummation—past, present and future. One preaches a gospel with no foundation if he neglects or distorts the creation, a gospel with no power if he omits the cross, and a gospel with no hope if he ignores or denies the coming kingdom. He preaches the gospel "according to the scriptures" only if all three are preached in fullness.

In light of these facts, how sadly mistaken are the great numbers of "evangelicals" (a word meaning "those who preach the gospel") who oppose or neglect the doctrine of creation. They tell us not to "waste time on peripheral controversies such as the evolution-creation question — just preach the gospel," not realizing that the gospel includes creation and *precludes* evolution! They say we should simply "emphasize saving faith, not faith in creation," forgetting that the greatest chapter on faith in the Bible (Hebrews 11) begins by stressing faith in the *ex nihilo* creation of all things by God's Word (verse 3) as preliminary to meaningful faith in any of His promises (verse 13). They advise us merely to "preach Christ," but ignore the fact that Christ was Creator before He became the Saviour, and that His finished work of salvation is meaningful only in light of His finished work of creation (Hebrews 4:3-10). They may wish, in order to avoid the offense of the true gospel, to regard creation as an unimportant matter, but God considered it so important that it was the subject of His first revelation. The first chapter of Genesis is the foundation of the Bible; if the foundation is undermined, the superstructure soon collapses.

Furthermore, in light of Revelation 14:6,7, it becomes more important to emphasize creation with every day that passes. Satanic opposition intensifies as the end approaches. The anti-Gospel of anti-Christ can be effectively corrected only by the true gospel of the true Christ.

The Anti-Gospel of Evolution

In contrast to the gospel according to the scriptures, the evolutionary system is a religion diametrically in contrast to Christianity. The true gospel is "good news:" evolution is "bad news." Christ offers purpose and hope for eternity; evolution proffers randomness and uncertainty forever.

In the true gospel, the Lord Jesus Christ is the omniscient Creator. In evolution, God is replaced by natural selection.

"Darwin pointed out that no supernatural designer was needed; since natural selection could account for any known form of life, there was no room for a supernatural agency in its evolution."[1]

"For the devout of past centuries such perfection of adaptation seemed to provide irrefutable proof of the wisdom of the Creator. For the modern biologist it is evidence for the remarkable effectiveness of natural selection."[2]

Natural selection, however, is powerless to create or change anything by itself, serving only to "select" and "save" those features generated by the remarkable phenomenon known as genetic mutations.

"The process of mutation ultimately furnishes the materials for adaptation to changing environments. Genetic variations which increase the reproductive fitness of a population to its environment are preserved and multiplied by natural selection."[3]

However, mutations are not creative either. They have no purpose or program, but occur strictly at random.

"It remains true to say that we know of no way other than random mutation by which new hereditary variation comes into being."[4]

Natural selection is believed by evolutionists to have eliminated the need for an intelligent Creator, but natural selection must wait for mutations, and mutations depend on chance! The gospel of Christ is one of creative purpose; evolution bids us worship the great god Chance!

The gospel of Christ is "according to the scriptures," which were recorded as "holy men of God spake as they were moved by the Holy Ghost" (II Peter 1:21). The anti-gospel of evolution also has its scriptures, but instead of Moses, David and Paul, its prophets have names like Darwin, Huxley and Dobzhansky — against whom none in the academic world dare speak lest they be excommunicated.

The anti-gospel of evolution, while often professing to be strictly empirical and scientific, is in reality a full-fledged religious system, complete with cosmology, soteriology, ethics and eschatology.

Since man is believed to be the highest achievement of evolution to date, its leading proponents have even elevated man to the position of deity. Evolution has become "incarnate" in man, and thus man can now worship himself, in a formal system of religion called humanism. He not only is the product of evolution but can now even control his future evolution, so he believes.

"Humanism is the belief that man shapes his own destiny. It is a constructive philosophy, a non-theistic religion, a way of life."[5]

"Man created himself even as he created his culture and thereby he became dependent upon it."[6]

"In giving rise to man, the evolutionary process has, apparently for the first and only time in the history of the Cosmos, become conscious of itself."[7]

316

That humanism is nothing but evolutionism formalized as man-worship is indicated by one of the founders of the Humanist Association, leading evolutionist Julian Huxley:

"I use the word humanist to mean someone who believes that man is just as much a natural phenomenon as an animal or plant; that his body, mind and soul were not supernaturally created but are products of evolution, and that he is not under the control or guidance of any supernatural being or beings, but has to rely on himself and his own powers."[8]

Another founding father of the American Humanist Association was John Dewey, the man more responsible than any other single individual for the secularization and antitheistic bias of the American public education system. Dewey was an evolutionary pantheist, regarding man as the most highly evolved animal and thus as the personification of evolution.

"There are no doubt sufficiently profound distinctions between the ethical process and the cosmic process as it existed prior to man and to the formation of human society. So far as I know, however, all of these differences are summed up in the fact that the process and the forces bound up with the cosmic have come to consciousness in man."[9]

Evolution, or evolutionary humanism, is thus in effect a state-established religion in which the true God of creation has been replaced by random forces and natural selection and then by man himself. That this is essentially the philosophy of the coming anti-Christ and his world government is indicated by many of the prophetic Scriptures.

"Who changed the truth of God into a lie, and worshipped and served the creature more than the Creator, who is blessed forever. Amen." (Romans 1:25).

" — there shall come a falling away first, and that man of sin be revealed — who opposeth and exalteth himself above all that is called God — ." (II Thessalonians 2:3,4).

"And he shall speak great words against the most High, — and think to change times and laws." (Daniel 7:25).

"Neither shall he regard the God of his fathers, nor the desire of women, nor regard any god: for he shall magnify himself above all. But in his estate shall he honor the God of forces." (Daniel 11:37, 38).

"And he opened his mouth in blasphemy against God, — and all that dwell upon the earth shall worship him." (Revelation 13:6,7).

In addition to its deification of man, evolutionary humanism incorporates all the other attributes of a complete system of religion. Consider the following facts.

(1) It is not merely a theory of biology or anthropology, but rather is a complete *cosmology,* embracing everything in space and time in its system.

"Evolution comprises all the stages of the development of the universe: the cosmic, biological, and human or cultural developments."[10]

"Most enlightened persons now accept as a fact that everything in the cosmos — from heavenly bodies to human beings — has developed and continues to develop through evolutionary processes."[11]

"Our present knowledge indeed forces us to the view that the whole of reality *is* evolution — a single process of self-transformation."[12]

In this picture of total evolution, the eternal God is replaced by *eternal matter,* which has through billions of years evolved itself from primeval randomly-moving particles into complex particular people and cultures. The process of "creation" is replaced by random mutations and natural selection.

(2) Evolutionary humanism incorporates a system of *soteriology* — that is, a doctrine of salvation. In the gospel of Christ, salvation is obtained by grave through faith in the substitutionary death of Christ for man's sins. The anti-gospel, however, proposes that man must save himself.

"Through the unprecedented faculty of long-range foresight, jointly serviced and exercised by us, we can, in securing and advancing our position, increasingly avoid the missteps of blind nature, circumvent its cruelties, reform our own natures, and enhance our own values."[13]

"Evolutionary man can no longer take refuge from his loneliness by creeping for shelter into the arms of a divinized father figure whom he himself has created."[14]

"No deity will save us; we must save ourselves."[15]

(3) Evolution also proposes and endorses a system of "scientific" *ethics*. The ethical system of the Christian gospel is based on love for Christ and one's fellow men. That of evolutionary humanism is based on whatever is judged, by the scientific and political establishments, to be conducive to further evolutionary progress in human societies. Since these establishments vary in space and time, so do their particular evolutionary ethical systems.

"Suffice it to mention the so-called Social Darwinism, which often sought to justify the inhumanity of man to man, and the biological racism which furnished a fraudulent scientific sanction for the atrocities committed in Hitler's Germany and elsewhere."[16]

"The law of evolution, as formulated by Darwin, provides an explanation of wars between nations, the only reasonable explanation known to us."[17]

The evolutionary basis of racism, imperialism, and economic exploitation are not commonly defended by evolutionists today, but modern evolutionists are no less ready to formulate their own ethical systems, usually in terms of evolutionary socialism.

"The foregoing conclusions represent, I believe, an outgrowth of the thesis of modern humanism, as well as of the study of evolution, that the primary job for man is to promote his own welfare and advancement, both that of his members considered individually and that of the all-inclusive group is due awareness of the world as it is, and on the basis of a naturalistic, scientific ethics."[18]

319

Christian standards of ethical behavior are, of course, codified and explained in the Bible, and are given by divine revelation for man's guidance and benefit. Evolutionary ethics can never be absolute, but must themselves evolve.

"Thus, human 'goodness' and behavior considered ethical by man societies probably are evolutionary acquisitions of man and require fostering, — An ethical system that bases its premises on absolute pronouncements will not usually be acceptable to those who view human nature by evolutionary criteria."[19]

(4) Evolution even has an *eschatology,* a doctrine of future things. To considerable degree, of course, this merges with its soteriology, since salvation is not believed to apply to any future life but to this life and this world only. Humanists believe, however, that by manipulation of the evolutionary process, both genetically and sociologically, a glorious future awaits mankind.

"We no longer need be subject to blind external forces but can manipulate the environment and eventually may be able to manipulate our genes."[20]

"Man's unique characteristic among animals is his ability to direct and control his own evolution, and science is his most powerful tool for doing this."[21]

Thus, exactly as does the Christian gospel, the anti-gospel of evolution also has a doctrine of origins, a system of morals and ethics, a way of salvation, and a doctrine of consummation, all of which are polar opposites of the corresponding aspects of the true gospel. Evolution is nothing but a naturalistic religious system, erected in opposition to the gospel of supernatural creation, conservation, and consummation centered in Christ and revealed in Scripture.

References

1. Julian Huxley, in *Issues in Evolution* Sol Tax, Editor; University of Chicago Press, 1960), p. 45.
2. Ernst Mayr, "Behaviour Programs and Evolutionary Strategies," *American Scientist* (Vol. 62, November-December, 1974), p. 650.

3. Francisco J. Ayala, "Genotype, Environment and Population Numbers," *Science,* Vol. 162, December 27, 1968, p. 1456.
4. C.H. Waddington, *The Nature of Life* (New York, Anthenium, 1962), p. 98.
5. Promotional brochure, American Humanist Association, distributed by Humanist Society of San Jose, California.
6. Rene Dubos, "Humanistic Biology," *American Scientist,* Vol. 53, March 1965, p. 8.
7. Theodosius Dobzhansky, "Changing Man," *Science,* Vol. 155, January 27, 1967, p. 409.
8. Julian Huxley, American Humanist Association promotional brochure, *op cit.*
9. John Dewey, "Evolution and Ethics," *Scientific Monthly,* Vol. 78, February, 1954, p. 66.
10. Theodosius Dobzhansky, "Changing Man," *Science,* Vol. 155, January 27, 1967, p. 409.
11. Rene Dubos, "Humanistic Biology," *American Scientist,* Vol. 53, March, 1965, p. 6.
12. Julian Huxley, "Evolution and Genetics," in *What Is Man?* (Ed. by J.R. Newman, New York, Simon and Schuster, 1955), p. 278.
13. H.J. Muller, "Human Values in Relation to Evolution," *Science,* Vol. 127, March 21, 1958, p. 629.
14. Julian Huxley, Keynote address at Darwin Centennial Convocation, University of Chicago, November 27, 1959.
15. 1974 Manifesto of American Humanist Association.
16. Theodosius Dobzhansky, "Evolution at Work," *Science,* May 9, 1958, p. 1091.
17. Arthur Keith, *Evolution and Ethics* (New York, G.P. Putnam's Sons, 1947), p. 149.
18. H.J. Muller "Human Values in Relation to Evolution," *Science,* Vol. 127, March 21, 1958, p. 629.
19. Arno G. Motulsky, "Brave New World?" *Science,* Vol. 185, August 23, 1974, p. 654.
20. *Ibid,* p. 653.
21. Hudson Hoagland, "Science and the New Humanism," *Science,* Vol. 143, January 10, 1964, p. 111.

more significant books for you...

Creation: Acts/Facts/Impacts, Vol. I

Edited by Henry M. Morris, Duane T. Gish,
George M. Hillestad

The Institute for Creation Research issues a monthly publication entitled "Acts and Facts" which carries articles about creationism and the work of the Institute in seminars, debates, and special meetings. This book is a compilation of important articles from June, 1972, through December, 1973, plus the entire "Impact" series no. 1 - no. 9. 193 pages, Quality Paperback.

Scientific Creationism   *Henry M. Morris, Editor*

An honest understanding of man and his world can only be acquired from accurate information. This valuable and wholly scientific handbook covers the subjects of origins and early earth history, and the entire field of the creationist alternative to evolution. Often used as a textbook for the study of origins. General Edition, *Includes Biblical Documentation.* 277 pages, Kivar; or Cloth. Public School Edition, *Non-Religious Text.* 217 pages, Kivar; or Cloth.

The Troubled Waters of Evolution

Henry M. Morris

The theory of evolution is a delusion and cannot be supported by the facts of science. It is a humanistic philosophy which requires more faith on the part of the believer than does belief in biblical creationism. Dr. Morris presents evolution as it is, an unsound scientific concept which has yet to be proven. Concerned and thinking people in all walks of life will want to read this controversial, revealing new book. 217 pages, Quality Paperback.

The Bible's Influence on American History

Tim F. LaHaye

An eloquent, concise presentation of the influence the Bible has had on American History and how it can affect our future if we let it. The content and special line drawings make it a fine gift book. 96 pages, Paper.

Many Infallible Proofs *Henry M. Morris*

A comprehensive and systematic handbook written as a survey of the unique truth and authority of biblical Christianity. Contains evidence from science, prophecy, history, internal structure, philosophy and common sense. Complete with questions and answers, an excellent reference for church and home study. 381 pages: Kivar, Cloth, or book and cassette Set.

The Remarkable Birth of Planet Earth

Henry M. Morris

An exciting journey back to our beginnings is in this concise introductory treatment of origins. Covers the amazing order of the universe, early history of all mankind, delusion of evolution, the worldwide flood and many other historical and prophetic confirmations of God's handiwork. 111 pages, Paper.

The Genesis Record

**A Scientific and Devotional Commentary
on the Book of Beginnings**

Henry M. Morris

Written as a narrative exposition, The Genesis Record is the only commentary on the complete book of Genesis written by a creationist scientist. Discussions on all important historical and scientific problems are woven into the narrative which holds the interest of the reader throughout. Convincing treatments are given to the record of an actual six-day special creation, the worldwide flood, the dispersion, and the lives of the patriarchs exactly as written in Genesis. 708 Pages, Cloth.

The Bible Has the Answer

Revised and enlarged

Henry M. Morris and Martin Clark

Bible answers to puzzling questions on the Bible-science, doctrine, Christian life, and behavior and relationships. Now you can have Bible-centered answers to the 150 most common and vexing questions on the Bible and the Christian life. About 400 pages, Quality Paperback.

Crash Go the Chariots
Clifford Wilson

Newly revised and enlarged, the original book of this title was the near million bestselling answer to von Daniken's theories concerning unexplained happenings and ruins. These revealing answers to mysterious and haunting questions will arouse your curiosity and at the same time provide sensible answers to von Daniken and his often absurd claims. About 156 pages, Paper.

East Meets West in
THE OCCULT EXPLOSION *Clifford Wilson*

Pagan and semi-religious movements are now sweeping Western culture with unusually successful results in securing converts. Spiritism, witchcraft, and other Satanic cults are on the one hand, and transcendental meditation, yoga, Hare Krishna and other eastern philosophic movements are springing up on the other hand. This evaluation is very timely and has real help for these very confusing times when Satanic power is being felt more than at any other time in history. About 156 pages, Paper.

Adventure on Ararat
John D. Morris

Mysterious, foreboding, unexplored Ararat! Will anyone ever discover the secrets of this majestic mountain? John Morris and others searched for Noah's Ark on this awesome mountain and kept a diary of their trip. Now you can read about this expedition with the many unexpected trials they encountered. 116 pages, Quality Paperback.

THE ARK ON ARARAT: the Search Goes On
Tim F. LaHaye and John D. Morris

The most complete and up-to-date exposition of all that is known about Noah's Ark, its modern sightings, and future prospects for discovery. Fully illustrated with beautiful color photographs. You can actually join the search if you desire with the section on things which you can do to help locate the Ark. 288 Pages, Quality Paperback.

EVOLUTION? The Fossils Say NO!

Duane T. Gish

The fossil record provides the critical evidence for or against evolution since no other scientific evidence can show the actual history of living things. The fossil record proves there has been no evolution in the past and none in the present. This important fact is conclusively documented by Dr. Gish in this critique of the evolutionary philosophy. 134 pages, Quality Paperback.

Has God Spoken?

A. O. Schnabel

God has given man ample evidence of His existence, His nature, and His communication with men through the ages. The purpose of this study is to accredit the testimony of the writers of this record, the Bible. 119 pages, Quality Paperback.